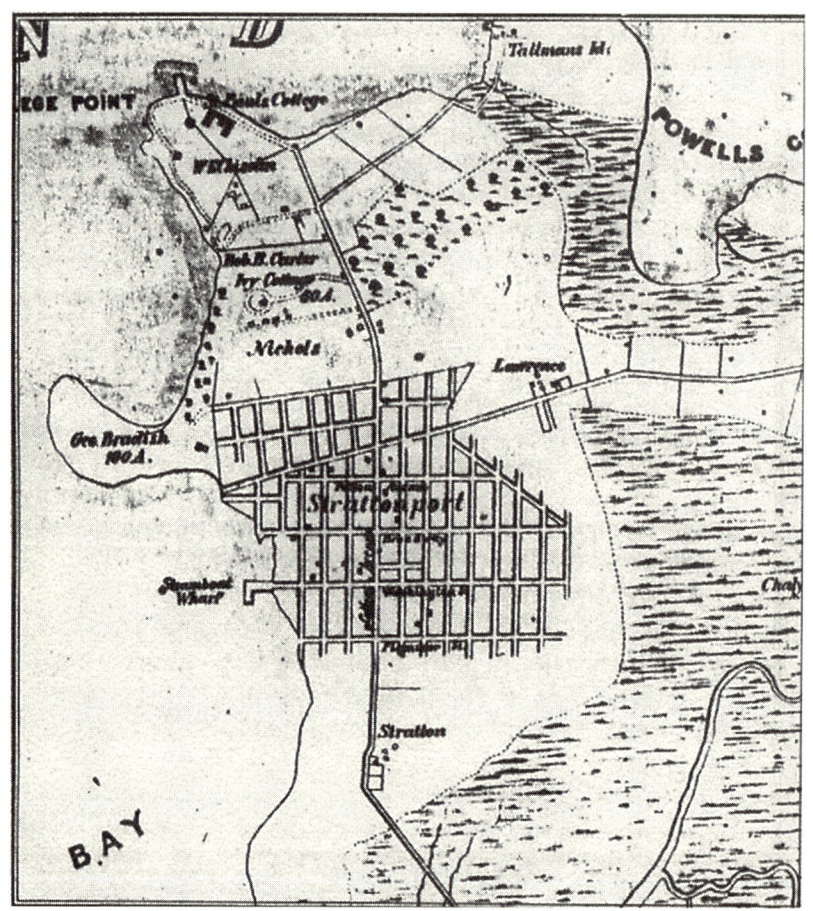

DRIPP'S MAP OF QUEENS COUNTY
College Point ca. 1852
Robert C. Friedrich Collection

This Gunner At His Piece

COLLEGE POINT, NEW YORK
& THE CIVIL WAR

With Biographies of the Men Who Served

James E. Haas

GATEWAY PRESS, INC.
Baltimore, MD   2002

Front and back cover photos of Post No. 451, GAR in 1898
Courtesy of the Poppenhusen Institute

Also by the author
Shout Hooray
Make A Joyful Noise
Praise the Lord
Eucharistic Prayer for Children
The Forgiving Christ
Liturgies for The Gift of Life
Rainbow Songs

"This Gunner at His Piece"
College Point, New York & The Civil War
With Biographies of the Men Who Served
Copyright © 2002 by James E. Haas

All rights reserved. Permission to reproduce in
any form must be secured from the author.

Please direct all correspondence and book orders to:
James E. Haas
P.O. Box 232
Millersville, MD 21108
or
www.jimhaasbooks.com

Library of Congress Control Number 2002111430

ISBN 0-9724139-0-1

Published for the author by
Gateway Press, Inc.
1001 N. Calvert Street
Baltimore, MD 21202-3897

Printed in the United States of America

For Lynne and Dan Haas and in Memory of Jim Haas, Jr.

Contents

Acknowledgements	viii
Foreword	ix
Process	xi
Tools and Resources	xv
College Point in 1860	1
The Flushing Journal	7
Adam Wirth Post No. 451, GAR	15
The Units In Which They Served	23
Census and Service Data	30
Introduction to the Biographies	81
Biographies	87
Postscript and Conclusion	261
Index to Units	265

Acknowledgments

I wish to recognize a number of persons who were very helpful in this project, especially Robert C. Friedrich, retired Senior Librarian at the Jamaica Branch of the Queensborough Public Library. His knowledge of College Point and its history is without parallel.

Vincent F. Seyfried is a noted Flushing and Long Island, New York Historian. His most recent book, *Flushing in the Civil War Era, 1837 to 1865*, tells the story of the larger town in Queens of which College Point was a part in the middle of the 19th Century.

Susan K. Brustmann, Executive Director of the Poppenhusen Institute in College Point, through whose efforts the work of the Institute and the legacy of Conrad Poppenhusen, is continued.

John Hyslop, Assistant Division Manager, Long Island Division of the Queensborough Public Library provided answers to numerous Queens-related questions, as well as a comprehensive list of men from the Borough who served during the war. That list was most helpful.

Mr. Jim O'Rourke, retired analyst for the National Security Agency, provided much appreciated editorial assistance. His eye for detail and probing questions helped to clarify many points. Any errors in the book, however, can be attributed solely to the author.

Mr. Henry Winkler, a long-time friend who many years ago helped me research the Pension File for my great, grandfather Burkhard Haas, who served in Company H of the 6th New York Heavy Artillery. A knowledgeable student of the Civil War, Henry contributed frequently to this work from his encyclopedic storehouse of information about the war and this period in our nation's history.

Foreword

The scope of this work has been limited to identifying the men who served from or who, following the Civil War, settled in College Point, New York, an easily defined geographical area in the borough of Queens. The notion of researching the Civil War era history of the town and identifying all the possible men who served as soldiers and sailors, has long fascinated me. I grew up there and am descended from of at least five veterans, three from College Point, of that national calamity.

Throughout the 140+ years that have passed since 1860, the population of College Point has increased, but the geography, for the most part, has remained a constant. Whereas the area was largely meadowland in 1860, the marshes have been filled in and the land, long since reclaimed, for the construction of homes and commercial buildings.

College Point was and remains a factory kind of town with a great deal of industry that created, and continues to create an on-going source of employment. As a result, descendants of many men who served in the Civil War still live, and even work in the area. Growing up there as I did in the 1940's, 50's, and 60's, many of the surnames researched for this book were very much in evidence then and are, to a certain extent, represented even today.

A much greater number of descendants, for obvious reasons, are scattered around the world and in the course of research, I have had the pleasure of communicating with a number of them. Beyond a shadow of a doubt there are many more. I hope to hear from them.

If nothing else, it has been a fascinating and rewarding experience that I hope will be of interest, not only to descendants in College Point, but also to descendants living in other areas of the United States, as not all veterans returned to the little village in Queens when their service was complete.

And there were those who served, but did not survive. Their names are inscribed on a monument that was solemnly dedicated on July 4, 1866 in Flushing on a busy thoroughfare called Northern Boulevard at the intersection of Linden Boulevard opposite what was then the Flushing Town Hall. As much as is known of their stories will be told and in the telling will they be remembered and their service, honored and revered.

Process

In the beginning of the project, I had made a copy of the relevant 66 pages of the 1860 Census comprising that small and isolated section of Flushing called at one time or another Strattonport, Flammersburg and, of course, College Point. It was Bob Friedrich who, based on his own College Point research, was able to provide me the 1860 Census page parameters, and that was very beneficial in the early stages of the research.

On each page I identified all males between the ages of 15 and 45 in the belief that the majority of those who eventually served in the war would fall within this age group, and such was the case with a very few exceptions.

Pages 689 to 755 contain the names of 2,840 people of which 676, or 24% of the total, were males between the ages of 15 and 45. Of the 676 males, 466, or 16% of the total, would fall in an age group between ages 15 and 35. It was from this group that the largest number of soldiers and sailors, 86, was drawn. By war's end, this number increased to 146, or about 30%.

On the basis of the number of available men of draft age, the percentage of them who went to the seat of war from College Point is noteworthy, and that topic will be touched on briefly in this work.

My objective then became to cross-reference all possible names within the 15-35 age group with verifiable Service Records and/or Pension Applications, if they could be found. When it appeared a soldier had not applied for a pension, it might have been because he hadn't done so, or because he had died without leaving a widow, or because he had moved outside of New York and blended into the emerging nation's population.

Unfortunately the pension records for a number of men could not be located when researched at the National Archives in Washington, DC. In those instances available Military Records were located, and as much data as they contained was incorporated into the individual biographies.

There were numerous challenges in researching this book, one of them being orthography or spelling, that in 1860 was a hit or miss affair with the census taker. Intending no slur, I believe the persons who performed the task of transcribing to paper what was heard, very likely had only a basic education. What they wrote frequently was a phoeneticized version of names spoken in heavily German-accented English. Thus the name *Jockers*, probably pronounced *Yockers*, was written on the page as what appears to be *Yiockers*. This occurred, not only in census records, but also in all the other documents I later reviewed. And there were many similar instances throughout the research.

Spellings were frequently changed or middle initials added at the time of military enrollment, or when the pension application was officially made. A number of men used *aliases* and that made for some interesting times.

Handwriting was also subject to both 19th Century norms, and the background of the individual taking the census, thus on census forms a capital S often appears as an L, the letters K and H are frequently indistinguishable, and the double S appears as SF, a standard way to write in 1860.

In addition to spelling and handwriting issues, the large number of candidates from the Census alone, 676, was substantial. It was also necessary to include in my research all of the names that appeared on lists in the *Flushing Journal*, in *Munsell's History of Queens County* and other documents referenced in the Tools and Resources section of this book.

There were many "common names" such as William Smith, and one man by this name did serve from College Point. Overall, 607 men named William Smith served from New York State, and 178 of them made applications for pension benefits. Daunting is one word that comes to mind.

In the list of College Point volunteers that appeared in the August 23, 1862 edition of the *Flushing Journal,* spelling inconsistencies abounded, and for many men there was either an incorrect unit designation or insufficient information provided as to the unit in which they supposedly served. In one or two instances the unit's numeric designation was provided, but not the state.

According to the *Flushing Journal* list, Jacob Keppler served in the 45th Regiment, but no state was identified. In actuality, *Jacob Keplar* served in the 45th Pennsylvania Infantry and he is our College Point veteran confirmed through other corroborating evidence.

The same list indicated that soldiers named George Montgomery and T. Quaid served in Sickle's Brigade, though no individuals by either name appear in the regimental roster of any unit of that esteemed fighting force.

Additionally two soldiers identified as Z. Baumeister and J. Broid supposedly served in the 79th New York Infantry, but efforts to locate either in any unit were unsuccessful.

Another soldier identified as Frederick Schuelzgover was named in a *Flushing Journal* article as having joined the Metropolitan Guard, but his name turned out to be Franklin Schultz.

Coming to grips with these challenges was made dramatically easier first through the use of the "wild card" option in much, but not all, of the computer-based research attempted.

Simply put, computerized data allows for the use of an asterisk *, a wild card as it were, to represent all possible letters in a given location. For example, if one was looking in a particular database for *William Smith*, but the spelling was not definite, one could type *Will*m Sm*th** and the computer would identify all individuals by the name of Smith in all of its variant spellings, along with the given name of William, including all possible typographical or transcription errors. William is frequently, if inadvertently, spelled *Willaim*.

Once a veteran was located, perhaps through searching a website, such as Ancestry.com, the list of soldiers in a particular regiment would then become accessible.

In the final analysis, the challenges presented the most enjoyable opportunities for research, and perhaps one day, the men who were not identified, will be found and their stories brought to light.

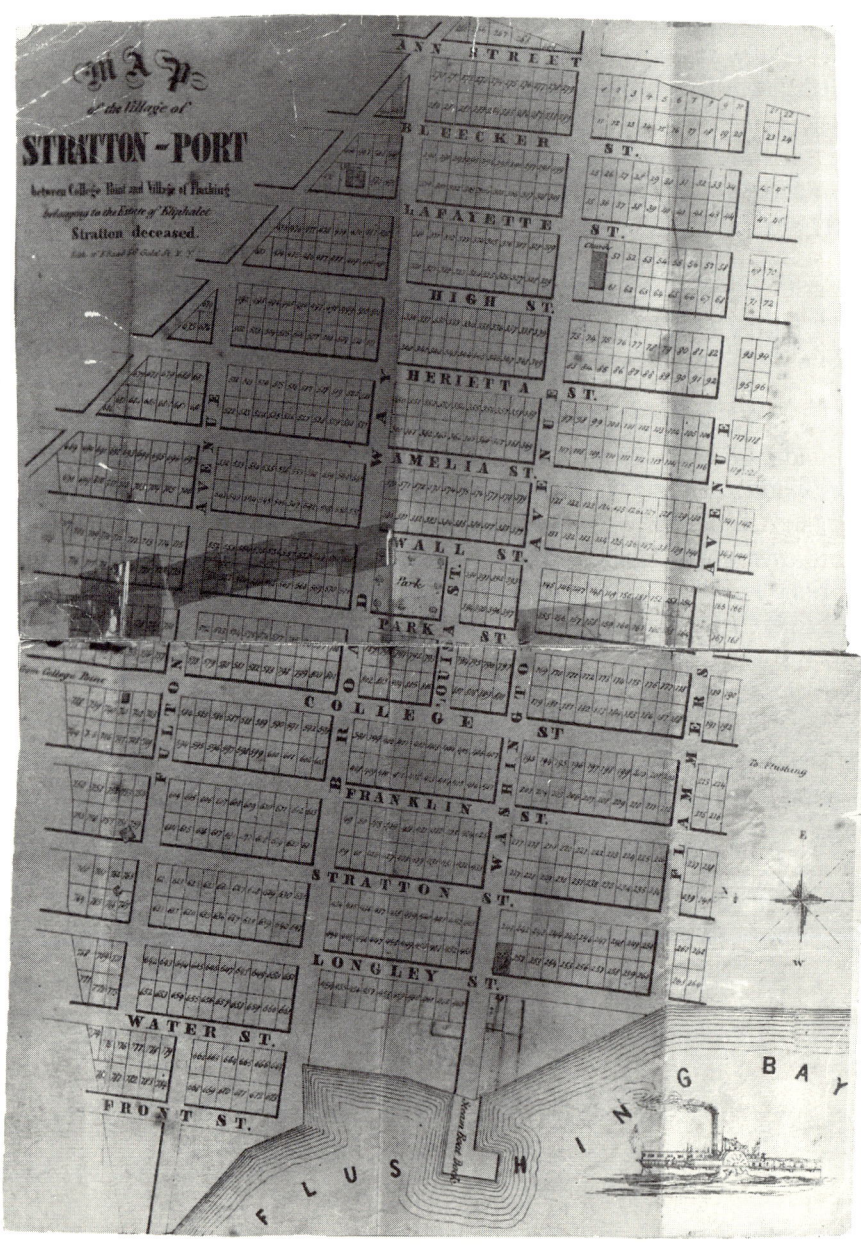

Stratton-Port Map
Courtesy of Robert C. Friedrich Collection

Tools & Resources

The computer age has made possible the availability and accessibility of vast amounts of data and historical information thus simplifying the task of doing research that in years past would have required spending countless hours in libraries, archives and other research facilities. Much of the initial research necessary to produce this work was done using a computer keyboard to access popular research websites.

Ancestry.com and its *Images On Line* technology made it possible to search for Military Records and Pension Applications for the soldiers. Once a file was located, additional research at the National Archives in Washington, DC was necessary to review the contents of any individual pension file.

Pension files for Civil War veterans often yield a great deal of information about the life of the individual before, during and after his service. In addition to detailed medical history, the files can contain much personal data including the names of parents, spouses, former spouses, children, dates of birth and death, countries of origin, addresses and employment histories.

Contained in files reviewed for this book were original letters from soldiers to parents, from pastors to the pension board, from fathers, seeking missing sons, sent to commanding officers. There were also original church marriage certificates, birth and death certificates and even one original Certificate of Discharge.

This information, or what was available, was incorporated into each biography and always was the wish that there would have been more.

Military Records, on the other hand, generally offered little in terms of personal information, however, in one instance just such a file yielded a gem; James C. Cornell's recommendation to be awarded the Congressional Medal of Honor. It was never awarded.

Using the *Images On Line* capability, it was also possible to access the actual pages for the various census records thus eliminating the former necessity of scrolling through reel upon reel of microfilm accessed at a remote site, again, such as an archive, library or research center.

The national census, taken every ten years in America since 1790, asked for different information at the beginning of each decade. Over the course of each ten-year period, many things changed. People died, spouses came and went, as did children. First names were altered as were the ages for individuals. It often appeared accuracy might not have been a criterion when the census taker called.

Nevertheless, each succeeding census offered a glimpse of what was taking place in the lives of the men identified in this book and the families of which they were a part.

For those who wish to delve deeper into census data, page references are offered throughout.

Since the objective of this book was to identify College Point men who fought in the Civil War, www.Civilwardata.com was a particularly helpful Civil War Research Database to locate a number of "hard to find" soldiers.

Other resources included:

The *1860 U.S. Federal Census Index* (AIS) for New York published in compact disk form by Ancestry.com.

The 1880 Census and National Index set of compact disks published by the Church of Jesus Christ of Latter Day Saints in Salt Lake City, Utah.

- The 1860 Federal Census of Flushing, Queens, New York, specifically pages 147/689 – 215/757. The Census used two parallel numbering systems, but I reference pages 689 - 757 in the assembled data.

- Analysis of 1860 College Point Census Data compiled and provided by Robert C. Friedrich

- Federal Census Records from 1850 through 1920 of Flushing and College Point and States other than New York. It is important to note that almost nothing of the 1890 Federal Census survived a massive fire, and that the 1910 Census for New York City is not indexed. As a result, research in these census years, though occasionally cited, is limited for this work.

- The 1870 Census of Flushing has two numbering systems as well and in this Census, College Point was not enumerated as a separate geographic entity. When applicable, reference is always made in the Biographies to the "Flushing" Census of 1870 with the individuals living in College Point. The pages that include College Point are 29/211 through 120/256. The second numbering system is referenced and it is important to note that for each page, there were actually two pages.

- The 1880 Census also has College Point as a subsidiary of the town of Flushing. In the list soldiers, to aid researchers I reference the Enumeration Districts (ED), 264 and 267. When applicable, in the Biographies I reference College Point as the Census place, and provide the appropriate page numbers.

- The *Flushing Journal* published a list of Volunteers from College Point printed in the August 23, 1862 edition. Vincent Seyfried provided a copy of this list, and it is reprinted in these pages. The list played an essential role in identifying the soldiers.

- Vincent Seyfried also transcribed a list of Union Volunteers from College Point, along with Membership Applications for the Adam Wirth Post No. 451, GAR in College Point. Margaret Testa, a direct descendant of Joseph Dockendorf, Co. G, 46th New York, provided a copy of this list. She is also a cousin.

- Susan Brustmann of the Poppenhusen Institute provided copies of original membership applications to Adam Wirth Post No. 451, and photographs of selected members reproduced in these pages.

- Robert C. Friedrich made available a copy of the original Roster of Adam Wirth Post No. 451 GAR that is reprinted in these pages.

- Friedrich also provided a copy of the Enrollment List for Strattonport, Flammersburg and College Point prepared on November 30, 1863 by the Office of the Provost Marshall in Jamaica, New York. This list was an effort to identify the men in Queens who were available for the draft.

- Friedrich also provided a list of Flushing and College Point soldiers that was printed in Munsell's *History of Queens County*.

- Seyfried, Friedrich and Brustmann provided copies of Civil War era newspaper articles from the *Flushing Journal*. The section on College Point in 1860 could not have been written without them.

- *The Flushing Battery: Reminiscences of the War of the Rebellion* by Jacob Roemer, Brevet Major, Battery L, 2nd New York Heavy Artillery, published by the Estate of Jacob Roemer, Flushing, NY, 1897, and printed by the Press of the *Flushing Journal*. This book is an essential resource for anyone researching this unit that became the 34th New York Light Artillery.

- To look deeper into a unit that attracted many men from the College Point area, a comprehensive retelling of the story of the 20th New York Infantry, written by Gary Kappesser, can be found at: http://gkkapp.home.infi.net/20NYSV.htm

- *Flushing in the Civil War Era, 1837 to 1865* by Vincent F. Seyfried, published in 2002 by the author. Seyfried has written 40 books that relate the history of the Borough of Queens in New York City. This is his most recent, and is essential to anyone interested in the town during this time period.

- *A History of College Point* written by Robert A. Hecht and published by the Bicentennial Committee of College Point in 1976. Available from the Poppenhusen Institute, this small volume is another essential resource for anyone seeking information about College Point from its earliest days. It contained the phrase that ultimately led to the research and writing of this book. In Chapter XII, *The Wars*, Hecht wrote: *"such a history* (of all the action seen by our servicemen) *would take several volumes"*.

When I read that in 1976, I made a commitment to one day write the Civil War portion of that story.

Throughout the course of research additional individuals have made contributions that have given life to individual biographies. Their contributions are appreciated and their names noted in the biographical sketches.

College Point in 1860

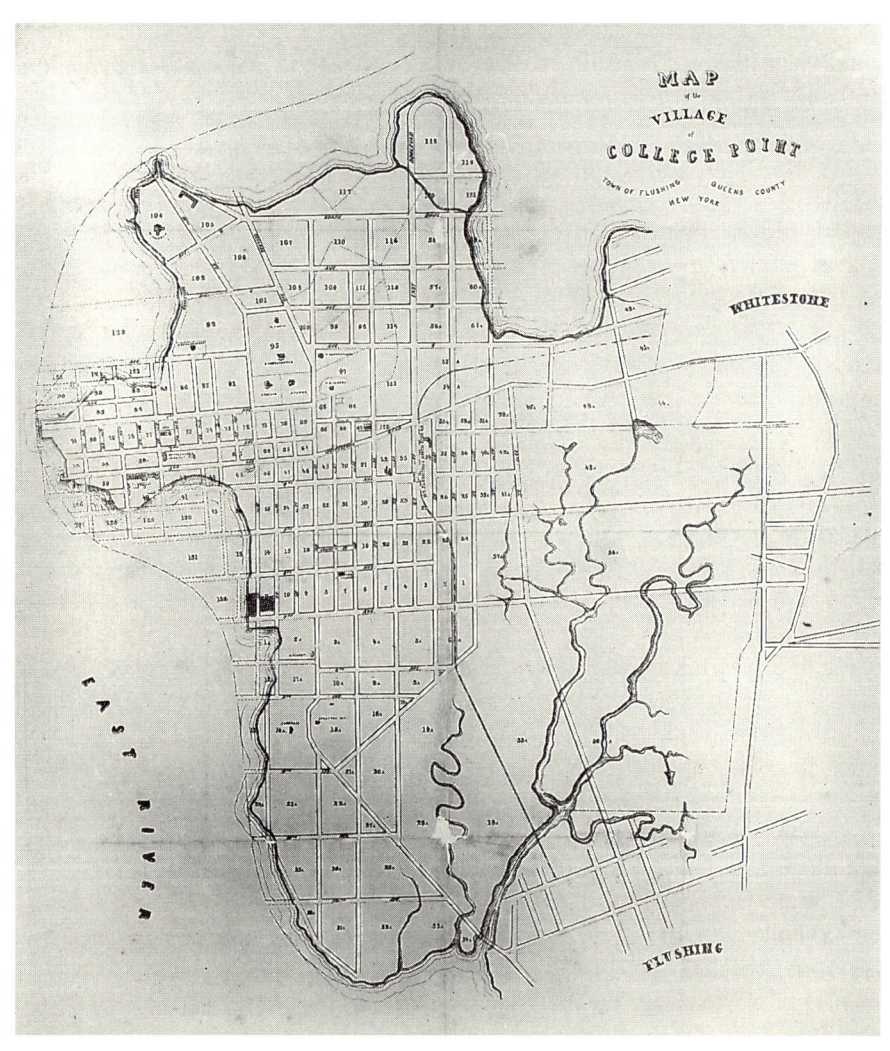

Robert C. Friedrich Collection

College Point in 1860

The area known today as College Point, a spit of land, peninsula actually, on the northern tip of Queens in New York City, was known in 1860 as Strattonport, Flammersburg and yes, College Point.

At that time, largely meadowland, College Point was a speculator's dream and real estate entrepreneurs, seeing the potential, created lot developments and advertised them for sale. It was and remains an area limited in size and in 1860 there were but two passable roads in and out of the town, the Whitestone Road so-called, today's 15th Avenue and a road that was known then as the "Causeway". Today, in the first decade of the 21st century, there are four roads and College Point remains a somewhat isolated community.

Robert C. Friedrich's statistical analysis of the 1860 Census, based on print out copies of the microfilmed original ledgers provided by Vincent Seyfried, identified 462 separate families living in the area, and a total population of 2,260, about 580 fewer than those listed on pages 689 to 755, the census pages used as a basis for my research. The discrepancy in total numbers may have come about as a result of the less than formal approach to the taking of the census by enumerators, of which there were two. It is entirely possible that not all of the 66 pages I used were, in fact, included in the original ledgers and the discrepancies, if in fact they exist, do not impact the statistical results of the research to any great extent.

According to Friedrich there were 1,119 males and 1,130 females, an almost equal representation and almost half of the total population, 1,223, were foreign-born with the largest majority, 956, having emigrated from a collection of German States and Principalities. There were 200 Irish-born residents, 37 from France, 24 from England, 16 from Switzerland and the remainder from various Western European countries. Three individuals claimed South America as their homeland.

Of the 1,119 males in Friedrich's analysis, a total of 479 could potentially be available for duty based on age alone, a significant figure in light of the numbers who would eventually serve in the military. Again, these numbers are at minimal variance from those noted above and the complete breakdown is as follows:

Heads of Family:

Male	20-29	30-39	40-49	Total
	68	186	111	365

Children:

Males	16-20	21+	Total
	84	30	114

The Black and Mulatto population, then as now, was small and the families lived in relative close proximity working primarily as stewards and servants with one individual listed as a boatman.

Conrad Poppenhusen employed approximately 75 men and women, the largest majority of the population, in his Enterprise Works of the India Rubber Comb Company. Poppenhusen, whose story is told more completely in Robert A. Hecht's *History of College Point, NY*, had relocated his factory from Williamsburgh in Brooklyn to College Point in 1854. As a result the area became a magnet for job-seeking immigrants, many of whom he had personally recruited on trips back to the country of his birth, Germany. Poppenhusen was Hamburg-born.

With a population dominated by Germans, it is not surprising that there were at least two breweries in 1860 and as many as twelve saloons in operation, some located in the homes of the residents. According to a report in *Flushing Past and Present: A Historical Sketch* by Rev. G. Henry Mandeville, published in 1860, three operating hotels served the needs of the fast-growing and ever-expanding, population.

The census rolls list 30 tailors; 24 shoe makers; 21 carpenters; 10 painters, masons, gardeners and cigar-makers; 8 bakers; 7 farmers and grocers; 6 blacksmiths and washerwomen; 4 butchers, basket-makers and barbers; 3 school teachers, chair-makers and pedlars (sic) and also 3 ministers of the Gospel with one of them being Father Joseph Huber, a German-born Catholic Priest who founded what became the Parish of St. Fidelis and another being Rev. August Heidmiller, *(sic)* the Pastor of St. John's Lutheran Church. The third clergyman enumerated is Henry M. Berse.

There were 2 each of milliners, seamstresses, dressmakers, milkmen, coopers, cartmen, florists, engravers and watchmakers. Rounding out these numbers there were 2 midwives, 2 physicians and 2 undertakers thus taking care of the populations' needs at birth, in life and at the time of death.

With the additional roles of druggist and optician, cook and confectioner, jeweler and glazer, piano-forte maker and telegraph operator being filled, College Point in 1860 could easily be described as a self-sustaining village, truly needing only two roads leading in and out of its confines. Still, Friedrich tells us there were no reported dealers in dry goods, hardware, ice, coal and/or lumber, wines, liquors or livery stable facilities, furniture stores or stationers, but I suspect these services were also delivered, and needs met, by the townspeople.

In the relatively short time between the taking of the 1860 Census and the start of hostilities in April, 1861, the population in College Point experienced an upward swing.

Of the 226 men who were identified for this book and who served, 83 are enumerated in the 1860 Census and 61 would move there and be included in the August 23, 1862 *Flushing Journal* list. Truly the village had experienced a population boom, due almost certainly, it is safe to say, to the availability of work there in Conrad Poppenhusen's rubber factory.

Bird's Eye View of College Point in 1876
Boston Public Library, Rare Books Department
Courtesy of the Trustees

The Flushing Journal

The Flushing Journal.

Devoted to News, Local Interests, Literature, Agriculture, Horticulture, Morality and Amus

Volunteers from College Point, Flushing, since the commencement of the War.

- Appel, Henry, 29th Regiment.
- Appel, Conrad, 29th Regiment.
- Brill, Chas. Sr. 2d. N. Y. Artillery.
- Brill, Chas. Jr. 2d. N. Y. Artillery.
- Behring, Fr. 58th Regiment.
- Bryody, R. 79th Regiment.
- Broid, J. 79th Regiment.
- Baumeister, Z. 79th Regiment.
- Bockler, C. 68th Regiment.
- Becker, Louis, 2d N. Y. Artillery.
- Baumann, John, 2d N. Y. Artillery.
- Copper, Wm. 2d N. Y. Artillery.
- Dillon, Michael, 10th Regiment.
- Doherty, John, 63rd Regiment.
- Doherty, Beruh, Lincoln Cavalry.
- Dockendorf, Fr. 20th Regiment.
- Dockendorf, Jos. 46th Regiment.
- Duerr, F. 8th Regiment.
- Egan, Patrick, 10th Regiment.
- Egan, Thomas, 10th Regiment.
- Frey, Joseph, 2d N. Y. Artillery.
- Fahner, T. 20th Regiment.
- Fritz, L. Wilson Zouaves.
- Freund, E. 20th Regiment.
- Frank, Louis, 2d N. Y. Artillery.
- Green, J. 2d N. Y. Artillery.
- Gunzert, Theodore, 58th Regiment.
- Gardiner, Rufus 48th Regiment.
- Gardiner, William 48th Regiment.
- Haubeil, Charles, 32 Reg. California.
- Haubeil, M. 74th. Reg. Sickles Brigade.
- Helfrich, Val. 58th Regiment.
- Howard, Wm. 2d N. Y. Artillery.
- Hoyne, Louis, 15th Regiment.
- Harrington, Thomas, 25th Regiment.
- Heilmann, Peter 2d N. Y. Artillery.
- Herle, John, 11th Connecticut.
- Haas, Dennis.
- Jokers, Adam, 20th Regiment.
- Kaufmann, J. 2d N. Y. Artillery.
- Koeckeritz, Bennoron, Lincoln Cavalry.
- Koch, Charles, 58th Regiment.
- Kabisch, F. 58th Regiment.
- Kang, John, 58th Regiment.
- Kang, R. Lincoln Cavalry.
- Kiernan, John, Lincoln Cavalry.
- Keppler, Jacob, 45th Regiment.
- Lasche, R. 20 Regiment.
- Montgomery, Geo. Sickles Brigade.
- Muller, Louis, 2d N. Y. Artillery.
- Muller, Louis, 20th Regiment.
- Muckey, E. 20th Regiment.
- Motz, G. 29th Regiment.
- Mahony, Michael, 29th Regiment.
- McGowan, Wm. Navy.
- Neumann, E. 29th Regiment.
- Nau, Michael, 2d N. Y. Artillery.
- Neumann, George, Sickles Brigade.
- Otto, H. 46th Regiment.
- Otto, H. Jr. 46th Regiment.
- Palmer, S. 2d N. Y. Artillery.
- Paschen, John, 2d N. Y. Artillery.
- Piereth, Val. 1st Reg. Delaware.
- Quaid, T. Sickles Brigade.
- Rubbel, H. 29th Regiment.
- Reinheimer, Danl., 2d N.Y. Artillery.
- Rein, Moritz Von, 7th Reg.
- Richter, Franz, 58th Reg.
- Richard, George.
- Rausch, Peter, 20th Reg.
- Snyder, Wm., Sickles Brigade.
- Schafer, Fr., 2d N.Y. Artillery.
- Schrader, Otto, 29th Reg.
- Shultz, D., 79th Reg.
- Steinbrucker, John, 2d N.Y. Artillery.
- Schumacher, Fr.,
- Schumacher, H., 20th Reg.
- Schubert, Emil, 41st Reg.
- Sternberg, H., 2d N.Y. Artillery.
- Sternberg, C. jr., "
- Sennewald, Theo., 20th Reg.
- Schierlitz, Paul Von, 29th Reg.
- Sparks, T., 10th. Reg.
- Steinbeck, Juls. 20th Reg.
- Straube, Henry,
- Stobbe, Nich. 57th Reg.
- Smith, Wm., 20th Reg.
- Shultz, Geo., Navy,
- Skinyon, Thos., 10th Reg.
- Smith, James, "
- Stader, Chas., 39th Reg.
- Stader, Geo, "
- Toot, Charles, Bricket's Artillery.
- Troy, John, U. S. Mortar Flotilla.
- Tyrrell, Willis, 11th Connecticut.
- Vix, G., 29th Reg.
- Wirth, Adam, 2d N.Y. Artillery.
- Warner, Hiram, Gunboat Perry.
- Weber, Beruh, 58th Reg.
- Werner, Jacob, 2d N.Y. Artillery.
- Winter, Adam, "
- White, Thos., "
- Wagner, H., Serrell's Engineers.
- Wilhelm, J., 68th Reg.
- Werner, F., 2d N.Y. Artillery.
- Wiessner, Val., "
- Zuberbier, Otto.
- Zeseler, Carl, 29th Reg.

The Flushing Journal

Published weekly on Saturday, the *Flushing Journal* was one of two local newspapers available in 1860 with the other being the *Long Island Times*. Together they chronicled the events of the war years and give us a fairly detailed picture of what occurred in and around College Point in those days.

Following the bombardment of Fort Sumter in South Carolina and President Lincoln's call for volunteers to put down the rebellion, the first of many war-related reports touching on College Point appeared in the April 27, 1861 edition of the *Flushing Journal*. It described a meeting that took place in Flushing and the optimistic enthusiasm of the townspeople to equip and organize the 15th Regiment of Volunteers.

"A standing committee was then adopted to solicit funds for supporting the families of those serving with the regiment. Conrad Poppenhusen then became the first by subscribing $2,000. Following the singing of the Star Spangled Banner, a call for a meeting of the village ladies was put forth for April 25th."

The expectation of this patriotic group of townspeople was that the war would be brief and that most soldiers would be returned to their homes and farms relatively quickly. According to the May 11th edition, *"The chances for our 15th Regiment to go to the seat of war is remarkably slim"*. With the benefit of hindsight, we know this was not to be the case.

Over the course of the war's first year there were numerous calls for financial support for the wives and children of the volunteers as in the May 18, 1861 edition.

"The collections made in this county for the equipment of the 15th Regiment, and for the support of soldiers' families, is about as follows, Flushing, $7500.00...", a substantial amount of money for the time

And as well there were not a few expressions of relief at the departure of some units as indicated by the headline and article in the July 6, 1861 edition. It read:

GOOD RIDDANCE: *"The 15th Regiment of Volunteers (*a regiment made up mainly of Queen's men, many of them from College Point) *under Col. J. McLeod Murphy... left last Saturday for the seat of war to the joy of the inhabitants who never saw their like before and never* wish to see their like again. With the exception of a few of the officers, the majority are held to be as hard a lot as can be scraped together anywhere..."

In a little over a year, on August 16, 1862, the paper would print a piece stating *"The College Point Election District in this town has sent more than one third of its legal voters to the war – mostly Germans. We doubt whether any Election District in the State has done better than this. Mr. Conrad Poppenhusen... contributes $15.00 additional bounty to every man that enlists and is accepted. The recruits from College Point and Strattonport mostly join old regiments in which the German element dominates."*

Then following on the August 23rd publication of the list of volunteers from College Point, the August 28, 1862 edition stated that,

"College Point and Strattonport are almost exhausted of recruits for the war, more than a third of its males having enlisted. The proprietors of the India Rubber Factory have pursued a most liberal and patriotic course, and have contributed largely to this result."

In the same edition under the headline *ENTERPRISE WORKS* a letter to the editor elaborated on the support given to volunteers:

The following notice appeared at the doors of the Enterprise Works: "All employees at the Enterprise Works are invited to a meeting held at the house of Mr. Kraemer... to contemplate proper steps for supporting families of those who possibly may be drafted into the United States service... and whose families would be deprived of their support by their absence."

The assembled association members agreed to pay *"$5 per week for every drafted man, $4 to an unmarried man having a mother or sister or other relative depending on him for support; $4 to a married man or widower having children with $.50 additional for each child."*

Messrs. Poppenhusen and Konig were thanked for their offer to pay 25% of all the monies the Association would expend while supporting the families of the drafted men then *"Three hearty cheers were then given for the Constitution of the United States and the meeting adjourned.*

Poppenhusen, the Benefactor of College Point, was obviously supportive of his workers and their families and in so doing created much good will throughout the community. Patriotism was still very prominent, but there were other things happening. With the war dragging on not everyone was anxious to go to the front.

July 21, 1862: *"The newspapers everywhere are noticing the great rush of men into fire departments evidently with the intention of escaping the draft.*

A week later a report followed describing the *"liberal"* bounties paid.

"The recruits from this county receives, when he passes medical examination and is mustered into service: From the state, $50, from the County, $15, from the United States $25, one month's pay in advance, $13, besides this the recruit is entitled to $2 if he manages his own enlistment, or $4 if he joins an old regiment."

One week later on August 9th, a piece stated: *"We have suddenly become a population of invalids. Our physicians are tormented from morning to night with applicants for certificates of physical disability... Opticians are run down by those who have suddenly discovered that they are near sighted. Cabinet makers are anticipating a rich harvest from crutches, and tin men from ear trumpets. Good heavens...."*

On March 14, 1863 yet another list appeared in the newspaper, this one containing the names of 38 deserters from the 34th New York Light Artillery also known as the Company L of the 2nd New York Heavy Artillery commanded by Captain Jacob Roemer. The majority of men in this and other units served with honor, some with distinction, but unfortunately, not all, and as many as four of the names on Roemer's list were those of College Point men, Ludwig Becker, Peter Heilmann, Valentine Wiessner and Otto Zuberbier.

Roemer afforded the deserters an opportunity of redemption and at least one, Heilmann, apparently took advantage of the offer thus enabling him to apply for and receive a veteran's pension later on in life. There is also some indication that a number of men reported as having deserted, actually resigned, and either entered other units, or joined the Navy, as did, apparently, John Troy.

During this month of March, because the need for added men to fight the war was critical, President Lincoln asked for a draft to be instituted in the Enrollment Act of March, 1863 and in doing so 776,000 men, ages 18 to 35, from every State in the Union, were put on notice.

Many were excused from service for legitimate reasons, mental or physical disabilities, or because they were the sole support of a widow, an orphan sibling or a motherless child. A large number of these men, up to 20%, simply left their respective area, and in the parlance of the day, *"skedaddled",* to Canada, out West or to other areas where they very likely assumed new identities.

It can be rightly assumed that a similar percentage of men from College Point who fell into these age categories, fled as well.

There were three additional drafts in 1864 and the names of the draftees were published for all to see. Some men were able to escape their military obligation by hiring a substitute and paying them a fee of up to several hundred dollars, a substantial sum when you consider that Army pay was set at $16.00 a month. The newspaper lists a number of prominent College Point men whose commutation fees were paid and an ancestral uncle of the author named Frank Dockendorf served in the capacity of *"substitute"* for a Delaware man.

The following June 6th the names of eight casualties including that of Adam Worth (*sic*), appeared. He was not only the first to die from the 34th New York, but he was also the first casualty from College Point. Years later in 1884, the College Point GAR post No. 451 would be named in his honor.

May 21, 1864 *"Wanted for the 15th Regiment, New York and National Guard for harbor defense duty, a number of substitutes, for whose services a good price will be paid"* This was a call for men to enlist for 30 days to garrison Fort Richmond in New York Harbor. At least 16 men from College Point responded to that call and one, John Stonebanks, lost his life in the service of his country.

Later in the summer of 1864 there were reports on dealing with relieving the sick and wounded soldiers in the hospital at Willets Point near Flushing, and another dealing with a 4th of July celebration at which dinners would be furnished to *"sick and wounded soldiers."* There was continued support three years into the war and a never-ending call for more volunteers as on September 24, 1864.

"THE DRAFT" Contrary to the expectations of many, we shall have to have a Draft in this District for about one thousand men... our

Supervisors have increased the bounties to about $500.00 to recruits, and $100.00 hand money to every person who brings an accepted recruit to the officer."

On October 1st the list of those drafted from Strattonport, 83 in number, was printed. Three weeks later on October 22nd the paper ran a short piece stating *"The quota for Queens County under the last call is full, consequently those who were drafted a few weeks since will not be called upon to do duty but will be discharged."*

Drafts continued through the end of 1864, and by early 1865 with the war dragging on, recruits were hard to come by. On March 11, 1865 *"The Editor notes that 30 or 40 of those drawn for the draft last month will have to provide their own substitutes or go to the front."*

And then the war was over and plans were begun to welcome home the warriors and honor those who had died.

July 29, 1865: *"The Soldiers Monument Association proposes holding a meeting in College Point next week in order to bring the matter before the people of that section of the town. Quite a number of soldiers from that locality have fallen in the war."*

A year went by and on June 6, 1866 another article appeared.

June 2, 1866: *Soldiers Monument-Names of Fallen Soldiers. To the Editors of the Journal. Dear Sir: The contract for the erection of a Soldier's Monument is signed (*with R. E. Launitz & Co. of New York*) and the work will be commenced within a week. In response to the request published some months ago, the following list was received from College Point. Will some of your readers living in that section be good enough to fill the vacancy in the first name of Mr. Richter and also note any errors or omission in the list and give us the full first names, as far as possible? I subjoin the list verbatim:*

*H. Appel**	*Robert Kans*	*Ch. Stader*
Jac. Buckley	*J. Keppler*	*J. Steinbrucker*
*J. Doherty**	*And. Reinhart*	*H. Sternberg**
*Ch. Erling**	*_____ Richter*	*Willys Tyrell*
J. Hefermehl	*Emil Schubert (doubtful)*	*Go. Vix**
Val. Helfrich	*David Schultz*	*Adam Wirth*

The letter did nothing to explain the meaning of the asterisk and two weeks later the amended list of College Point casualties appeared and added the following names written here as they appeared in the article signed by L. Bradford Prince:

Capt. Louis Brisky	*Thomas Conner*	*John Dogerty*
Jurgen Steinberg	*John Stonebanks*	

The creator of the list was correct to express doubts in the matter of Emil Schubert as he lived to apply for a pension from his home in the District of Columbia. Nevertheless his name is on the monument.

Richter's first name was Franz and at least five soldiers who lost their lives while serving, or shortly after the war, are not included on the 32-foot high, Quincy Granite, monument. They are: Patrick Maher, George McDonald, Thomas Skinnon, Leopold Wenzler, and Frederick Werner.

Flushing Monument Photo Courtesy Vincent F. Seyfried

Adam Wirth Post No. 451, GAR

MEMORIAL DAY EXERCISES. 1928

ORIGINAL ROSTER OF ADAM WIRTH POST, No. 451, G. A. R.

Name	Rank	Regiment
BENZ, LOUIS H.,	Drummer	U. S. M. Band
GRANT, FRED.,	Private	Co. K, 12th Reg. Maine Vol.
NIEMEYER, ANDREW,	Corp.	C. C. N. Y. Vol.
HARVEY, ANDREW,	Carpenter's Mate	Ship Black Hawk
MARX, CHARLES,	Private	Co. G, 15th Vol. N. Y.
HAUSER, JOHN,	Corporal	Co. B, 5th Artillery, N. Y.
COFFIN, LOWELL,	Private	Co. C, 46th Infantry, Mass.
STEINBECK, JULIUS,	Private	Co. I, 2nd Infantry, N. Y.
COLONS, JOHN,	Private	Co. K, 1st and 26th Artillery, Conn.
FOWLER, CORNELIUS,	Private	Co. F, 65th Vol. N. Y.
CORNELL, JAMES,	Sergeant	Co. 34 V. V. Battery
MONTANYE, WASHINGTON,	Corporal	Co. I, 13th N. Y. Heavy Art.
MILLER, FREDERICK,	Private	Co. H, 1st Del. Vol.
LARK, JOSEPH,	Musician	Co. D, 5th U. S. Art.
SCHNEEMAN, JOSEPH,	Corporal	Co. D, 20th N. Y. Vol.
HICKMAN, RICHARD T.,	Private	Co. C, 210th Penn. Vol.
STRAUBE, HENRY,	Private	Co. I, 20th N. Y. Vol.
JOCKERS, ADAM,	Corporal	Co. D, 20th N. Y. Vol.
RAUSSMULLER, CHARLES,	Capt.	Co. B, 54th N. Y. Vol.
MAHLENTHAL, EMANUEL,	Private	Co. C, 90th N. Y. Vol.
BAUMAN, FREDERICK,	2nd Lieut.	Co. K, 103rd N. Y. Vol.
DRAKERT, FRANK J.,	Corporal	Co. F, 6th N. Y. Vol.
FOWLER, GEORGE O.,	Private	Co. F, 37th N. Y. Vol.
GEAR, SAMUEL W.,	Private	Co. F, 1st Conn. Vol.
DENNO, TRUFFIL,	Private	Co. C, Vermont Inft.
WILKENS, FREDERICK,	Privte	Co. A, 29th N. Y. Vol.
GELBART, THEO. F.,	Private	Co. B, 20th N. Y. Vol.
McMANUS, ROBT.,	Private	1st Conn. Vol.
NAU, MICHAEL,	Private	Co. I, 2nd Artillery, N. Y.
DOCKENDORF, JOSEPH,	Private	Co. C, 46th Vol. N. Y.
STARKINS, JOHN H.,	1st Sergeant	Co. L, 2nd Artillery, N. Y.
HOENIG, WM.,	Corporal	Co. C, 133rd N. Y. Vol.
WINKLER, JOHN L.,	Private	Co. B, 52nd Vol. N. Y.
BUSER, CHARLES,	1st Sergeant	Co. B, 15th Artillery, N. Y.
DIETRICH, GEORGE,	Private	Co. I, 32nd Infantry N. Y.
LUTTERS, ERNEST,	Private	Co. F, 131st Infantry N. Y.
BERTSCHINGER, GUSTAV, G. O.		No. 94 War Dept.
LUDWIG, WILLIAM,	Corporal	Co. L, 2nd Infantry N. Y.
ACKERKNECHT, FREDERICK,	Private	Co. K, 59th Vol. N. Y.
MOTZ, PHILIP,	Bugler	Co. D, 1st U. S. Artillery
SUTOROIOUS, JACOB,	Corporal	Co. L, 2nd Artillery N. Y.
EMMERICH, JOHN,	Landsman	U. S. Navy
ENGELHARDT, CHARLES R.,	Private	Co. A, 14th Vol. Conn.
LUDWIG, CARL,		Co. L, 2nd Artillery N. Y.
WURTZ, HENRY,	Private	Co. 3, N. Y. Ind. Battery
HOELLE, JOHN,	Sergeant	Co. C, 11th Vol. Conn.
DUER, FRANK,	Sergeant	Co. B, 8th Vol. Infantry N. Y.
ROONEY, THOMAS,	Corp.	Co. C, 74th Vol. N. Y.
SNYDER, EDWIN A.,	Musician	Co. B, 2nd Vol. Penn.
SCHUMACHER, HENRY,	Private	Co. I, 2nd Vol. N. Y.
JOHNSTON, DANIEL L.,	Private	Co. L, 2nd Artillery N. Y.
LINDECKER, WILLIAM,	Private	Co. K, 5th Vol. Infantry, Mich.
LANE, CHARLES,	Seaman	North Carolina, U. S. Navy
LARK, PETER,	Private	Co. A, Battery A, U. S. Engineers
FARREL, HENRY,	Private	Co. 20, Ohio Battalion
BERNDT, WILLIAM,	Private	Co. 34, 2nd Battery N. Y.
PLUEMACHER, CHARLES F.,	Private	Co. I, 20th N. Y. Vol.
DOCKENDORF, F. W.,	Private	Co. I, 20th N Y. Vol.
ARNOLD, WILLIAM,	Seaman	U. S. Navy
HOBSON, JOSH C.,	Private	Co. C, New Jersey Vol.
MAY, WILLIAM,	Sergeant	Co. C, 68th N. Y. Vol.
WIRTH, ADAM,	Sergeant	Co. L, 2nd Battery, N. Y.

Adam Wirth Post No. 451, GAR

Chartered on February 21, 1884, the Adam Wirth Post No. 451 was one of over 7000 Posts created in the decades following the Civil War.

In the words of President Lincoln, they were established to care for *"those who have borne the burden, his widow and orphans"*, and by 1890 there were over 400,000 Grand Army of the Republic members including five presidents, Grant, Hayes, Garfield, Harrison and McKinley.

As a matter of history the GAR came about very quickly following the war when groups of men banded together for fellowship. Membership was limited to those who had served between April 12, 1861 and April 9, 1865, had been honorably discharged, and had not taken up arms against the United States since the end of the war.

Official organization of Posts began in earnest as early as 1866 and most had a number and name. The person for whom the Post was named had to be deceased, as was Adam Wirth, the College Point soldier who died on September 25, 1862 as a result of wounds suffered at the Second Battle of Bull Run on August 30, 1862.

Early on, candidates for membership were recommended by a current member and were voted upon using the Masonic system of casting black or white balls. More than one black ball was required for a candidate to be rejected and if that occurred, the rejection was reported to what was called the Department, consisting of all of the Posts within a state. Additionally the rejections were maintained at the local Post written, as it were, in a "Black Book".

This system was not liked very much resulting in a decline in membership. The system was abandoned and membership increased dramatically.

The GAR was first and foremost a veteran's organization that met regularly and encouraged its members to share memories, sing old songs and tell tales of wartime experiences from bygone days, but the GAR had a more serious role as well in giving support to widows and those orphaned by the war, by paying housing, medical, as well as other numerous other reasonable and expected expenses.

The GAR also took care of its aging and indigent veterans through the establishment of Soldier's Homes in many states, where a number of College Point veterans spent time, and at which a number lived out their final days.

Through GAR efforts, memorials and monuments, statues and other reminders were erected throughout the United States in honor of the soldiers' sacrifices. Cannons were placed in front of courthouses and in public parks. Museums, local historical societies, and veteran's organizations were presented with a variety of artifacts; flags and other war-related ephemera.

Toward the end of the 19th century and into the 20th, the organization had gained considerable political clout, so much so that candidates for office regularly sought out their support. It was commonly held that it was impossible to be nominated on the Republican ticket without the endorsement of the GAR voting block.

Perhaps the most lasting legacy of the GAR is the annual celebration of Memorial Day, traditionally held on May 30th and originally called Decoration Day. A few years following war's end in 1868, General John Logan, Commander in Chief of the GAR, asked that on May 30th of that year, members of all Posts decorate the graves of their fallen comrades with flowers. The practice caught on very quickly and continues to the present day in communities across the country honoring the dead, not only from the Civil War, but also from all wars in which the United States has taken part.

In almost every one of the pension records reviewed for this book there were numerous letters and affidavits prepared by GAR members in support of their comrades' applications for invalid or, in many cases, widow's benefits. The affidavits attested to many things such as a veteran's health prior to and after the war, marriage validity and faithfulness, children's' names and a whole host of replies to questions posed by the Pension Board.

Many times the letters helped to bring about a positive result and the awarding of benefits. At other times, benefits were refused based on technicalities about which the petitioning woman could do nothing. A number of women who believed themselves to be widows were refused benefits due to their husbands having contracted previous marriages that had not been ended by either death or divorce.

Bureaucracy reigned then as it does now in our current times, but happily in these pages, there are photographs of a number of the men taken both before and after the war, in youth and in old age, in uniform and in dress clothes.

In 1896, members of Adam Wirth Post No. 451, GAR posed for professional photographer Jacob Wieners, Jr., son of veteran Jacob F. Wieners. They appear in their double-breasted, dark blue coats with bronze buttons wearing a wide-brimmed, black slouch hat, and on the brim rests a gold wreath GAR insignia and cord.

The badge pinned near the left breast pocket shows an eagle and below it hangs a small representation of a flag, and below it, a five-point star that shows a soldier and sailor clasping hands in front of a figure of Liberty.

They called each other *"Comrade"*, while others, for reasons unexplained, derisively called them *"bronze button heroes"*, whatever that meant.

There were sixty-two original members of Post 451 in 1884. Reproduced in these pages is that original roster as prepared for Memorial Day Exercises in 1928. Most certainly there had to have been additional members in the intervening years, but no records of their names are currently known to exist.

A newspaper article dated May 12, 1928, just two weeks prior to the publication of the original membership list, indicated that veteran Frederick Wilkens had died in the morning of that day. The article identified him as being the last member of the Post to pass away. In actuality, two other members, Tuffeil Denno and Joseph Roessel, lived longer. Denno lived on another ten months and died in Woodside on March 27, 1929. Roessel died in late December 1935 and was truly the last surviving member.

Following those deaths, the Post was officially disbanded and many of the records and artifacts passed into the hands of members of the Oscar Amman Post No. 853 of the American Legion in College Point, but another organization called the Sons of Union Veterans of the Civil War, continued to pass on the heritage of the men who had served, their fathers.

In College Point, on Saturday evening, December 10, 1887, the David Schultz Post #29 of the Sons Union Veterans, held its First Grand Ball at Frank Duer's Town Hall. Duer was himself a veteran, and a copy of the program from that event, provided by Bob Friedrich, is reproduced in these pages, and points to it as having been a grand and glorious affair.

Over the course of the evening there was music played by Boller's Orchestra with the dances, including waltzes, schottisches and quadrilles, being dedicated to a host of Post leaders and to visiting Posts as well. And there was what had to be a magnificent supper. College Point was, after all, a town with numerous German hotels and restaurants, Duer's being one of them.

David Schultz, for whom the Post was named, was a member of the 79th New York Infantry, called the *Highlanders*. He took part in the Battle of Knoxville on November 29, 1863, and lost his life while trying to capture a rebel flag.

During a festive occasion in College Point probably around 1889, the Sons of Union Veterans held its second annual picnic and summernight festival at Charles Freygang's Bay View Park, another of College Point's renowned facilities also owned by another veteran.

According to an undated newspaper article *"The park presented a brilliant appearance. It was literally filled with Grand Army men and many war reminiscences were recalled. An interesting feature of the affair was the presentation of an American flag, the donor being Mrs. Schultz, the mother of the young soldier after whom the post is named. The veterans formed a circle in the hall and Mrs. Schultz, accompanied by her son-in-law, Mr. James Hallahan, stepped forward and spoke in a very feeling manner and said it was her pleasing duty to present the post with a slight token of her esteem and appreciation. Mrs. Schultz then handed the American flag to the Commander of David Schultz Post, Mr. Jacob F. Wieners, Jr. who in return and in behalf of the post presented Mrs. Schultz with a fine crayon of her son, elaborately framed and which was taken from a small tintype by Photographer, Jacob F. Wieners. Tears filler her eyes when Mrs. Schultz was presented with this munificent gift."*

In this same newspaper article there appears the only known list of members of the organization, but it very likely an incomplete list. Two men whose names are included are C, for Charles, Hemminger, and F, for Fred, Thurston. From all that could be found, these two individuals apparently moved to College Point as adults. Their fathers, Charles Hemminger, Sr., and Thomas Thurston, did serve, and their stories are told in the Biographies section of the book. Their names, however, do not appear in the Census and Service Data section, as they were not from College Point, nor did they ever live in the town following the war.

While Post No. 29 no longer exists, the Sons of Union Veteran's Organization, Oliver Tilden Camp, No. 26, of New York City, continues to this very day.

There were other GAR auxiliary organizations including the Women's Relief Corps, started in 1883, the Ladies of the Grand Army of the Republic begun in 1896 and the Daughters of Union Veterans of the Civil War who work to establish and improve veterans' facilities.

Adam Wirth Photo
Courtesy of the Poppenhusen Institute

Ink drawing of Jacob Roemer
From the author's collection

Placard calling for volunteers that appeared in the *Flushing Journal*
shortly after the outbreak of the Civil War
Vincent F. Seyfried Collection

The Units in Which They Served

Badly damaged wetplate of Hamilton's Light Artillery, Company L, 2nd New York Heavy Artillery. This is the only known photo of this unit shown here drawn up in a battle line near Washington, DC.

Photo courtesy of the National Archives

The Units in Which They Served

At the beginning of the war, for obvious reasons, the largest majority of College Point men enlisted in units that were soliciting volunteers, consisting mostly of German immigrants, some who had already been in the military in Germany. That they would come to America, many after 1860, and volunteer for service in a war to which they had little patriotic connection, says a great deal about the times in which they lived, and possibly about the individuals themselves.

Instinctively, perhaps, these men were aware of the basic or essential inherent value of human life. If they were cognizant of the broader issues of what it meant to be the *"United States of America"*, is not known, nevertheless they did volunteer.

What is obvious is that a number of units attracted the largest percentage of men and, for whatever reasons, other units held sway.

Their service represented every branch possible, including the infantry, from many states, the artillery, heavy and light, from many states, and in United States Regiments as well. They joined Engineer and Cavalry Regiments, the Marine Band, the Navy, Militia and/or National Guard units.

Of all the units in the list that follows, the one that attracted the most volunteers was the 34th Regiment of New York Light Artillery. In all 42 men from College Point served with Jacob Roemer in a unit with roots rich in American military history.

According to Roemer in his book **The Flushing Battery,** *"The "Flushing Guard", the earliest uniformed military organization in Flushing, was mustered into the New York State Militia, November 1, 1839, as Light Artillery. In February 1843, the company was changed from infantry to artillery and in 1845 it was again changed to Light Horse Artillery, Lieutenant Charles A. Hamilton commanding."*

Roemer enlisted in the unit in 1845 and by 1851 had attained the rank of First Sergeant. In 1859 he was promoted to First Lieutenant.

"The Battery at the time was commanded by Captain Thomas L. Robinson and was attached to the 15th Regiment of New York State Militia" in which it remained until 1861 and the outbreak of hostilities. The unit was mustered into service for three years and assigned to the 2nd New York Heavy Artillery Company L. It left Flushing on December 2, 1861 under command of Captain Robinson, and served initially in the Washington, DC area.

On November 19, 1863, the Battery, which had served detached from the regiment since March 1862 as light artillery, was permanently detached and officially designated the 34th Regiment of New York Light Artillery.

The regiment saw service in major battles throughout the conflict among them Second Bull Run, Antietam, Fredericksburg, Vicksburg, the Siege of Knoxville, the Wilderness and the Siege of Petersburg.

On May 23, 1862 Captain Thomas L. Robinson was discharged from the service and Roemer, promoted to Captain on the same day, took formal charge of the unit.

"In consequence of the dismissal of Captain Robinson, Roemer writes, *some twenty-seven men who were in sympathy with him deserted the Battery. Before Captain Robinson left the Battery he had given these men to understand that they had a right to leave because they had enlisted to serve under him and not under his successor. They were not well posted in Army Regulations. Five of the poor fellows were caught, brought back, court-martialed and sentenced to the Rip Raps."*

Roemer believed the men were not to blame for their actions and placed it squarely on the head of Robinson and as a result they avoided major punishment as a result of having deserted. Three of those twenty-seven men, Ludwig Becker, John P. Heilmann and John Steinbecker were from College Point. Becker and Steinbecker failed to return, but Heilmann took advantage of the offer. Still, other members of this unit deserted at different times throughout the war.

The battery continued in service until June 21, 1865 and was honorably discharged at Hart's Island in New York Harbor. Two of its members, Carl Ludwig and John Starkins, were awarded the Congressional Medal of Honor. The actions of a third member, James C. Cornell, were recognized as deserving of the honor, but the Medal was never awarded.

The second unit to attract a large number of volunteers from College Point never saw action in any theater of the war, and existed only for thirty days. Nevertheless one of its members, John Stonebanks, did lose his life.

The 15th Regiment of New York State Militia was organized on June 6, 1864 to garrison Fort Richmond on the East Coast of Staten Island in New York Harbor. Today Fort Richmond, incorporated into what is now Fort Wadsworth, is found on the Staten Island side of the Verrezano Narrows Bridge.

In the early part of the war what was the "old" Fort Richmond, was rebuilt as a five-foot thick, three-tiered battlement with gun and rifle ports. It was to this "new" Fort Richmond that the 15th was detailed for protective purposes, and the engineer, upon whose 1840 recommendation the fort was refitted, was Captain Robert E. Lee.

It appears that members of this unit were not eligible to apply for pension benefits, but census and other records tell a small portion of their lives and times. The unit was mustered out on July 7, 1864.

Seventeen men from College Point enlisted in the 20th Regiment of New York Infantry, most in Company I, organized in Brooklyn, Williamsburgh, and College Point. Colonel Max Weber was the commanding officer.

The unit was organized on May 1, 1861 and was known as the *United Turner Rifles*, the Turners being a German Fraternal Organization founded in Berlin in 1811 to promote patriotism and nationalism through gymnastics. It was composed of volunteers from members of the Turner Societies in New York City and the surrounding area and left for Fortress Monroe in Virginia the following June 13th.

The 20th was present at the Battles of New Market, Savage Station, Chancellorsville and Fredericksburg in Virginia, and Antietam in Maryland.

In the last days of April 1863, just before the Battle of Chancellorsville, about 200 members of the unit laid down their arms in the belief that the terms of their service had expired. They were subject to Court Martial, found guilty, and dishonorably discharged from the service. In August a pardon was granted through the intervention of the Turner Societies and President Lincoln.

A fuller description of this event, called a mutiny, appears in the biography of Frederick Dockendorf elsewhere in this book. For more details the link that follows will be very helpful.
http://gkkapp.home.infi.net/20NYSV.htm

Eleven College Pointers enlisted for two years in the 29th New York Infantry commanded by Colonel Adolph Von Steinwehr, it being another of the German regiment, this one called the *First German Infantry*.

The regiment left New York on June 21, 1861 for Washington, DC, and fought at both Battles of Bull Run in 1861 and 1862, and at Chancellorsville and Gettysburg as well, in 1863.

Henry Apel, John Steinbrucker and George Vix served in this unit and all lost their lives although Apel was a member of the 7th New York Infantry at the time of his death as was Steinbrucker. The 29th New York was mustered out on June 20, 1863.

Eleven men served in various capacities in the United States Navy, but it appears none applied for pension benefits. As a result, not a great deal is known about most of these individuals.

Finally, nine men served in the 58th New York Infantry, known also as the *Morgan Rifles*. It took part in battles at Cross Keys, Second Bull Run and Chancellorsville in Virginia and at Gettysburg, Pennsylvania.

The Units in Which They Served

Among its members, College Point men Valentine Helfreich and Franz Richter, would die of disease while in service.

As has already been noted, the remainder of the men served in a large number of units and it is not the intention of this book to retell the stories of those units, many of which have been better told in other books.

That which follows is an overview look at the service data for all of the men who have been identified to date, with the information coming, for the most part, from the Adjutant General's Report published between 1894 and 1906. Most men or their widows filed for pension benefits and an X indicates those who did. Additionally, for those who might wish pursue any individual for genealogical purposes, wherever possible I have referenced census data as available.

Finally, an asterisk * appears in front of the names of those individuals who moved to College Point after the war or those who were original members of the Adam Wirth Post No. 451, GAR.

To facilitate the work of researchers in the future, there is an index of the unit-by-unit breakdown, as comprehensive as possible to date, in the final pages of this book.

✶PROGRAMME✶

PART I.

1. Overture,   Boller's Orchestra
2. Grand Entree, *David Schultz Post S. O. V.*   Boller
3. Lanciers,—*Marquis*,   To the Commander-in-Chief
4. Waltz,—*Little Boy Blue*,   Adam Wirth Post, G. A. R.
5. Quadrille,—*Festival*,   Cum on Kate
6. Schottische,—*Souvenier*,   Jas. A. Garfield Post No. 27
7. Quadrille Waltz,—*Winchester*,   To our Commander
8. Polka,—*My Favorite*,   Kneisly 'round the Horn
9. Lanciers,—*Concentration*,   Gen. Thomas Post No. 16
10. Waltz,—*Old Factory Bell*,   To the Surgeon General
11. Glide Lanciers,—*Plymouth*   To our Quartermaster
12. Schottische,—*Homestead*,   To the Depart. Commander
13. Quadrille,—*Village Queen*,   To our Surgeon
14. Waltz,—*Joys of Youth*,   To our Sen. Vice Commander
15. Quadrille—March,   Mike's Water Melon Party

SUPPER.

PART II.

1. Re-Entree,   *To Our Guests*,   Boller
2. Lanciers,—*Brigadier*,   To R. T. Lincoln Post No. 7
3. Waltz,—*Life's Story*,   If I live I go
4. Quadrille Waltz—*Euclid*,   To our Jun. Vice Commander
5. Schottische,—*Magnolia*,   To Huntsman Post. G. A. R.
6. Lanciers,—*Ruddygore*,   To our Chaplain
7. Polka,—*O' Kolona*,   Wird ya Flat
8. Quadrille,—*Acme*,   To Abel Smith Post No. 5
9. Waltz,—*Ma Belle*,   To our Photographer
10. Lanciers,—*Delegation*,   To our Officer of the Day
11. Schottische,—*Grace Irene*,   Thieves in the Yard
12. Caledonians,—*Scotch Gems*,   To the Tammanys
13. Galopp,—*Adjudants*,   To our Adjutant
14. Lanciers,—*Pyramid*,   To our Officer of the Guard
15. Waltz,—*Happy Thoughts*,   Katzenjammer

BON JOUR.

First ✦ Grand ✦ Ball
— OF —
David Schultz Post
No. 29, SONS OF VETERANS,
— AT —
Frank Duer's Turn Hall,
— ON —
Saturday Evening, December 10th, 1887.

MUSIC BY PROFESSOR CHARLES BOLLER.

OFFICERS:

OSCAR WEISS, Commander,
H Dillmann, Sen Vice-Com.,   Jacob Fink, Chaplain,
John Miller, Jun. Vice-Com.,   C. Wurtz, Officer of the Guard
G. Wieners, Officer of the Day;   William Johann, Adjutant;
George Duer, Quartermaster,   J. F Wieners Jr, Inside Sentinel
Louis Marx, Surgeon,   Adam Nau, Outside Sentinel.

QUEENS COUNTY FREIE PRESSE PRINT.

FLOOR MANAGER:
OSCAR WEISS.

ASSISTANT FLOOR MANAGERS:
H. DILLMANN,   **JOHN MILLER.**

FLOOR COMMITTEE:
J. F. WIENERS, Jr.,   M. ENGELHARDT,
H. L. STRAUBE, Jr.,   G. VOLLBRACHT,
G. A. S. WIENERS,   GEORGE DUER.

RECEPTION COMMITTEE:
WM. H. JOHANN, Chairman,

Ferd. Gentner,	Peter Johann,
Charles Weiss, Jr.,	Paul Steinbeck,
Jacob Fink,	Ed. Straube,
Henry Fritz,	John Rooney,
Wm. Satorious.	Louis Marx,
Adam Nau.	Chas. Wurtz,
Julius Heilmann,	J. Ackerknecht.

Courtesy of Robert C. Friedrich Collection

Census and Service Data

Name	Unit	Rank	Date	Age	Event	Pension
1. *Ackerknecht, Frederick	Co. K, 58th NY	Pvt.	10/19/61 10/01/65- 02/21/84 1880	22	Enlisted in New York City Discharged at Nashville, TN Original Roster of Adam Wirth Post No. 451, GAR College Point, NY Census, ED 264, Page 238D	X
2. Apel, Conrad	Co. E, 29th NY	Pvt.	1860 05/15/61 06/04/61 08/30/62 06/20/63	19	Flushing, NY Census, Page 741 Enlisted in New York City Enlisted in Unit Wounded Discharged	X
3. Apel, Henry	Co. E, 29th NY Co. E, 7th NY	Pvt. Pvt.	1860 05/15/61 06/04/61 08/23/62 06/20/63 07/29/64 04/02/65 04/04/65 06/02/66 1870 1882	42 44	Flushing, NY Census, Page 741 Enlisted in New York City Enlisted in Unit *Flushing Journal*/ List of Volunteers Discharged at New York City Enlisted in Unit Wounded Died of Wounds *Flushing Journal*/ List of Casualties Flushing, NY Census, Page 245, widow Mary and children *History of Queens County*	X
4. *Arnold, William	U.S. Navy	Seaman	08/18/62 07/18/64 02/21/84	36	South Atlantic Squadron Discharged Original Roster of Adam Wirth Post No. 451, GAR	

Census and Service Data

5. *Baumann, Frederick
   Co. K, 103rd NY — Sgt. — 24 — X
   - 11/11/61 — Enlisted in Unit
   - 06/08/63 — Promoted to 2nd Lieutenant
   - 12/03/64 — Discharged
   - 1880 — Long Island City Census, Page 120D
   - 02/21/84 — Original Roster of Adam Wirth Post No. 451, GAR

6. Baumann, John
   Co. L, 2nd NYHA — Pvt. — 20 — X
   34th NYLA
   - 10/19/61 — Enlisted in Flushing, NY
   - 10/23/61 — Enlisted in Unit
   - 11/19/63 — Unit Designation Changed
   - 06/21/65 — Discharged at Hart's Island, NY Harbor, NY
   - 1860 — Flushing, NY Census, Page 726
   - 1870 — Flushing, NY Census, Page 224
   - 1880 — College Point, NY Census, ED 267, Page 295B

7. Baumeister, Z
   79th NY
   - 08/23/62 — Flushing Journal List of Volunteers

8. Beardslee, Frederick E.
   U.S. Signal Corps — 2nd Lieut. — X
   - 1860 — Flushing, NY Census, Page 699
   - 1870 — Flushing, NY Census, Page 221
   - 1882 — History of Queens County

9. Becker, Ludwig
   Co. L, 2nd NYHA — Pvt. — 43
   34th NYLA
   - 09/07/61 — Enlisted in Flushing, NY
   - 10/01/61 — Enlisted in Unit
   - 06/04/62 — Deserted from Camp Barry, DC
   - 08/23/62 — Flushing Journal List of Volunteers
   - 11/19/63 — Unit Designation Changed

10. Behring, Friedrich Co. C, 58th NY	Pvt.	42	1860 10/04/61 08/23/62 05/02/63 10/22/64	Flushing, NY Census, Page 719 listed as *Behringer* Enlisted in New York City *Flushing Journal* List of Volunteers Prisoner of War after Chancellorsville Discharged at Stevenson, AL
11. *Benz, Louis			02/21/84	U.S. Marine Band Original Roster of Adam Wirth Post No. 451, GAR
12. Beresheim, Jacob 15th NYSM	Pvt.	41	1860 11/30/63 06/06/64 1870 1880 1882	Flushing, NY Census, Page 737 Provost Marshall's List 30-day enlistment Flushing, NY Census, Page 220, spelled *Bersheimer* College Point, NY Census, ED 267, Page 297B widow and family appear *History of Queens County*
13. *Berndt, William Co. L, 2nd NYHA 34th NYLA	Pvt.	22	09/09/61 11/19/63 09/30/64 02/21/84	Enlisted in Flushing, NY Unit Designation Changed Reported KIA at Pegram Farm, VA – Not true X Original Roster of Adam Wirth Post No. 451, GAR
14. *Bertschlinger, Gustav			1880 02/21/84	College Point, NY Census, ED 267, Page 309B Original Roster of Adam Wirth Post No. 451, GAR
15. Beyerly, Peter 15th NYSM	Pvt.	38	1860 11/30/63 06/06/64 1880	Flushing, NY Census, Page 741 Provost Marshall's List 30-day enlistment College Point, NY Census, ED 267, Page 298C

Census and Service Data   33

# / Name / Unit	Dates	Rank	Age	Notes	
16. Bisky, Louis Co. C, 45th NY	1860 09/01/61 11/04/61 03/11/62 01/12/63 05/02/63 06/23/66	Lt. 2nd	43	New York City Census, 14th Ward, Division 3, Page 691 Enlisted in New York City Commissioned Promoted to Lieutenant, 1st Class Promoted to Full Captain Died of wounds at Chancellorsville *Flushing Journal* List of Casualties	X
17. Bockler, Christolomus Co. C, Morgan Rifles Co. C, 58th NY	10/04/61 11/23/61 10/22/64 08/23/62 1880	Pvt.	44	Enlisted in New York City Transferred to Unit Disability discharge, Nashville, TN *Flushing Journal* List of Volunteers College Point, NY Census, ED 267, Page 313B	X
18. Bracken, John Co. L, 2nd NYHA 34th NYLA	10/01/61 08/23/62 11/19/63 12/31/64	Pvt.	22	Enlisted in New York City *Flushing Journal* List of Volunteers, spelled *Paschen* Unit Designation Changed Reported Deserted, but he applied for a pension	X
19. Brill, Christian, Jr. Co. L, 2nd NYHA 34th NYLA	09/07/61 10/01/61 08/23/62 11/19/63 10/30/63 12/11/64 04/03/65	Pvt.	18	Enlisted in Flushing, NY Enlisted in Unit *Flushing Journal* List of Volunteers Unit Designation Changed Prisoner of War at Andersonville, GA Paroled at Charleston, SC Discharged at New York, NY	
20. Brill, Christian, Sr. Co. L, 2nd NYHA 34th NYLA	1860 09/01/61 11/19/63 09/30/64	Pvt.	22	Flushing, NY Census, Page 701 Enlisted in Flushing, NY Unit Designation Changed Discharged at Hart's Island, NY Harbor, NY	X

21. Briody, Richard Co. K, 79th NY	05/13/61 05/28/61 07/21/61 05/24/62 08/23/62	Pvt.	20	Enlisted in New York City Enlisted in Unit Prisoner of War Discharged at Washington, DC *Flushing Journal* List of Volunteers	x
22. Broid, J. 79th NY	08/23/62			*Flushing Journal* List of Volunteers	
23. Buckley, John U.S. Navy	1860 11/05/63 06/23/66			Flushing, NY Census, Pages 701 and 744 Enlisted Died at Charleston Harbor *Flushing Journal* List of Casualties	
24. Buhl, Peter 15th NYSM	1860 11/06/61 06/06/64 1870	Pvt.	47	Flushing, NY Census, Page 717 spelled *Puhl* Name mentioned in *Flushing Journal* article 30-day enlistment Flushing, NY Census, Page 212	
25. *Buser, Charles Co. B, 15th NYHA	09/01/61 02/03/64 08/14/65 08/22/65 02/21/84	Pvt.	19	Enlisted in Philadelphia, PA Promoted to Full Sergeant Promoted to Lieutenant, 2nd Class Discharged at Washington, DC Original Roster of Adam Wirth Post No. 451, GAR	x
26. *Coffin, Lowell Co. C, 46th MA	09/24/62 09/25/62 07/29/63 02/21/84	Pvt.	19	Enlisted Enlisted in Unit at Camp Banks, MA Discharged in Hampden Park, Springfield, MA Original Roster of Adam Wirth Post No. 451, GAR	

Census and Service Data

#	Name / Unit	Date	Rank	Age	Notes	X
27.	*Colvin, John Co. K, 1st CTHA	1850 05/23/61 07/28/65 02/21/84	Pvt.	21	New York City Census, Page 273 Enlisted in East Haddam, CT Discharged Original Roster of Adam Wirth Post No. 451, GAR Flushing, NY Census, Page 287C	X
28.	Conners, Thomas Co. K, 61st NY	1860 09/08/62 07/02/63 06/23/66	Pvt.	22	Flushing, NY Census, Page 696 Enlisted in New York City Died of wounds at Gettysburg *Flushing Journal* List of Casualties	X
29.	Cooper, William Co. L, 2nd NYHA	08/28/61 03/04/62 08/23/62 10/08/62 1870 1880	Sgt. 1st	30	Enlisted In Flushing, NY Promoted to Lieutenant, 2nd Class *Flushing Journal* List of Volunteers Discharged by Surgeon's Certificate # 284 Flushing, NY Census, Page 237 College Point, NY Census, ED 267, Page 315A	X
30.	Cordier, Daniel 15th NYSM	1850 1860 11/30/63 06/06/64	Pvt.	34	New York City Census, 16th Ward, Page 191 Flushing, NY Census, Page 720 Provost Marshall's List 30-day enlistment	
31.	*Cornell, James C. Co. L, 2nd NYHA 34th NYLA	1860 08/06/61 08/30/62 11/19/63 04/30/64 01/01/65 06/21/65 02/21/84	Pvt.	18	Flushing, NY Census, Page 579 Enlisted in Flushing, NY Wounded in Action Unit Designation Changed Promoted to Full Corporal Promoted to Full Sergeant Discharged at Hart's Island, NY Harbor, NY Original Roster of Adam Wirth Post No. 451, GAR	X

32. *Denno, Tuffeil Co. C, 9th VT	08/22/64 06/13/65 02/21/84	Pvt.		Enlisted in Orwell, VT Discharged X Original Roster of Adam Wirth Post No. 451, GAR
33. *Dietrich, George Co. I, 82nd NY	09/01/62 02/13/63 02/21/84	Pvt.	19	Enlisted in New York City Discharged from Convalescent Camp, Alexandria, VA X Original Roster of Adam Wirth Post No. 451, GAR
34. Dillon, Michael Co. E, 10th NY	10/04/61 08/23/62 04/26/63 04/27/63	Pvt.	19	Enlisted in New York City *Flushing Journal* List of Volunteers Transferred Deserted at Falmouth, VA
35. *Dillman, Henry 13th NYNG	1860 06/96/63 11/30/63 1870 1880	Cpl.	35	Flushing, NY Census, Page 715 Enlisted in Unit Provost Marshall's List Flushing, NY Census, Page 254 College Point, NY Census, ED 267, Page 306D Son John will be active in the Sons of Union Veterans
36. Dockendorf, Francis Co. H, 1st DE	1860 12/29/64 1870 1880	Pvt.	17	Flushing, NY Census, Page 720 Enlisted as Substitute for John Swain of Delaware Flushing, NY Census, Page 211 College Point, NY Census, ED 264, Page 242C

Census and Service Data

37. Dockendorf, Frederick Co. I, 20th NY	1860 06/01/61 08/23/62 06/01/63 1870 1880 02/21/84	Pvt.	24	Flushing, NY Census, Page 720 Enlisted in Williamsburg, NY *Flushing Journal* List of Volunteers Discharged at New York City Flushing, NY Census, Page 249 College Point, NY Census, ED 264, Page 241B Original Roster of Adam Wirth Post No. 451, GAR	X
38. Dockendorf, Joseph Co. G, 46th NY	1860 09/03/61 08/23/62 07/28/65 1880 02/21/84	Pvt.	18	Flushing, NY Census, Page 720 Enlisted in New York City, spelled *Doggendorf* *Flushing Journal* List of Volunteers Discharged at Delaney House, Washington, DC College Point, NY Census, ED 264, Page 241B Original Roster of Adam Wirth Post 451, GAR	X
39. Doherty, Bernard Co. B, 1st NY Cavalry	1860 09/19/61 08/23/62 06/29/63 07/03/64 10/22/64 03/01/65 06/27/65	Pvt.	20	Flushing, NY Census, Page 701 Enlisted in New York City *Flushing Journal* List of Volunteers Promoted to Full Corporal Prisoner of War Promoted to Sergeant Paroled Discharged at Alexandria, VA	
40. Dougherty, John Co. F, 63rd NY	02/20/62 04/03/62 08/23/62 09/17/62 06/23/66	Pvt.	23	Enlisted in New York City Enlisted in Unit *Flushing Journal* List of Volunteers Died of wounds at Battle of Antietam in Maryland *Flushing Journal* List of Casualties	X

#	Name / Unit	Dates	Rank	Age	Notes	X
41.	*Drakert, Francis J. Co. F, 6th NY	04/25/61 05/25/61 06/25/63 1880 02/21/84	Pvt.	19	Enlisted in New York City Enlisted in Unit Discharged in New York City College Point, NY Census, ED 267, Page 304D Original Roster of Adam Wirth Post No. 451, GAR	X
42.	Duer, Franz Co. B, 8th NY	04/23/61 06/08/62 08/23/62 09/13/62 10/15/62 04/23/63 1880 02/21/84	Pvt.	28	Enlisted in New York City Prisoner of War after Battles of Cross Keys in VA *Flushing Journal* List of Volunteers Paroled Returned to Unit Discharged College Point, NY Census, ED 267, Page 303B Original Roster of Adam Wirth Post No. 451, GAR	X
43.	Egan, Patrick Co. H, 10th NY	04/30/61 08/23/62 05/07/63	Pvt.	21	Enlisted in New York City *Flushing Journal* List of Volunteers Discharged at New York City	X
44.	Egan, Thomas Co. H, 10th NY	01/03/62 08/23/62 03/13/63	Pvt.	17	Enlisted in New York City *Flushing Journal* List of Volunteers Deserted	
45.	*Ehm, Jacob 15th NYSM	1860 11/30/63 06/06/64 1870 1880 1882	Pvt.	40	Flushing, NY Census, Page 733 Provost Marshall's List 30-day enlistment Flushing, NY Census, Page 230 College Point, NY Census, ED 267, Page 300D *History of Queens County* Son George will be active in the Sons of Union Veterans	

Census and Service Data

46. Emmerich, John	U.S. Navy		21	1860 08/23/62 08/24/63 11/30/63 08/24/64 1870 1880 02/21/84	Flushing, NY Census, Page 699 *Flushing Journal* List of Volunteers Landsman, Brooklyn Navy Yard Provost Marshall's List Discharged, Brooklyn Navy Yard Flushing, NY Census, Page 214 College Point, NY Census, ED 264, Page 238C Original Roster of Adam Wirth Post 451, GAR
47. *Englehardt, Charles R. Co. A, 14th CT		Pvt.	39	08/07/62 08/20/62 09/17/62 02/08/63 1870 1880 02/21/84	Enlisted in Bridgeport, CT Enlisted in Unit Wounded at Battle of Antietam in Maryland X Disability discharge Flushing, NY Census, Page 223 College Point, NY Census, ED 267, Page 299A Original Roster of Adam Wirth Post 451, GAR
48. Erling, Charles Co. D, 11th MA		Pvt.	36	08/13/63 05/05/64 06/23/66 1880	Enlisted Died of wounds at the Wilderness X *Flushing Journal* List of Casualties Widow and Family in New Brunswick, NJ Census, Page 125D
49. Fahner, Jacob Co. I, 20th NY		Pvt.	28	05/03/61 05/06/61 08/23/62 06/01/63 11/30/63 1870 1880	Enlisted in College Point, NY Enlisted in Unit *Flushing Journal* List of Volunteers Discharged at New York City Provost Marshall's List Flushing, NY Census, Page 230 College Point, NY Census, ED 267, Page 300C

#	Name / Unit	Dates	Rank	Age	Notes	
50.	*Farrell, Henry 20th OHLA	10/29/62 07/13/65 02/21/84	Pvt.	18	Enlisted Discharged at Camp Cleveland, OH Original Roster of Adam Wirth Post No. 451, GAR	
51.	Feuerbacher, August Co. C, 45th NY	1860 09/10/61 07/01/63 07/01/65 1870 1880	Pvt.	36	Flushing, NY Census, Page 706-spelled *Felebeazeher* Enlisted in New York City Wounded in action at Gettysburg Discharged at New York City Kings, NY Census, 19th Ward, Page 404 Son appears in Brooklyn, NY Census, Page 454A	X
52.	Fink, John Co. R, 15th NYSM	1860 06/06/64 1870 1880 1882	Cpl.	38	Flushing, NY Census, Page 719 30-day enlistment Flushing, NY Census, Page 218 College Point, NY Census, ED 267, Page 309B *History of Queens County*	
53.	Fisher, John Co. B, 15th NY Eng.	05/09/61 06/25/63	Pvt.	21	Enlisted In Unit Discharged Member of Adam Wirth Post 451, GAR	X
54.	Foster, Samuel, Jr. 34th NYLA 4th NYLA	1860 08/06/61 10/01/61 05/14/64 05/14/64 1880	Pvt.	18	Flushing, NY Census, Page 751 Enlisted in Flushing, NY Enlisted In Unit Promoted to Full Lieutenant Commissioned in unit Father in Brooklyn, NY Census, 17th Ward, Page 553 A	X

Census and Service Data 41

55. *Fowler, Cornelius		1850		Flushing, NY Census, Page 303
		1860		Flushing, NY Census, Page 655
Co. K, 61st NY	Sgt.	11/17/62	28	Enlisted in New York City
		05/01/63		Promoted to Full Sergeant
		06/19/64		Wounded at Petersburg, VA
		05/27/65		Disability discharge
		1870		Flushing, NY Census, Page 207
		1880		Flushing, NY Census, Page 275C
		02/21/84	x	Original Roster of Adam Wirth Post No. 451, GAR
56. *Fowler, George		05/05/61		Enlisted in Astoria, NY
		06/20/61		Enlisted in Unit
Co. F, 67th NY	Pvt.	02/04/63	19	Disability discharge, Convalescent Camp, VA
		02/21/84	x	Original Roster of Adam Wirth Post 451, GAR
57. Frank, Lewis		1860		Flushing, NY Census, Page 705
		09/05/61		Enlisted in Flushing, NY
	Pvt.	10/01/61	25	Enlisted in Unit
Co. L, 2nd NYHA		08/23/62		*Flushing Journal* List of Volunteers
		09/15/63		Transferred to Veteran's Reserve Corps
58. Franke, Anton				Enlisted
Co. C, Morgan Rifles		10/04/61		Transferred to Unit
Co. C, 58th NY	Pvt.	11/23/61	25	Provost Marshall's List
		11/30/63		Flushing, NY Census, Page 236
		1870		
		1880		College Point, NY Census, ED 267, Page 303B

59. Freund, Edward Co. I, 20th NY		Pvt.	23	05/06/61 05/20/61 08/23/62 05/04/63 05/15/63 06/01/63 1870 1880	Enlisted Enlisted in Unit *Flushing Journal* List of Volunteers Taken Prisoner of War at Chancellorsville Paroled Discharged at New York City X Flushing, NY Census, Page 216 College Point, NY Census, ED 264, Page 242C
60. Frey, Joseph Co. L, 2nd NYHA 34th NYLA		Pvt.	35	1860 09/06/61 10/01/61 11/19/63 06/21/65 1870	Flushing, NY Census, Page 733 Enlisted in Flushing, NY Enlisted in Unit Unit Designation Changed X Discharged at Hart's Island, NY Harbor, NY Flushing, NY Census, Page 253
61. Freygang, Charles Co. R, 15th NYSM		Pvt.	34	06/06/64 1870 1880 1882	30-day enlistment Flushing, NY Census, Page 262 College Point, NY Census, ED 264, Page 241B, *Julius* *History of Queens County*
62. Fritz, Louis Co. K, 6th NY		Pvt.	18	1860 06/05/61 10/09/61 08/23/62 06/25/63 1880 1882	Flushing, NY Census, Page 740 Enlisted at Staten Island, NY Wounded at the Battle of Santa Rosa Island *Flushing Journal* List of Volunteers Discharged at New York City X College Point, NY Census, ED 267, Page 311B *History of Queens County* Son Henry will be active in the Sons of Union Veterans

Census and Service Data

#	Name / Unit	Rank	Age	Dates	Notes	X
63.	Gardner, Rufus Co. D, 48th NY	Pvt.	19	1860 08/12/61 08/21/61 07/29/62 08/23/62 11/30/63	Flushing, NY Census, Page 723 Enlisted in Gardnertown, Orange County, NY Enlisted in Unit Disability discharge *Flushing Journal* List of Volunteers Provost Marshall's List	
64.	Gardner, Savillian Co. K, 48th NY	Cpl.	20	1860 08/12/61 08/16/61 08/23/62 08/01/63 09/16/64	Flushing, NY Census, Page 723 Enlisted in Newburgh, Orange County, NY Enlisted in Unit *Flushing Journal* List of Volunteers, named *William* Promoted to Full Sergeant Discharged	X
65.	*Gear, Samuel Co. F, 1st CT	Pvt.	22	04/18/61 04/22/61 07/31/61 02/21/84	Enlisted Mustered into Unit Discharged at New Haven, CT Original Roster of Adam Wirth Post No. 451, GAR	
66.	*Gelbart, Theodore Co. B, 20th NY	Pvt.	23	05/03/61 05/06/61 05/03/63 09/17/62 05/03/63 02/21/84	Enlisted in New York City Enlisted in Unit Discharged in Baltimore, MD Wounded at Battle of Antietam in Maryland Disability discharge Original Roster of Adam Wirth Post No. 451, GAR	X
67.	Gentner, Nicholas Co. R, 15th NYSM	Pvt.	43	1860 11/30/63 06/06/64 1870 1880	Flushing, NY Census, Page 742 Provost Marshall's List 30-day enlistment Flushing, NY Census, Page 252 College Point, NY Census, ED 267, Page 293A Son Ferdinand will be active in the Sons of Union Veterans	

#	Name / Unit	Dates	Rank	Age	Notes	X
68.	Glaeser, Charles Co. R, 15th NYSM	1860 11/30/63 06/06/64 1870 1882	Sgt.	35	Flushing, NY Census, Page 706 Provost Marshall's List 30-day enlistment Flushing, NY Census, Page 230 History of Queens County	
69.	*Grant, Fred Co. K, 13th ME	06/10/63 08/20/65 02/21/84	Pvt.	19	Enlisted in New Orleans, LA Discharged at Savannah, GA Original Roster of Adam Wirth Post No. 451, GAR	X
70.	Green, John 34th NYLA	09/02/61 08/23/62 03/12/64	Pvt.	22	Enlisted in Flushing, NY Flushing Journal List of Volunteers Deserted in Flushing, NY	
71.	*Griffin, Albert Co. L, 2nd NYHA 34th NYLA	10/09/61 11/19/63 01/01/65 06/21/65	Pvt.	18	Enlisted in Flushing, NY Unit Designation Changed Promoted to Full Sergeant Discharged at Hart's Island, NY Harbor, NY Member of Adam Wirth Post 451, GAR	X
72.	Gunzert, Theodore Co. D. Morgan Rifles Co. D. 58th NY	10/16/61 10/30/61 08/23/62 10/31/62 11/01/63 01/01/65 10/01/65 1870 1880	Pvt.	31	Enlisted in New York City Transferred to Unit Flushing Journal List of Volunteers Taken prisoner at Manassas Junction, VA Promoted to Full Quartermaster Sergeant Promoted to Full Lieutenant 1st Class Discharged at Nashville, TN Flushing, NY Census, Page 232 New York City Census, 8th Ward, 15th Dist. P. 305B	X

Census and Service Data

#	Name / Unit	Dates	Rank	Age	Notes	
73.	Harrington, Thomas Co. H, 25th NY & US Navy	05/13/61 06/14/61 07/10/63 1870 1880	Sgt.	23	Enlisted in New York City Enlisted in Unit Discharged at New York City Pepperell, MA Census, Page 274 Pepperell, MA Census, Page 386B	x
74.	*Harvey, Andrew U.S. Navy	1880 02/21/84			Served on the Ship *Blackhawk* Flushing, NY Census, Page 193A Original Roster of Adam Wirth Post No. 451, GAR	x
75.	Haubell, Charles Co. E, 32nd NY	1860 06/06/61 05/19/62 08/23/62 1880 1882	Pvt.	24	Flushing, NY Census, Page 727 Enlisted in New York City Hospitalized at White House, VA *Flushing Journal* List of Volunteers New York, NY Census, Page 251D *History of Queens County*	
76.	Haubell, Martin Co. C, 74th NY Co. M, 15th NYHA	1860 06/01/61 07/07/61 08/23/62 02/17/63 03/04/64 08/22/65 1880 1882	Pvt. Pvt.	18 21	Flushing, NY Census, Page 727 Enlisted in Flushing, NY Enlisted in Unit *Flushing Journal* List of Volunteers Disability discharge, Convalescent Camp, VA Enlisted in New York City Discharged at Washington, DC Flushing, NY Census, Page 88 *History of Queens County*	
77.	Hebel, Jacob Co. R, 15th NYSM	1860 06/06/64 1870 1880	Pvt.	53	Flushing, NY Census, Page 706 30-day enlistment Flushing, NY Census, Page 254 College Point, NY Census, ED 267, Page 307A	

#	Name	Rank	Age	Dates	Notes	X
78.	Hefermehl, John Co. D, 15th NYHA	Pvt.	17	1860 12/26/63 03/10/64 1870 1880	Flushing, NY Census, Page 734 Enlisted in New York City Died of disease at Fort Lyon, VA Flushing, NY Census, Page 230 Father in NYC Census, 8th Ward, Dist. 9, Page 245C	
79.	Heilmann, John, P. 34th NYLA	Pvt.	32	1860 09/17/61 10/16/61 06/29/62 1870 1880	Flushing, NY Census, Page 740 Enlisted in Flushing, NY Enlisted in Unit Deserted at Tennallytown, MD, probably not true Flushing, NY Census, Page 250 College Point, NY Census, ED 267, Page 308D Son Julius will be active in the Sons of Union Veterans	
80.	Helfreich, Valentine Co. C, Morgan Rifles Co. C, 58th NY	Pvt.	36	1860 10/04/61 11/23/61 10/19/62 06/23/66 1880	Flushing, NY Census, Page 722 Enlisted in New York City Transferred to Unit Died of disease at Sperryville, VA *Flushing Journal* List of Casualties Wife appears in Brooklyn, NY Census, Page 256A	X
81.	Herbig, Hieronymus Co. F, 31st NY	Pvt.	29	05/08/61 05/27/61 08/27/61 07/01/62 06/04/63 1880	Enlisted Enlisted in Unit Promoted to Corporal Promoted to Sergeant Discharged at New York City College Point, NY Census, ED 264, Page 237B	X

Census and Service Data 47

82. Heyne, Lewis			1860	New York City Census, 14th Ward, 2nd Dist. Pg. 434
			05/09/61	Enlisted in New York City
		Pvt.	06/17/61	Enlisted in Unit
			08/23/62	*Flushing Journal* List of Volunteers, listed as *Hoyne*
			06/25/63	Discharged
Co. F, 15th NY Eng.		36	1880	Philadelphia Census, 1st Ward, Dist. 21, Page 320C X
83. *Hibson, Joseph			08/21/61	Enlisted in Yorkville, NY
			01/31/63	Promoted to Full Private
		Pvt.	07/18/63	Wounded at Fort Wagner in South Carolina X
			1880	New York City Census, 21st Ward, District 10, Page 68A
Co. A, 48th NY		19		Member of Adam Wirth Post 451 GAR
84. *Hickman, Richard			09/10/64	Enlisted using an alias of *John T. Richey*
		Pvt.	05/30/65	Discharged in Washington, DC X
210th PA		20	02/21/84	Original Roster of Adam Wirth Post No. 451, GAR
85. *Hobson, Josh				
Co. C, NJ Volunteers			02/21/84	Original Roster of Adam Wirth Post No. 451, GAR
86. Hoelle, John			09/27/61	Enlisted
			10/25/61	Enlisted in Unit
			08/23/62	*Flushing Journal* List of Volunteers, written as *Herle*
		Cpl.	12/18/62	Promoted to Full Sergeant
			07/30/64	Wounded in action
			11/15/64	Discharged
			1880	College Point, NY Census, ED 267, Page 298C X
Co. C, 11th CT		23	02/21/84	Original Roster of Adam Wirth Post No. 451, GAR

87. Hoenig, William　　　Pvt.　19　Enlisted in New York City
　　Co. C, 133rd NY
　　　08/13/62　　　　　*Flushing Journal* List of Volunteers
　　　08/23/62　　　　　Enlisted in Unit, name appears as *William Haenig*
　　　09/24/62　　　　　Discharged at Washington, DC　　　　　　　X
　　　06/06/65　　　　　College Point, NY Census, ED 264, Page 240C
　　　1880
　　　02/21/84　　　　　Original Roster of Adam Wirth Post No. 451, GAR

88. Hollweg, August　　　Pvt.　23　Flushing, NY Census, Page 713
　　Co. B, 15th NYHA
　　　1860　　　　　　　Enlisted In New York City
　　　08/06/62　　　　　Enlisted in Unit
　　　09/30/63　　　　　Promoted to Full Corporal
　　　09/01/64　　　　　Discharged
　　　06/05/65

89. Horn, Michael　　　Pvt.　20　Flushing, NY Census, Page 719
　　Co. I, 20th NY
　　　1860　　　　　　　Enlisted in College Point, NY
　　　05/03/61　　　　　Discharged by order of Col. M. Weber, Commander
　　　05/06/61　　　　　Flushing, NY Census, Page 249
　　　1870　　　　　　　College Point, NY Census, ED 264, Page 245A
　　　1880

90. Horstman, Charles　　Pvt.　27　Enlisted in New York City
　　Co. E, 133rd NY
　　　08/27/62　　　　　Enlisted in Unit, Name written as *Hoffman*
　　　09/24/62　　　　　Provost Marshall's List
　　　11/30/63　　　　　Discharged at Frederick, MD　　　　　　　　X
　　　05/31/65　　　　　*History of Queens County*
　　　1882

91. *Houser, John　　　Pvt.　28　Enlisted in New York City
　　Co. G, 5th NYHA
　　　08/16/62　　　　　Wounded in Winchester, VA
　　　09/19/64　　　　　Discharged at Fort Duncan, Harper's Ferry　X
　　　06/22/65　　　　　Great Neck, NY Census, Page 312C
　　　1880
　　　02/21/84　　　　　Original Roster of Adam Wirth Post No. 451, GAR

Census and Service Data

92. Howard, William, J.

		1860		Flushing, NY Census, Page 711
Co. L, 2nd NYHA	Pvt.	08/06/61	36	Enlisted in Flushing, NY
		10/16/61		Enlisted in Unit
		08/23/62		*Flushing Journal* List of Volunteers
34th NYLA		11/19/63		Unit Designation Changed
		06/21/65		Discharged at Hart's Island, NY Harbor, NY X
		1870		Flushing, NY Census, Page 253
		1880		College Point, NY Census, ED 267, Page 292C

93. Illerd, Dennis *aka* Dennis Mahon

		09/09/61		Enlisted in Flushing, NY
Co. L, 2nd NYHA	Pvt.	10/01/61	19	Enlisted in Unit
		08/23/62		*Flushing Journal* List of Volunteers written as *Illand*
		08/30/62		Wounded in Action at Centreville, VA
34th NYLA		11/19/63		Unit Designation Changed
		06/21/65		Discharged at Hart's Island, NY Harbor, NY X

94. Jockers, Adam

		1860		Flushing, NY Census, Page 710, spelled *Yiockers*
		05/03/61		Enlisted in New York City
Co. D, 20th NY	Pvt.	05/06/61	19	Enlisted in Unit
		08/23/62		*Flushing Journal* List of Volunteers written *Jokers*
		02/15/63		Promoted to Full Corporal
		06/01/63		Discharged at New York City X
		1870		Flushing, NY Census, Page 216
		1880		College Point, NY Census, ED 267, Page 295B
		02/21/84		Original Roster of Adam Wirth Post No. 451, GAR

95. Johann, Matthew

Co. I, 5th NYNG	Sgt.	06/18/63	25	30-day enlistment
		1870		Flushing, NY Census, Page 240
		1880		College Point, NY Census, ED 267, Page 302D
				Son William will be active in the Sons of Union Veterans

96. *Johnston, Daniel S. Co. L, 2nd NYHA 34th NYLA	10/05/61 11/19/63 1880 02/21/84	Pvt.	18	Enlisted in Flushing, NY Unit Designation Changed College Point, NY Census, ED 267, Page 314D Original Roster of Adam Wirth Post No. 451, GAR	X
97. Kabisch, Friedrich Co. G, 7th NY	04/23/61 08/23/62 09/17/62 05/08/63 1880	Pvt.	26	Enlisted in New York City *Flushing Journal* List of Volunteers Wounded at the Battle of Antietam Discharged at New York City New York, NY Census, Page 115A	X
98. Kanz, John Co. C, Morgan Rifles Co. C, 58th NY	10/07/61 11/23/61 08/23/62 10/01/65	Pvt.	20	Enlisted in Unit Transferred to Unit *Flushing Journal* List of Volunteers Discharged at Nashville, TN	X
99. Kanz, Robert Co. H, 52nd NY	11/06/61 06/28/62 08/23/62 06/02/66	Pvt.	30	Enlisted in unit Died of disease at Fair Oaks, VA *Flushing Journal* List of Volunteers *Flushing Journal* List of Casualties	X

Census and Service Data

100. Kaufmann, John 34th NYLA	Pvt.	30	1860 08/06/61 10/01/61 11/01/61 08/23/62 01/01/65 06/21/65 1870	Flushing, NY Census, Page 717 Enlisted in Flushing, NY Enlisted in Unit Promoted to Full Sergeant *Flushing Journal* List of Volunteers Promoted to Full Quartermaster Sergeant Discharged at Hart's Island, NY Harbor, NY x Flushing, NY Census, Page 250
101. Kelly, Cornelius Co. C, 15th NY Eng. Co. A, 15th NY Eng.	Pvt.	40	1860 09/05/62 06/18/63 02/01/65 07/02/65 1870 1880 1882	Flushing, NY Census, Page 724 Enlisted in Flushing, NY Transferred Promoted to Full Artificer Discharged in Washington, DC x Flushing, NY Census, Page 223 College Point, NY Census, ED 264, Page 235A *History of Queens County*
102. Keppler, Jacob Co. K, 45th PA	Pvt.		10/22/61 08/23/62 09/14/62 06/23/66	Enlisted at Harrisburg, PA *Flushing Journal* List of Volunteers Died in Battle of South Mountain, MD x *Flushing Journal* List of Casualties
103. Kiernan, John 34th NYLA	Pvt.	23	1860 09/06/61 10/01/61 08/23/62 04/03/63 1870 1880	Flushing, NY Census, Page 696 Enlisted in Flushing, NY Enlisted in Unit *Flushing Journal* List of Volunteers serving in *Lincoln Cavalry* Deserted at Covington, KY Flushing, NY Census, Page 255 Flushing, NY Census, Page 264A

104. Kiernan, Patrick 1860 Flushing, NY Census, Page 692
    Co. L, 2nd NYHA 10/10/61 Pvt. 18 Enlisted in Flushing, NY
    34th NYLA 10/16/61 Enlisted in Unit
    11/19/63 Unit Designation Changed
    09/30/64 Wounded in Action at Petersburg, VA
    01/01/65 Promoted to Full Corporal
    06/21/65 Discharged at Hart's Island, NY Harbor, NY X
    1880 Flushing, NY Census, Page 319A
    1882 *History of Queens County*

105. Koch, Charles 1860 Flushing, NY Census, Page 717
    Co. C, Morgan Rifles 10/04/61 Pvt. 41 Enlisted in New York City
    Co. C, 58th NY 11/23/61 Transferred to Unit
    08/23/62 *Flushing Journal* List of Volunteers
    10/22/64 Discharged X

106. *Kulle, Albert G.
    08/25/62 Pvt. 18 Enlisted in Jamaica, NY
    Co. C, 158th NY 08/31/62 Enlisted in Unit
    09/29/64 Wounded at Chaffin Farm, VA
    06/30/65 Discharged at Richmond, VA X

107. Landt, Henry 1860 Flushing, NY Census, Page 712
    08/25/62 Pr. 22 Enlisted in New York City
    Co. C, 162nd NY 09/11/62 Enlisted in Unit known as the Metropolitan Guard
    09/01/63 Promoted to Full Sergeant 1st Class
    07/26/64 Prisoner of War after the Battle of New Market, VA
    10/15/64 Paroled
    05/26/65 Promoted to Lieutenant, 1st Class
    10/12/65 Discharged at Savannah, GA X
    1880 Wife *Philipina* in New York, NY Census, Page 614A

Census and Service Data

#	Name / Unit	Rank	Age	Dates	Notes	
108.	*Lane, Charles			03/17/62	Enlisted & Served on *North Carolina* and *Morning Light*	
	U.S. Navy			07/07/65	Discharged	
				02/21/84	Original Roster of Adam Wirth Post No. 451, GAR	X
109.	*Lark, Joseph					
	5th US Art.				Original Roster of Adam Wirth Post No. 451, GAR	
110.	*Lark, Peter	Pvt.	18	10/10/60	Enlisted in Unit in New York City	
	Co. A, US Eng.			07/11/64	Re-enlisted	
				07/11/64	Discharged at West Point, NY	
				1880	Whitestone, NY Census, Page 229B	
				02/21/84	Original Roster of Adam Wirth Post No. 451, GAR	
111.	Lasche, Robert	Pvt.	21	05/03/61	Enlisted in Williamsburg, NY	
	Co. I, 20th NY			05/06/61	Enlisted in Unit	
				07/11/61	Promoted to Full Corporal	
				05/01/62	Promoted to Full Sergeant	
				08/23/62	*Flushing Journal* List of Volunteers	
				09/17/62	Wounded at Battle of Antietam in Maryland	
				06/01/63	Discharged at New York City	
					Commissioned Lt. 1st Class	
	Co. H, 35th WI			02/14/65	Promoted to Full Captain, Co. K	
	Co. K, 35th WI			02/14/65	Transferred to Unit	
				07/17/65	Discharged at Nashville, TN	
				1880	Milwaukee, WI Census, Page 150B	X
112.	Leppert, John	Pvt.	19	04/26/61	Enlisted in Unit	
	Co. E, 10th NY			05/07/63	Discharged at New York City	
				1880	College Point, NY Census, ED 267, Page 306D	X

#	Name	Rank	Age	Dates	Notes
113.	*Lindecke, William Co. K, 28th MI	Pvt.	36	09/15/64 10/17/64 06/05/66 1880 02/21/84	Enlisted at Houghton, MI Enlisted in Unit Discharged in Raleigh, NC Babylon, NY Census, Page 47D Original Roster of Adam Wirth Post No. 451, GAR	x
114.	Ludwig, Carl Co. L, 2nd NYHA 34th NYLA	Pvt.	20	09/05/61 10/01/61 11/19/63 04/30/64 06/22/64 06/21/65 1870 1880 1882 02/21/84	Enlisted in Flushing, NY Enlisted in Unit Unit Designation Changed Promoted to Full Corporal Wounded at Battle of the Wilderness Discharged at Hart's Island, NY Harbor, NY Flushing, NY Census, Page 212 College Point, NY Census, ED 267, Page 311B *History of Queens County*, spelled *Rudwick* Original Roster of Adam Wirth Post No. 451, GAR	x
115.	Ludwig, William Co. L, 2nd NYHA 34th NYLA	Pvt.	22	09/05/61 10/01/61 11/19/63 05/12/64 01/01/65 06/21/65 1870 1880 1882 02/21/84	Enlisted in Flushing, NY Enlisted in Unit Unit Designation Changed Wounded at Gaines Mill, VA Promoted to Full Corporal Discharged at Hart's Island, NY Harbor, NY Flushing, NY Census, Page 229 College Point, NY Census, ED 267, Page 315A *History of Queens County*, spelled *Rudwick & Ludwig* Original Roster of Adam Wirth Post No. 451, GAR	x

Census and Service Data

#	Name / Unit	Rank	Age	Dates	Notes	X
116.	Lutters, Ernst Co. F, 131st NY	Pvt.	19	1860 04/07/65 07/26/65 1880 02/21/84	Flushing, NY Census, Page 725 Enlisted in Milford Discharged in Savannah, GA, alias *John H. Gray* College Point, NY Census, ED 267, Page 314D Original Roster of Adam Wirth Post No. 451, GAR	X
117.	Maher, Patrick Co. C, 74th NY	Pvt.	30	1860 08/21/62 08/26/63 1880	Flushing, NY Census, Page 692 Enlisted in Flushing, NY Disability discharge, Convalescent Camp, VA Flushing, NY Census, Page 327A	X
118.	*Mahlenthal, Emmanuel Co. C, 90th NY	Pvt.	25	10/01/64 06/03/65 1880 02/21/84	Enlisted at New York City Discharged at New York City Census, District 16, Page 264D Original Roster of Adam Wirth Post No. 451, GAR	
119.	Mahoney, Michael 34th NYLA	Pvt.	37	09/02/61 10/01/61 05/29/62 08/23/62	Enlisted in Flushing, NY Enlisted in Unit Disability discharge, Camp Barry, Washington, DC *Flushing Journal* List of Volunteers spelled *Mahony*	
120.	*Mandeville, George Co. G, 4th NY	Pvt.	27	05/24/61 01/01/62 09/17/62 05/23/63 1880	Enlisted in Unit Promoted to Sergeant Wounded at Battle of Antietam in MD Discharged at New York, NY College Point, NY Census, ED 264, Page 238C	

121. Marx, Charles
    Co. D, 15th NJ   Pvt.   29   11/30/63   Provost Marshall's List
    Co. E, 2nd NJ   03/11/65   Enlisted at Newark, NJ
                                    06/21/65   Transferred to Unit   X
                                    08/23/65   Discharged in Newark, NJ
                                    1870   Flushing, NY Census, Page 108
                                    1880   College Point, NY Census, ED 267, Page 715
                                    02/21/84   Original Roster of Adam Wirth Post No. 451, GAR
                                                Son Louis will be active in the Sons of Union Veterans

122. *May William
    Co. C, 68th NY   Pvt.   23   08/30/62   Enlisted
                                    05/14/63   Promoted to Corporal
                                    07/01/63   Prisoner of War after Gettysburg
                                    11/19/63   Rejoined Regiment
                                    08/22/64   Promoted to Sergeant
                                    06/17/65   Discharged at Chattanooga, TN   X
                                    02/21/84   Original Roster of Adam Wirth Post No. 451, GAR

123. *McClymont, George
    Co. H, 4th NY   Pvt.   18   07/06/61   Enlisted in New York City
                                    08/30/65   Discharged at Washington, DC   X
                                                Member of Adam Wirth Post 451 GAR

124. McCormick, Daniel
    Co. U, 3rd NY   Pvt.   30   1860   Flushing, NY Census, Page 689
                                    03/13/65   Enlisted in Brooklyn, NY
                                    1880   Brooklyn, NY Census, Page 588C

125. McDonald, George
    Co. C, 63rd NY   Corp.   36   1860   Flushing, NY Census, Page 749
                                    08/21/61   Enlisted in New York City
                                    09/17/62   Died of wounds at Battle of Antietam in Maryland

Census and Service Data

126. McGowan, William
  U. S. Navy

  08/23/62
  1882

  Landsman on the ship *Wabash*
  Flushing Journal List of Volunteers
  History of Queens County

127. *McManus, Robert
  Co. A, 1st CT

  Pvt. 21

  04/16/61
  07/31/61
  1880
  02/21/84

  X

  Enlisted in Unit
  Discharged at New Haven, CT
  Brooklyn, NY Census, Page 296D
  Original Roster of Adam Wirth Post No. 451, GAR

128. Metzger, Charles

  1860

  Flushing, NY Census, Page 717, age 34 *or*
  Flushing, NY Census, Page 745, age 43
  One of these two is the actual veteran

  15th NYSM

  06/06/64
  1880
  1882

  30-day enlistment
  College Point, NY Census, ED 267, Pages 300D & 307A
  History of Queens County

129. Michel, Charles
  U.S. Navy

  Sgt.

  1860

  08/16/62
  1880
  1882

  Flushing, NY Census, Page 723
  U.S. Sloop *Ossipee*
  Name appears in *Flushing Journal*
  College Point, NY Census, ED 264, Page 235B
  History of Queens County

130. Miller, Frederick
  Co. H, 1st DE

  Pvt. 17

  1860
  1865
  1880
  1882
  02/21/84

  X

  Flushing, NY Census, Page 712, age 12
  Enlisted in Unit
  College Point, NY Census, ED 264, Page 239A
  History of Queens County
  Original Roster of Adam Wirth Post No. 451, GAR

#	Name / Unit	Dates	Rank	Age	Notes
131.	Miller, Lewis 34th NYLA	1860 08/29/61 10/01/61 08/23/62 11/15/63 06/21/65 1880 1882			Flushing, NY Census, Page 712 Enlisted in Flushing, New York Enlisted in Unit *Flushing Journal* List of Volunteers, spelled *Muller* Discharged at Lenoir Station, TN Discharged at Hart's Island, NY Harbor, NY x College Point, NY Census, ED 267, Page 312D *History of Queens County*
132.	Miller, Louis Co. I, 20th NY	1860 05/03/61 05/06/61 07/17/62 08/23/62 06/01/63	Pvt.	19	Flushing, NY Census, Page 712 Enlisted in Williamsburg, NY Enlisted in Unit Promoted to Full Corporal *Flushing Journal* List of Volunteers, spelled *Muller* Discharged in New York City
133.	*Montanye, Washington Co. A, 83rd NY	05/27/61 10/22/62 1880 02/21/84	Pvt.	26	Enlisted in Unit Disability discharge, Finlay Hospital, Washington, DC New York City Census, 16th Ward, District 4, Page 395C Original Roster of Adam Wirth Post No. 451, GAR
134.	Montgomery, George Sickle's Brigade				No one by this name in any unit of Sickle's Brigade
135.	*Motz, Jacob 15th NYSM	11/30/63 06/06/64 1870 1880			Provost Marshall's List 30-day enlistment Flushing, NY Census, Page 238 College Point, NY Census, ED 267, Page 313B

Census and Service Data 59

136. Motz, Philip Co. D, 1st US Art.	01/21/65 01/01/68 1880 02/21/84			X	Enlisted in Unit Discharged, applied for pension alias *Philip Morse* College Point, NY Census, ED 264, Page 234D Original Roster of Adam Wirth Post No. 451, GAR
137. Muecke, Englebert Co. I, 20th NY	1860 05/03/61 05/06/61 08/23/62 06/01/63 1880	Pvt.	20	X	Flushing, NY Census, Page 716 Enlisted in Williamsburg, NY Enlisted *Flushing Journal* List of Volunteers Discharged in New York City College Point, NY Census, ED 264, Page 226D Divorced father & sons listed
138. Mutz, Gustav Co. E, 29th NY	05/15/61 06/04/61 08/23/62 06/20/63	Musician	24	X	Enlisted in New York City Enlisted in Unit *Flushing Journal* List of Volunteers Discharged in New York City
139. Nau, Michael 34th NYLA	10/24/61 10/26/61 08/23/62 06/21/65 02/21/84	Pvt.	24	X	Enlisted in Flushing, NY Enlisted in Unit *Flushing Journal* List of Volunteers Discharged at Hart's Island, NY Harbor, NY Original Roster of Adam Wirth Post No. 451, GAR Son Adam will be active in the Sons of Union Veterans
140. Naumann, George 15th NYSM	1860 11/06/61	Lieut.			Flushing, NY Census, Page 706 Death noted in *Flushing Journal*; Never went to war

141. Newman, Edward			1860	Flushing, NY Census, Page 739 name spelled *Niman*	
	Co. A, 121st NY	Pvt.	05/15/61	Enlisted in New York City	
	Co. E, 29th NY		06/04/61	Enlisted in Unit	
			08/23/62	*Flushing Journal* List of Volunteers	
			10/15/62	Deserted, but not true	
			07/17/65	Discharged at Halls Hill, VA	x
			1870	Flushing, NY Census, Page 212	
			1880	College Point, NY Census, ED 264, Page 246C	
142. Newman, George					
	Co. E, 73rd NY	Pvt.	01/22/62	Enlisted in New York City	
			05/05/62	Wounded at Fair Oaks, VA	
			08/23/62	*Flushing Journal* List of Volunteers	
			01/20/64	Discharged in Convalescent Camp, VA	x
143. Neimeier, Andrew					
	Co. C, 74th NY	Pvt.	08/12/62	Enlisted in Flushing, NY	
	Co. G, 40th NY		08/03/64	Transferred to Unit	
			1880	Whitestone, NY Census, Page 219B	
			02/21/84	Original Roster of Adam Wirth Post No. 451, GAR	x
144. *Noss, Adam					
	Co. K, 39th NY	Pvt.	08/23/62	*Flushing Journal* List of Volunteers	
			01/04/64	Enlisted in New York City	
			07/01/65	Discharged at Alexandria, VA	x
			1880	College Point, NY Census, ED 267, Page 300D	

Census and Service Data

145. Otto, Hermann

	1860		Flushing, NY Census, Page 744
Co. B, 46th NY	08/05/61	Cpl.	Enlisted in New York City
	08/23/62		*Flushing Journal* List of Volunteers
	10/01/62		Promoted to Full Sergeant
	09/15/64		Discharged
Co. C, 46th NY	02/15/65	Pvt.	Re-enlisted in Unit in New York City
	07/28/65	37	Discharged in Washington, DC
	1870		Flushing, NY Census, Page 231
	1880	42	College Point, NY Census, ED 267, Page 311B x

146. Palmer, Samuel

	1860		Flushing, NY Census, Page 613
Co. L, 2nd NYHA	08/28/61	Sgt.	Enlisted in Flushing, NY
	10/01/61		Enlisted in Unit
34th NYLA	08/23/62		*Flushing Journal* List of Volunteers
120th Co. 2nd Btty. VRC	11/19/63		Unit Designation Changed
	12/15/63		Transferred to Unit
	09/30/64	40	Discharged x

147. Pfortner Vonder Holle, Max

Co. A. 68th NY	07/25/61	Pvt.	Enlisted in New York City
	08/01/61		Enlisted in Unit
	08/31/62		Discharged
	1880		College Point, NY Census, ED 267, Page 294D x

148. Piereth, Christian

	1860		Flushing, NY Census, Page 732, spelled *Bureth*
15th NYSM	11/30/63	Pvt.	Provost Marshall's List
	06/06/64		30-day enlistment
	1870		Flushing, NY Census, Page 227
	1880	46	College Point, NY Census, ED 267, Page 296C
	1882		*History of Queens County*

#	Name / Unit	Date	Rank	Age	Notes
149.	Piereth, Valentine Co. C, 1st DE	1860 12/16/61 08/23/62 06/26/63 09/30/64	Pvt.	19	Flushing, NY Census, Page 732, spelled *Bureth* Enlisted in Unit *Flushing Journal* List of Volunteers Wounded Discharged at Petersburg, VA
150.	*Plitt, George 15th NYSM	11/06/61 11/30/63 1870 1880 1882			Named in *Flushing Journal* article as belonging to Unit Provost Marshall's List Flushing, NY Census, Page 228 College Point, NY Census, ED 267, Page 307B *History of Queens County*
151.	Pluemacher, Charles Co. I, 20th NY	07/20/61 06/30/62 08/05/62 08/23/62 06/01/63 1880 02/21/84	Pvt.	24	Enlisted in New York City Prisoner of War at White Oak Swamp, VA Paroled at Aikens Landing, SC *Flushing Journal* List of Volunteers x Discharged in New York City Norristown, PA Census, Page 472A Original Roster of Adam Wirth Post No. 451, GAR
152.	Propfer, Augustus 15th NYSM	1860 11/30/63 06/06/64 1870 1880 1882	Pvt. Pvt.	37	Flushing, NY Census, Page 736 Provost Marshall's List 30-day enlistment Flushing, NY Census, Page 46 Flushing, NY Census, ED 267, Pg. 297A, Barbara appears *History of Queens County*
153.	Quaid, T. Sickle's Brigade				No one by this name in any unit of Sickle's Brigade

Census and Service Data

#	Name / Unit	Date	Rank	Age	Notes	X
154.	Rausch, Peter Co. H, 20th NY	05/03/61 05/06/61 08/23/62 06/01/63	Pvt.	22	Enlisted in New York City Enlisted in Unit *Flushing Journal* List of Volunteers Discharged in New York City	X
155.	*Rausmuller, Charles Co. K, 54th NY	10/16/61 06/23/63 09/01/65 04/14/66 02/21/84	Pvt.	24	Enlisted at Hudson City, NJ Promoted to 1st Lieutenant Promoted to Captain Discharged at Charleston, SC Original Roster of Adam Wirth Post No. 451, GAR	X
156.	Reinhard, Andrew Co. B, 11th NY Cav. "Scott's 900"	1860 01/11/64 10/04/64 06/02/66	Pvt.	18	Flushing, NY Census, Page 721 Enlisted in New York City Died of disease in New Orleans, LA Hospital *Flushing Journal* List of Casualties	X
157.	Reinheimer, Daniel Co. L, 2nd NYHA 34th NYLA	1860 09/02/61 10/01/61 06/05/62 08/23/62 11/19/63 1870 1880 1882	Pvt.	37	Flushing, NY Census, Page 716 Enlisted in Flushing, NY Enlisted in Unit Disability discharge, Washington, DC *Flushing Journal* List of Volunteers Unit Designation Changed Flushing, NY Census, Page 238 College Point, NY Census, ED 264, Page 226C *History of Queens County*, listed incorrectly as 15th NYHA	X

158. Rhein, Moritz
    Co. I, 7th NY — Pvt. — 40
    - 04/29/61 — Enlisted in New York City
    - 05/10/61 — Promoted to Full Sergeant
    - 09/01/61 — Promoted to Full Lieutenant, 2nd Class
    - 10/03/61 — Transferred to Co. K
    - 01/23/62 — Transferred to Co. E, promoted to Full Lieutenant, 1st Class
    - 03/21/62 — Transferred to Co. D and promoted to Full Captain
    - 08/23/62 — *Flushing Journal* List of Volunteers
    - 05/08/63 — Discharged in New York City

159. Richard, George — Pvt. — 23
    - 1860 — Flushing, NY Census, Page 705
    - 08/31/61 — Enlisted in Flushing, NY
    Co. L, 2nd NYHA
    - 10/01/61 — Enlisted in Unit
    - 08/23/62 — *Flushing Journal* List of Volunteers
    - 11/19/63 — Unit Designation Changed
    34th NYLA
    - 09/30/64 — Discharged in New York City   x

160. Richter, Franz — Pvt. — 41
    Co. D, Morgan Rifles
    - 10/15/61 — Enlisted in New York City
    - 11/23/61 — Transferred to Unit
    Co. D, 58th NY
    - 08/23/62 — *Flushing Journal* List of Volunteers
    - 10/02/64 — Died of disease in Bridgeport, AL
    - 06/23/66 — *Flushing Journal* List of Casualties   x

161. *Roessel, Joseph — Pvt. — 22
    - 08/24/62 — Enlisted
    Co. C, 29th NJ
    - 09/20/62 — Enlisted in Unit
    - 07/06/63 — Discharged at Freehold, NJ
    - 1880 — College Point, NY Census, ED 267, Page 303B

Census and Service Data

162. *Rooney, Thomas Co. C, 74th NY	Pvt.	18	06/01/61 07/07/61 08/01/63 07/06/64 1880 02/21/84	Enlisted in Flushing, NY Enlisted in Unit Promoted to Full Corporal Discharged in Petersburg, VA Flushing, NY Census, Page 260A Original Roster of Adam Wirth Post No. 451, GAR	x
163. Rubel, Henry Co. E, 29th NY	Pvt.	23	05/15/61 06/04/61 08/23/62 11/08/62 1870 1880	Enlisted in New York City Enlisted in Unit Flushing Journal List of Volunteers Disability discharge, Washington, DC Flushing, NY Census, Page 212 College Point, NY Census, ED 264, Page 240D	x
164. Schafer, Nicholas 34th NYLA	Pvt.	19	08/23/62 06/12/63 07/12/64 06/21/65 1880	*Flushing Journal* List of Volunteers, listed as *Fr.* Enlisted in New York City Enlisted in Unit Discharged at Hart's Island, NY Harbor, NY New York, NY Census, Page 62C	x
165. Schaefer, Peter Co. L, 2nd NYHA	Pvt.	42	1860 08/28/61 03/05/62 1870 1880	Allegheny County, PA Census, Town of Reserve Enlisted in Flushing, NY Disability discharge, Washington DC Flushing, NY Census, Page 231 College Point, NY Census, ED 267, Page 316A	
166. Schermerhorn, Louis Co. G, 7th NY	Pvt.	20	1860 05/25/62 09/05/62 11/30/63 1880	Flushing, NY Census, Page 689 30-day enlistment Discharged in New York City Provost Marshall's List Flushing, NY Census, Page 175A	x

167. Schierlitz, Paul		Pvt.	23	
Co. E, 29th NY	05/15/61			Enlisted in New York City
	06/04/61			Enlisted in Unit
	08/23/62			*Flushing Journal* List of Volunteers
	11/06/62			Promoted to Full Corporal
	05/02/63			Wounded
	06/20/63			Discharged in New York City X
168. *Schneemann, Joseph		Pvt.	22	
Co. D, 20th NY	05/03/61			Enlisted in New York City
	05/06/61			Enlisted in Unit
	03/13/63			Promoted to Full Corporal
	06/01/63			Discharged at New York, NY
	02/21/84			Original Roster of Adam Wirth Post No. 451, GAR X
169. Schrader, Otto		Sgt.	36	
	1860			Flushing, NY Census, Page 737
	05/15/61			Enlisted in New York City
Co. E, 29th NY	06/04/61			Enlisted in Unit
2nd NYLA	08/01/61			Unit Designation Changed
	08/23/62			*Flushing Journal* List of Volunteers
	07/23/63			Transferred to hospital
	1870			Flushing, NY Census, Page 220
	1882			*History of Queens County*
170. Schubert, Emil		Sgt. 1st Class	32	
Co. A, 41st NY	06/06/61			Enlisted in New York City
	09/01/61			Promoted to Full Lieutenant, 2nd Class
9th NYLA	09/01/61			Commissioned in Unit
	04/05/62			Promoted to Full Lieutenant, 1st Class
	08/23/62			*Flushing Journal* List of Volunteers
	12/12/62			Promoted to Full Captain
	06/13/64			Discharged in New York City X
	06/23/66			*Flushing Journal* List of Casualties, but not true

Census and Service Data

#	Name / Unit	Dates	Rank	Age	Notes	
171.	Schultz, Franklin 133rd NY	08/16/62			According to *Flushing Journal*, he enlisted in the unit	
172.	Schultz, David A. Co. K, 79th NY	1860 05/13/61 05/28/61 08/23/62 11/29/63 1880 1886	Pvt.	22	Flushing, NY Census, Page 739 Enlisted in New York City Enlisted in Unit *Flushing Journal* List of Volunteers Killed in Action in Knoxville, TN College Point, NY Census, ED 264, Page 244D, Mother is listed Sons of Union Veterans Post # 29 named in his honor	X
173.	Schultz, George Navy	08/23/62			*Flushing Journal* List of Volunteers	
174.	Schultz, Henry Co. R, 15th NYSM	1860 11/30/63 06/06/64 1882	Cpl.		Flushing, NY Census, Page 705 Provost Marshall's List 30-day enlistment *History of Queens County*	
175.	Schumacker, Frederick Co. L, 2nd NYHA 34th NYLA	1860 08/06/61 08/23/62 11/19/63 06/21/65	Pvt. Bugler	33 33	Flushing, NY Census, Page 700 Enlisted in Flushing, NY *Flushing Journal* List of Volunteers Unit Designation Changed Discharged at Hart's Island, NY Harbor, NY	X
176.	Schumacher, Henry Co. I, 20th NY	05/03/61 05/06/61 08/23/62 06/01/63 1880 02/21/84	Pvt.	18	Enlisted in Williamsburg, NY Enlisted in Unit *Flushing Journal* List of Volunteers Discharged in New York City Newtown, NY Census, Page 245B Original Roster of Adam Wirth Post No. 451, GAR	

177. Sennewald, Theodore Co. I, 20th NY	Pvt.	18	05/03/61 05/06/61 05/01/62 11/16/62 1870 1880	Enlisted in College Point, NY Enlisted in Unit Promoted to Full Bugle Major Discharged X Iberville Parish, LA Census, Ward 6, Plaquemine St. Martin Parish, LA Census, Page 46A
178. Skinnon, Thomas Co. E, 10th NY	Pvt.	21	04/30/61 06/27/62 08/23/62	Enlisted in New York City Died of wounds at Gaines Mill, VA X *Flushing Journal* List of Volunteers spelled *Skinyon, T.*
179. Smith, James R. Co. E, 10th NY	Sgt.	20	04/26/61 04/30/61 09/21/61 06/27/62 08/23/62 12/04/62	Enlisted in New York City Enlisted in Unit Promoted to Full Lieutenant, 2nd Class Wounded at Gaines Mill, VA *Flushing Journal* List of Volunteers Resigned as a result of wounds X
180. Smith, William Co. I, 20th NY	Pvt.	22	1860 05/01/61 08/23/62 06/01/63	Flushing, NY Census, Page 725 Enlisted at Williamsburgh, NY *Flushing Journal* List of Volunteers Discharged in New York City
181. *Snyder, Edwin Co. B, 31st PA Co. A, 191st PA	Musician		01/22/62 06/16/64 06/28/65 1880 02/21/84	Enlisted in Unit Transferred into Unit Discharged at Washington, DC College Point, NY Census, ED 264, Page 237A Original Roster of Adam Wirth Post No. 451, GAR

Census and Service Data

182. Snyder, William H.			1860	Flushing, NY Census, Page 740
Co. C, 74th NY	Pvt.	25	06/15/61	Enlisted in Camp Scott, Flushing, NY
			07/06/61	Enlisted in Unit
			08/23/62	*Flushing Journal* List of Volunteers
			01/07/63	Disability discharge
			1882	*History of Queens County*
183. Sparks, John				Enlisted in New York City
Co. E, 10th NY	Pvt.	20	04/26/61	Enlisted in New York City
			04/30/61	Enlisted in Unit
			08/23/62	*Flushing Journal* List of Volunteers
			05/07/63	Discharged in New York City x
184. Stader, Charles			1860	Flushing, NY Census, Page 715
Co. C, 39th NY	Pvt.	18	05/20/61	Enlisted in New York City
			08/23/62	*Flushing Journal* List of Volunteers
			12/02/63	Prisoner of War in Andersonville
			08/02/64	Died of disease at Andersonville Prison in Georgia
			06/23/66	*Flushing Journal* List of Casualties
185. Stader, George			1860	Flushing, NY Census, Page 715
Co. C, 39th NY	Pvt.	25	05/15/61	Enlisted in New York City
			10/02/62	Disability discharge
			1880	New York City, NY Census, Page 41A x
186. Stader, John			1860	Flushing, NY Census, Page 715
15th NYSM			06/06/64	30-day enlistment
			1870	Flushing, NY Census, Page 228
			1880	Flushing, NY Census, ED 267, Page 301A, spelled *Stadler*

#	Name / Unit	Rank	Age	Dates	Notes	X
187.	*Starkins, John H. Co. L, 2nd NYHA 34th NYLA	Pvt.	19	10/07/61 10/09/61 10/17/63 11/19/63 11/13/64 06/21/65 1880 02/21/84	Enlisted in Flushing, NY as a Blacksmith Enlisted in Unit Promoted to Full Sergeant Unit Designation Changed Promoted to Full Sergeant First Class Discharged at Harts Island, NY Harbor College Point, NY Census, ED 267, Page 305B Original Roster of Adam Wirth Post No. 451, GAR	X
188.	Steinbeck, Julius Co. I, 20th NY	Pvt.	27	05/03/61 05/06/61 08/23/62 06/01/63 1870 1880 02/21/84	Enlisted in Williamsburg, NY Enlisted in Unit Flushing Journal List of Volunteers Discharged in New York City Flushing, NY Census, Page 216 College Point, NY Census, ED 264, Page 242D Original Roster of Adam Wirth Post No. 451, GAR Sons Paul and Julius will be active in the Sons of Union Veterans	
189.	Steinbecker, John Co. L, 2nd NYHA 34th NYLA	Pvt.	31	09/06/61 04/01/62 06/25/62 08/23/62 11/19/63	Enlisted in Flushing, New York Reduced to Private Deserted in Tennallytown, MD Flushing Journal List of Volunteers Unit Designation Changed	
190.	Steinbrucker, John Co. E, 29th NY	Pvt.	31	1860 05/15/61 06/04/61 06/18/61 06/02/66	Flushing, NY Census, Page 738 Enlisted in New York City Enlisted in Unit Reported as deserted, but actually died in battle Flushing Journal List of Casualties	X

Census and Service Data

191. Sternberg, Casper			1860	Flushing, NY Census, Page 697
	Co. L, 2nd NYHA	Pvt.	18	Enlisted in Flushing, NY
			09/09/61	Enlisted in Unit
			10/01/61	Promoted to Full Bugler
			11/15/62	Unit Designation Changed
	34th NYLA		11/19/63	
			06/21/65	Discharged at Hart's Island, NY Harbor, NY X
192. Sternberg, Jurgon			1860	Flushing, NY Census, Page 697
	Co. L, 2nd NYHA	Pvt.	45	Enlisted in Unit
			09/06/61	*Flushing Journal* List of Volunteers, listed as *H. Sternberg*
			08/23/62	
			01/19/63	Died of disease, Windmill Point, VA in Aquia Creek Hospital X
193. Stobbe, Nicholas				Enlisted in New York City
	Co. A, 57th NY	Cpl.	25	Enlisted in Unit
			10/01/61	
			10/16/61	Promoted to Full Sergeant
			01/01/62	Promoted to Full Sergeant, First Class
			01/01/63	Transferred to Unit, promoted to Full Lieutenant, 2nd Class
	Co. B, 57th NY		08/30/64	
			09/23/64	Discharged in Petersburg, VA X
194. Stonebanks, John			1860	Flushing, NY Census, Page 739
	Co. D, 15th NYNSM	Pvt.	20	30-day enlistment
			06/06/64	Died at Fort Richmond, NY Harbor
			07/64	*Flushing Journal* List of Casualties
			06/23/66	Flushing, NY Census, Page 251, Father & family appear
			1870	College Point, NY Census, ED 267, siblings on 291B & 294C
			1880	
195. Stratton, Alfred				Enlisted in Dunkirk, NY
	Co. G, 147th NY	Pvt.	18	
			08/19/63	
			09/27/64	Discharged because of wounds; lost both arms X

196. Straube, Henry		Pvt.	21	1860 05/03/61 05/06/61 08/23/62 06/01/63 1870 1880 02/21/84	Flushing, NY Census, Page 718 Enlisted in Williamsburg, NY Enlisted in Unit *Flushing Journal* List of Volunteers Discharged in New York City Flushing, NY Census, Page 237 College Point, NY Census, ED 264, Page 240D Original Roster of Adam Wirth Post No. 451, GAR Sons Henry, Jr. and Edward will be active in the Sons of Union Veterans	X
Co. I, 20th NY						
197. Sutorius, Jacob		Pvt.	22	09/06/61 10/01/61 04/30/64 06/30/65 1880 02/21/84	Enlisted in Flushing, NY Enlisted in Unit Promoted to Full Corporal Discharged at Hart's Island, NY Harbor, NY College Point, NY Census, ED 267, Page 301A Original Roster of Adam Wirth Post No. 451, GAR	X
34th NYLA						
198. Thomas, George		Pvt.	21	1860 09/05/62 01/18/63 06/29/65	Flushing, NY Census, Page 752 Enlisted in Flushing, NY Transferred to Unit Discharged in Washington, DC	X
Co. F, 163rd NY Co. I, 73rd NY						
199. Thompson, Edward		Pvt.	21	08/16/62 08/25/62 08/27/63 1860 1880	*Flushing Journal* article announces his enlistment Enlisted in New York City Disability discharge Flushing, NY Census, Page 742 College Point, NY Census, ED 267, Page 293A	
Co. K, 61st NY						

Census and Service Data

200. Todt, Charles E.
  32nd NYLA

Date	Rank	Age	Notes
1860		36	Flushing, NY Census, Page 712
12/18/61	Pvt.		Enlisted in New York City
12/18/61	Lt. 2nd Class		Commissioned

  29th NYLA

06/01/62			Transferred to Unit
06/07/62			Disability discharge ✗
08/23/62			*Flushing Journal* List of Volunteers, listed as Toot
1880			Brooklyn, NY Census, Page 106A widow Mary appears

201. Troy, John
  34th NYLA

09/06/61	Pvt.	20	Enlisted in Flushing, NY
09/22/61			Reported as deserted, but he actually joined the Navy
08/23/62			*Flushing Journal* List of Volunteers

202. Tyrrell, Willis H.
  Co. E, 11th CT

10/24/61	Pvt.	25	Enlisted
10/25/61			Enlisted in Unit
01/02/62			Promoted to Full Corporal
08/23/62			*Flushing Journal* List of Volunteers
09/17/62			Wounded at Battle of Antietam in Maryland
02/09/63			Promoted to Full Sergeant
08/25/63			Died of wounds at Hampton Hospital, VA ✗
06/23/66			*Flushing Journal* List of Casualties

203. Underhill, John
  Co. C, 65th NY
  Co. H, 65th NY

1860		18	Flushing, NY Census, Page 690
07/11/61	Pvt.		Enlists in New York City
09/10/64			Transferred to Unit
07/17/65			Discharged in Hall's Hill, VA ✗

73

#	Name / Unit	Rank	Age	Dates	Notes	X
204.	Vix, George Co. E, 29th NY	Musician	21	1860 05/15/61 08/23/62 08/30/62 06/02/66 1880	Flushing, NY Census, Page 713 Enlisted in New York City *Flushing Journal* List of Volunteers Killed at the Second Battle of Bull Run *Flushing Journal* List of Casualties College Point, NY Census, ED 264, Page 240C, father and family appears	X
205.	Vogt, Jurgon Co. L, 2nd NYHA 34th NYLA	Pvt.	26	09/02/61 10/01/61 11/19/63 08/12/64 06/21/65	Enlisted Enlisted in Unit Unit Designation Changed Wounded at Deep Bottom Run, VA Discharged at Hart's Island, NY Harbor, NY	X
206.	*Vollbracht, William Co. C, 45th NY	Pvt.	22	09/26/61 09/27/61 07/25/62 1880	Enlisted in New York City Enlisted in Unit Disability discharge at Cumberland, MD New York City Census, District 25, Page 307C Son George will be active in Sons of Union Veterans	X
207.	Von Kockeritz, Benno Co. L, 1st NY Cav. Co. U, 13th NY Cav.	Lt. 2nd Class Pvt.	41 38	05/29/61 08/22/61 09/12/61 08/23/62 12/05/62 03/11/63 03/27/63	Enlisted in New York City Commissioned Transferred *Flushing Journal* List of Volunteers Discharged at Oldtown, MD Enlisted in New York City Enlisted in Unit	

Census and Service Data

#	Name / Unit	Dates	Rank	Age	Notes	
208.	Wagner, Henry Co. D, 1st NY Eng.	08/22/61 08/30/61 08/23/62 06/03/63 1880	Pvt.	22	Enlisted Enlisted in Unit *Flushing Journal*/ List of Volunteers Disability discharge, Hilton Head, SC Flushing, NY Census, Page 281C	X
209.	Warner, Hiram U.S. Navy	1860 08/23/62			Flushing, NY Census, Page 740 Served on Gunboat *Perry* *Flushing Journal*/ List of Volunteers	
210.	Weber, Bernhard Co. G, 39th NY	1860 05/28/61 06/08/62 08/23/62 03/16/63 1870	Pvt.	20	Flushing, NY Census, Page 622 Enlisted in New York City Wounded at Battle of Cross Keys, VA *Flushing Journal*/ List of Volunteers as serving in 58th NY Disability discharge, Centreville, VA Brooklyn, NY Census, 10th Ward, Page 661	X
211.	Weiss, Charles Co. I, 11th NYSM	06/16/63 06/18/63 11/30/63 1870 1880	Pvt.		Enlisted in New York City 30-day enlistment Provost Marshall's List Flushing, NY Census, Page 249 College Point, NY Census, ED 267, Page 312C Sons Oscar and Charles active in Sons of Union Veterans	
212.	Wenzler, Leopold 34th NYLA	02/27/64 09/01/64	Pvt.	40	Enlisted in Jamaica, NY Died of Disease in Alexandria, VA	
213.	Werner, Frederick 34th NYLA	10/01/61 10/06/61 09/12/63	Pvt.		Enlisted in Jamaica, NY Enlisted in Unit Died of Typhoid Fever	

#	Name / Unit	Rank	Age	Dates	Notes	X
214.	White, Thomas Co. L, 2nd NYHA 34th NYLA	Pvt.	24	09/09/61 10/01/61 08/23/62 11/19/63 06/21/65 1882	Enlisted in Flushing, NY Enlisted in Unit *Flushing Journal* List of Volunteers Unit Designation Changed Discharged in Hart's Island, NY Harbor, NY *History of Queens County*	X
215.	*Wieners, Jacob Co. E, 69th NYSM	Pvt.	19	06/22/63 1870 1880	30-day enlistment Flushing, NY Census, Page 80 College Point, NY Census, Page 225B	
216	Wiessner, Valentine Co. L, 2nd NYHA 34th NYLA	Pvt.	40	1860 09/09/61 10/01/61 08/23/62 11/19/63 05/26/64	Flushing, NY Census, Page 726 Enlisted in Flushing, NY Enlisted in Unit *Flushing Journal* List of Volunteers Unit Designation Changed Deserted in North Anna River, VA	
217	Wilhelm, Johann Co. B, 68th NY	Pvt.	27	07/29/61 08/01/61 08/16/61 06/25/62 08/23/62	Enlisted in New York City Enlisted in Unit Promoted to Full Musician Discharged *Flushing Journal* List of Volunteers	X
218	*Wilkens, Frederick Co. C, 39th NY	Pvt.	20	05/20/61 05/28/61 06/24/64 02/21/84	Enlisted in New York City Enlisted in Unit Discharged in New York, NY Original Roster of Adam Wirth Post No. 451, GAR	X
219	Wilson, William Co. K, 61st NY	Pvt.	25	08/16/62 08/27/62 11/29/63	*Flushing Journal* article announces his enlistment Enlisted in New York City Deserted at David's Island, NY	

Census and Service Data

220. *Winkler, John Co. B, 52ⁿᵈ NY	Pvt.	31	08/09/61 11/01/61 03/08/62 1870 1880 02/21/84	Enlisted in New York City Enlisted in Unit Disability discharge Flushing, NY Census, Page 219 College Point, NY Census, ED 267, Page 296D Original Roster of Adam Wirth Post No. 451, GAR	x
221. Winter, Adam Co. K, 41ˢᵗ NY	Wagoner	28	06/06/61 06/09/61 05/30/62 08/23/62 11/16/62 02/21/84	Enlisted in New York City Enlisted in Unit Promoted to Full Corporal Flushing Journal List of Volunteers Disability discharge, Convalescent Camp, VA Member of Adam Wirth Post 451 GAR	x
222. Wirth, Adam 34ᵗʰ NYLA	Pvt.	20	1860 09/09/61 10/01/61 11/01/61 05/27/62 08/23/62 08/30/62 09/25/62 07/21/66 1870 1871 1880 02/21/84	Flushing, NY Census, Page 699 Enlisted in Flushing, NY Enlisted in Unit Promoted to Full Corporal Promoted to Full Sergeant *Flushing Journal* List of Volunteers Wounded in 2ⁿᵈ Battle of Bull Run Died in Georgetown, DC *Flushing Journal* List of Casualties Flushing, NY Census, Page 221, father and brother, Page 103, brother David College Point, NY Census, ED 264, Page 246D & 234C, GAR Post 451 named in his honor	x
223. Woener, John J. 34ᵗʰ NYLA	Cpl.	43	08/28/61 10/02/61 05/15/62 08/23/62	Enlisted in Flushing, NY Enlisted in Unit Disability discharge, Washington, DC *Flushing Journal* List of Volunteers listed as *Jacob Werner*	

224. Wurtz, Henry			1860	Flushing, NY Census, Page 748
	Co. A, 20th NY	Pvt.	20	Enlisted in New York City
	5th NYLA		08/15/62	Transferred to Unit
	3rd NYLA		05/07/63	Transferred to Unit
			01/28/64	Discharged in New York City X
			06/24/65	
			1870	Flushing, NY Census, Page 218
			1880	College Point, NY Census, ED 267, Page 294C
			02/21/84	Original Roster of Adam Wirth Post No. 451, GAR
				Son Conrad will be active in the Sons of Union Veterans
225. Zerberbiers, Otto			1860	Brooklyn, NY Census, 6th Ward, Page 894, spelled *Saharbenrer*
		Pvt.	18	
			09/02/61	Enlisted in Flushing, NY
	Co. L, 2nd NYHA		10/01/61	Enlisted in Unit
			08/23/62	*Flushing Journal* List of Volunteers spelled *Zuberbier*
			10/11/62	Deserted at Cliffeburn General Hospital, Washington, DC
226. Ziessler, Charles				
	Co. E, 29th NY	Pvt.	37	Enlisted in Unit
			06/04/61	*Flushing Journal* List of Volunteers listed as *Zeseler*
			08/23/62	Disability discharge, Washington, DC X
	1st NJLA		10/20/62	Enlisted in Unit in Newark, NJ
			12/21/63	Discharged at Sickle US Army General Hospital
			06/15/65	

Photo Section

S.O. 710/1.

APPLICATION FOR CHARTER.

Adam Wirth Post. No. 451

TO BE SITUATED IN

Town of *College Point*

County of *Queens* N.Y.

Headquarters, Department of N. Y., G. A. R.

Charter Issued *Feby 20th* 1884

By order of Dep't Commander.

George D. Squires

Assistant Adjutant General.

Organized, *Feby 21st* 1884

By *Geo. C. Field Post 51*.

DIRECTIONS.

1. Posts are formed by authority of the Department Commander, on application of not less than ten persons eligible to membership in the Grand Army of the Republic. The application for a Charter shall be accompanied by a Charter Fee of ten dollars.

2. If, on the receipt of such applications, the Department Commander shall be satisfied that it is for the interest of the Grand Army of the Republic to form such a Post, he shall either in person or by some officer of his staff, admit the applicants into the Grand Army of the Republic, superintend the election of Post officers for the remainder of the current year, and complete the organization of the Post.

3. *Eligibility.*—Soldiers and Sailors of the United States Army, Navy, or Marine Corps, who served in the suppression of the late Rebellion, and those having been honorably discharged therefrom after such service, shall be eligible to membership in the Grand Army of the Republic. And no person shall be eligible to membership who has at any time borne arms against the United States.

OBJECTS.—The objects to be accomplished by this organization are as follows:

1. To preserve and strengthen those kind and fraternal feelings which bind together the soldiers, sailors and marines who united to suppress the late rebellion, and to perpetuate the memory and history of the dead.

2. To assist such former comrades in arms as need help and protection, and to extend needful aid to the widows and orphans of those who have fallen.

3. To maintain true allegiance to the United States of America, based upon a paramount respect for, and fidelity to the National Constitution and laws; to discountenance whatsoever tends to weaken loyalty, incites to insurrection, treason or rebellion, or in any manner impairs the efficiency and permanency of our free institutions; and to encourage the spread of universal liberty, equal rights and justice to all men.

Assistant Adjutant General of the Department of New York,
Grand Army of the Republic.

We, the undersigned honorably discharged Soldiers and Sailors of the Army and Navy of the United States, now residents of College Point, County of Queens, State of New York, do respectfully apply for a **CHARTER** for a Post of the Grand Army of the Republic, under the jurisdiction of the Department of New York, G. A. R., subject to the regulations of the Grand Army of the Republic, and the Department of New York thereof.

NAMES	RESIDENCE	RANK	CO.	REGIMENT OR SHIP
William Hoenig	College Point	Corp.	C	133d N.Y. Vols
John H. Starkins	"	1st Sgt	34	N.Y. 2nd Battery, N.Y.
Georg Dietrich	"	Private	I	82d N.Y. Vol
George Manteuker	"	Private	C	4 Reg N.Y.V. Scott L.I.
Ernst Lutter	"	Private	F	131 N.Y.V.
Fritz Silberknoll	"	"	K	58 N.Y. Vols
Michael Nau	"	"	"	34 N.Y. 2nd Battery N.Y.
William Ludwig	"	Corp		
John L. Winkler	"	Private	B	52d N.Y. Vols
Aug. Berger	-	"	B	4 Th. Cav.
Jos Dorkendorff	"	"	G	46 N.Y.V.
Chas Buser	"	1st Sergt	B	15 N.Y. A

Courtesy of the New York State Archives

Carl Ludwig
Poppenhusen Institute

John Starkins
Poppenhusen Institute

Joseph Dockendorff
Courtesy of Elsa Dockendorf Kaiser, Granddaughter of Joseph Dockendorff

Frederick Dockendorf
Poppenhusen Institute

Tuffeil Denno
Poppenhusen Institute

Frederick Wilkens
Poppenhusen Institute

Julius Steinbeck
Julia Steinbeck-Reeves

Frederick Behring
Julia Steinbeck-Reeves

Alfred Stratton
Poppenhusen Institute

William Berndt
Poppenhusen Institute

William Hoenig
Poppenhusen Institute

Henry Farrell
Poppenhusen Institute

Charles Marx
Poppenhusen Institute

Andrew Harvey
Poppenhusen Institute

Frederick Baumann
Poppenhusen Institute

Emmanuel Mahlenthal
Poppenhusen Institute

Theodore Gunzert
Army Military History Institute

Louis Bisky
Courtesy of the National Archives

Introduction to the Biographies

Introduction to the Biographies

"By recreating the past we are calling on the same magic as our forebears did with stories of their ancestors round the fires under the nights skies. The need to do this, to keep earth in its place, lies deep in human nature, and the art of biography rises from that need. This is its justification." So said Michael Holroyd in his *Works on Paper: The Craft of Biography and Autobiography Writing.*

The majority of the men whose stories, told in outline form, follow, would not for the most part, be looked upon as candidates for the writing of an individual biography unless of course, it were to be written by a descendant with a particular genealogical interest.

But these men did take part in a defining moment in American History, the Civil War, and they were in the forefront of a greater global event, the Industrial Revolution.

They came to College Point to work in Conrad Poppenhusen's rubber factory before, during, and after the war. By 1854 Poppenhusen had acquired the time-limited, initial sole rights to the use of Charles Goodyear's process for hardening rubber, a process that enabled him to manufacture buttons, combs and other accoutrements that would be used in support of the war effort and to meet the general population's requirements.

Poppenhusen was known as the *"Benevolent Tycoon"* and from the mid 1850's, was a primary moving force in College Point. Attracting large numbers of German and Irish immigrant workers for his factory, he built houses, paved roads, and did everything he could to set in place the infrastructure that would make his enterprise a success.

A first-class entrepreneur, he brought the railroad to town through the acquisition in 1870 of what was then called the North Shore Railroad that ran at the time only from Long Island City to Flushing.

Eventually he would become President of what became the Long Island Rail Road, but as ahead of his time as he was, was he also subject to the financial ups and downs of the era. The line went into receivership in 1877 and Poppenhusen returned to Germany to reorganize finances.

His many accomplishments included the establishment of the first free kindergarten ever operated in the United States and officially opened on July 1, 1870. It was housed at the Poppenhusen Institute where immigrants were taught their new language and could even learn a trade. Poppenhusen also created a library at the Institute and made a substantial donation of $30,000 to help build the First Reformed Church in College Point that incidentally, still exists today.

Poppenhusen died in 1883 and in 1884 the citizens of College Point erected a monument in his honor on a triangle of land on College Point Boulevard. Even more importantly, the Poppenhusen Institute, founded in 1868, continues to function in his honor as a living history museum located at 114-04 14th Road in College Point.

In the years following the war, silk mills came to town and the entertainment industry, with its attendant hotels and bars that were already there in the 1860's, flourished. College Point's many fabled breweries, among them Joseph Thaler's and Hirsch & Co., provided the liquid refreshment, and it was a long-standing belief that the town had more bars per capita than any town of similar size in the entire United States.

The Civil War serves as a backdrop to the lives of all these men who enlisted and served, were captured, imprisoned, and in the case of some, but not all, paroled. Many were wounded, and many died as a result of illness or the wounds received in battle.

They wrote letters, some quoted from in these pages, and letters were written about them, in support of them, and they were poignant letters, indeed, pleading letters.

A few names appear with frequency on marriage records and in letters they wrote in support of applications for pension benefits filed for by widows. One such name is that of Rev. Joseph Huber, the founding pastor of the Catholic Church in College Point, Saint Fidelis. Another is Lutheran Pastor August Ebendick from St. John's Church, also in College Point.

Introduction to the Biographies

Germany, site of the Reformation, was both strongly Catholic as well as Lutheran, and since College Point had such a large German-born population, both ministers of the Gospel would have had prominent roles to play in the lives of these men and their families. Huber ministered to the Catholic members of the community from 1856 though 1888 and Ebendick, whose ministry to the Lutheran members of community began in the village in 1864, preached his final sermon on September 10, 1910.

Many of the men worked for forty years or more in the *"rubber factory"* also called at times, the *"comb factory"*. They married, raised children and buried children, buried wives and remarried and their lives are traced through military and pension files, census records and as many sources for information as could be found.

In many cases the information is scant, while for some it is entirely non-existent due possibly to their not having applied for pensions, due possibly to their deaths, or due simply to not being able to find them in any census records after the war. It is logical to assume that among those who had deserted, there would be little interest in responding to the census taker's questions.

For the largest number of men, pension and military files, provide a great deal in addition to an individual's age, height, complexion, eye and hair color at the time of enlistment, and as much as could be learned is passed on in these mini-biographies, some of which could serve as the basis for some interesting novels, such is life.

As noted previously, a large number of the men who served had been born in Germany, and the pension files often provided the name of the specific town or village of birth. The names of those towns are spelled as they appeared in the pension records.

For purposes of clarity, the biographies of the soldiers who came to College Point following the war begin with the phrase "GAR member" and their individual stories then follow with as much information as could be found. In a very few instances former soldiers moved to the village, but apparently never joined Adam Wirth Post No. 451.

As has been said before, a number of their descendants continue to live and work in College Point and some have contributed to the information thus far compiled and recorded here.

One final note, there were a number of men in the 1860 Census of Flushing living in College Point who could very possibly have served, but whose service could not be definitively documented. As a result their stories are not included here, but may appear in subsequent editions of this book should their service ever be documented.

Biographies

Biographies

Ackerknecht, Frederick

GAR member Frederick Ackerknecht was born in the village of Witzenburg, Germany in June 1836 and came to America in 1860. He was a cobbler by trade.

On October 19, 1861 he enlisted in Company K of the 51st New York Infantry and was discharged on October 1, 1865.

Four years after his discharge he married 20 year-old Ann Melusina Tofler at the First German Presbyterian Church on Rivington Street in New York City. Pastor Schneider performed the ceremony and at some point the family moved to College Point where they are found in the 1880 Census on page 238D. Fritz, as he was known, is a laborer, Anna keeps house and there are five children; Julius, born in 1872, Paulina, February 11, 1872, Frederick, August 20, 1874, Edward, March 14, 1877, Anna, August 17, 1879. Two more children will be born; Emil in November 1882, and Herman on September 11, 1889.

The family appears in the 1900 Census in College Point with all of the children living at home except Julius and Frederick. By 1920 only Herman yet lives in College Point and he is found on page 58-A in Enumeration District 193 of that Census.

Frederick was admitted to the National Soldiers' Home in Elizabeth City, North Carolina on January 22, 1904 and the record says he was discharged twelve years later on October 11, 1916. Two months later he died, at the age of 80, at 309 11th Street in College Point.

Apel, Conrad

Conrad is the 18 year-old, blacksmith son of war casualty Henry Apel, and his wife Mary who appears with them in the 1860 Census of Flushing on page 741. He has a sister Amelia who is 15 and working as a *"factory girl"*, but the nature of her labor is not explained no further. She also has a brother William who is 12.

Conrad Apel was born in Saxony in Germany ca. 1842 and enlisted in Company E of the 29th New York Infantry on May 15, 1861. In 1862 he was wounded then discharged on June 20, 1863 to come home to work in the rubber factory. He died from typhoid pneumonia in College Point on October 19, 1873, a single man, and is buried in Flushing Cemetery with his mother Mary, sometimes called Marie, who passes away on November 4, 1874, some fourteen months later.

Apel, Henry

Henry Apel married his wife Mary in the Lutheran Church in the village of Reibersdorf in Saxony, Germany on April 11, 1841. They came to America sometime in the early 1850's and settled in College Point where in the 1860 Census of Flushing, the family is found on page 741. There are three children; Amelia, 15, Conrad, 18 and a blacksmith, and William, who is 12.

On May 15, 1861 at the age of 42, Henry enlisted along with his son Conrad, in Co. E of the 29th New York Infantry and served for two years, mustering out on June 20, 1863 only to reenlist a year later on July 29, 1864 in Company E of the 7th Infantry Veteran Regiment.

In one of war's cruel twists of fate, on April 2, 1865, exactly one week before Confederate General Robert E. Lee asked for armistice at Appomattox, Apel was wounded while on picket duty, suffering a fatal gunshot wound to the left lung. He died two days later on April 4th at Armory Square Hospital in Washington, DC, one week shy of his 24th wedding anniversary and ten days before John Wilkes Booth would assassinate President Abraham Lincoln.

Armory Square, one of the largest Civil War hospitals, was located where the present National Air and Space Museum stands today. The 1000-bed hospital had 12 pavilions, overflow tents, and was spread out across the Washington Mall. During his time in the military, Henry had been detailed a number of times as a nurse, perhaps even at this hospital.

Henry's name is etched on the Flushing Memorial to Civil War casualties.

On July 31, 1865 Marie applied for and was granted widow's benefits. She appears in the 1870 Census of Flushing on Page 245 with son Conrad, who works in the rubber factory and a second son William, a 22 year-old baker. Mary is keeping house and has an annual income of $5,000.

As noted earlier, she died on November 4, 1874 and is buried in Flushing Cemetery.

Arnold, William

GAR member William Arnold served in the Atlantic Squadron of the U.S. Navy according to the information available. He does not appear in either 1880 or 1900 Census records in College Point and nothing else is known of this individual.

Baumann, Frederick

GAR member Frederick Baumann was born in Germany ca. 1837 to Philip and Rosina Billert Baumann.

In 1856, according to his pension file, he was living in Havana, Cuba and landed in New York Harbor in March 1857. He lived with his parents at 41st Street and 9th Avenue in New York City until the day he enlisted.

On that day, November 11, 1861, he stood 5'9", had brown hair, gray eyes and was working as a laborer in a brickyard at Croton Point. On December 3, 1864 he was mustered out of Company K of the 103rd New York Infantry and returned to New York City.

He was married twice; the first time to Anna Marie Brueckner, probably right after the war. They had three children; Peter, born March 23, 1866, Edward, 1867 and Frederick, April 19, 1869. Anna Marie died on March 29, 1871 in New York City. She was 24 years old.

A short while later on June 8th he married Eva Ohl at St. Francis Catholic Church on West 31st Street. Rev. Andrew Pfeifer performed the ceremony and the couple had five children; Francis Joseph, born February 19, 1872, Caroline Emma, August 3, 1876, Adam John, September 19, 1880, Julia, April 5, 1882 and Philip Jacob, January 12, 1884.

In his pension application he claimed that while marching from White House Landing to Hanover Court house in Virginia he suffered sunstroke resulting in deafness.

The family is enumerated in the 1880 Census. Frederick is a junk dealer and Eva is keeping house.

Frederick is an original member of the GAR in College Point where he dies on July 22, 1911. Eva lives on until April 27, 1918 when she dies while living at 964 6th Avenue.

Baumann, John

John Baumann was born in the town of Frankenberg in Hesse, Germany on November 5, 1843 to John and Anna Baumann who came to America in 1855. His mother's maiden name was Gross and the family appears in the 1860 Census of Flushing on page 726, living in a house on present day 119th Street between 20th and 22nd Avenues. John is enumerated with his father, mother and two sisters; 22 year-old Catherine and 15 year-old Mary. Both sisters are working as *"Factory Girls"* undoubtedly at Conrad Poppenhusen's Rubber Factory.

In the years to come Mary will marry Charles Metz and be widowed around 1891. Catherine will be wed to College Point Civil War veteran Michael Nau and she dies on October 27, 1879.

On enlistment day, October 19, 1861, John, a comb-maker, stood 5'5", had a dark complexion with gray eyes and sandy hair. During his time in the 34th New York Light Artillery, he was hospitalized a number of times. The first took place in Cincinnati, Ohio in April, 1863, then in Covington, Kentucky from August 31st to October 23rd of the same year and twice more before the end of December. As did many soldiers, he suffered from bouts of diarrhea.

John served through the war and following his discharge on June 21, 1865, he married Adeline Piereth, daughter of veteran Christian Piereth, and sister to veteran Valentine Piereth. It is likely the ceremony took place at St. John's Lutheran Church.

They were parents to Mary and Bathsheba, twins born October 23, 1868, Catherine, May 3, 1870, Rosalie, September 6, 1871, John, April 20, 1874, Christian, June 9, 1876, Wilhelm, December, 1878, Conrad, October 19, 1879, Margaretha, March 3, 1883 and Adeline, February 6, 1888.

In 1870 his parents and unmarried sister Mary appear in the Flushing Census on page 224. John and Adeline are enumerated on page 56 with the twins and baby Kate. John works at the rubber factory.

John's wife Adeline, died in College Point on April 4, 1892. A pension document submitted on April 1, 1898 indicates by their absence that Mary, Christian and Conrad may also have died in preceding years, but dates are not given.

Seventeen months after Adeline's death, John married Sophia Koch on August 25, 1893 in a ceremony performed by Pastor Ebendick at St. John's Lutheran Church and they appear in the 1900 Census of College Point. Sophie died in the years to come and John married a third time at St. John's on March 14, 1908, Marie Haas, the widow of one Louis Schneider. Pastor Ebendick once again performed the ceremony.

At age 66 in the 1910 Census John is still employed as a rubber worker.

Nine years later John Baumann died on October 18, 1919 and is buried in Flushing Cemetery. At least one of his descendants, Bonnie Tustin, lives yet in College Point. Her grandmother was Margaretha, the daughter born to John and Adeline in 1883.

Baumeister, Z

A thorough search of all known resources resulted in a number of individuals with this surname, but none with a name beginning with the letter "Z" or any in the 79th New York Infantry. He, along with J. Broid of the same unit, will remain a mystery.

Beardslee, Frederick E.

Frederick appears in the 1860 Flushing Census on page 699, the 19 year-old son of George W. Beardslee, an electrician. Frederick has two siblings; Caroline, 15 and George L., 13. Two Irish servants are also enumerated, Mary Nolan, 25, and Mary Powers, 19, a seamstress.

His father had invented a successful magneto-electric generator, patented in 1859. An article in the May, 1976 edition of the *Civil War Times Illustrated* states: *"The inventor had been manufacturing his magneto machines commercially for several years at College Point, Long Island with financial backing from the firm of Poppenhusen and Konig, dealers in gutta-percha and India rubber."*

The Army had been seeking a portable source of electricity to power the telegraph in the field and Beardslee's invention, with modifications, made it possible.

Frederick became a 2nd Lieutenant in the United States Signal Corps, certainly because of his background and familiarity with the field. After his service he returned to College Point and appears on page 221 in the 1870 Census, unmarried and working as an Assistant Inspector on the railroad.

On March 13, 1876 he married Laura Dingee in Brooklyn at a Methodist Episcopal Church. A child named Lester Eugene is born on January 6, 1878 in Mexico where Frederick had relocated to work as an electrician. He is later baptized at the Park Avenue Primitive Methodist Church in Brooklyn on September 20, 1879.

After the family returned to the U.S., Frederick had a number of jobs according to his cousin William F. Beardslee, whose signed affidavit was included in the pension file.

Frederick was an accomplished electrician and had no difficulty finding work. He did, however, have difficulties that lead to his suicide on September 3, 1888 at the age of 44. He had been depressed according to pension documents, and his death certificate indicates that he poisoned himself at 76 Beekman Street. The certificate also confirmed that he was an electrician and, indeed, the son of George W. Beardslee.

Frederick is buried at Green-Wood Cemetery in Brooklyn and Laura remained in Brooklyn living at 421 Henry Street. It is not known when she passed away.

Becker, Ludwig

Ludwig or Louis Becker, age 43, enlisted in Flushing on September 7, 1861 and deserted the 2nd New York Heavy Artillery the following June 4th at Camp Barry in Washington, DC. His name was included in the August 23, 1862 list of men from College Point that appeared in the *Flushing Journal*. Nothing else is known.

Behring, Friedrich

Friedrich or Frederick Behring was born ca. 1821 in Obenheim, Schwarzburg, Saxony in Germany and appears in the 1860 Census of Flushing on page 719, a 39 year-old laborer married to Caroline, whose maiden name may have been Lippman. They have three children; Amelia, born September 17, 1841, Christina, September 25, 1843, and Paul, 12, all born in Germany. It appears also that Friedrich's mother, Elizabeth, lives with them.

Friedrich was included in the August 23, 1862 list of volunteers from College Point that appeared in the *Flushing Journal*. On October 4, 1861 he enlisted in Co. C of the 58th New York Infantry and was wounded at the Battle of Cross Keys in Virginia. He was also taken prisoner of war following the Battle of Chancellorsville in May 1863. For reasons unknown, he did not apply for a pension.

It is known that daughter Christine married veteran Edward Freund and daughter Amelia married another veteran, Julius Steinbeck. Paul is in the 1880 Census, married and living in New York City.

According to Tania Steinbeck-Reeves, a descendant of Julius and Amelia, Caroline died on April 24, 1873; Friedrich two years later on May 15, 1875.

Benz, Louis

No military service or pension record of GAR member Louis Benz was found, nor is he enumerated in any Census in College Point. Other than his membership in Post No. 451, nothing else is known.

Beresheim, Jacob

Jacob appears in the 1860 Census of Flushing on page 737, a 37 year-old baker from Bavaria married to Catherine who is 33, and also from Bavaria. They have two children; Jacob, 3 and Eugene, 2. The name is spelled *Bershein*.

Jacob is listed in Munsell's *History of Queens County* as having served in the 15th New York Heavy Artillery, but it was actually a 30-day enlistment in the 15th New York Regiment of National Guard Infantry from June 6, 1864 through July 7, 1864. In this instance his name is spelled *Berensheimer*.

In the 1870 Census of Flushing the family name is found on page 220 with the surname spelled *Bersheimer*. Jacob is a teamster, and it appears baby Eugene has died. Five additional children have been born; Lena, 10, Adam, 7, George, 6, Frank, 4 and Kate who is but 1 month old.

In the 1880 Census of College Point, Catherine is listed on page 297B as a widow. Her eldest son Jacob is a farmer. All of the children from 1870 are enumerated and the name is spelled *Bershein* as it was in 1860.

By 1900 the name is spelled *Beresheim* and Catherine tells us she was born in December 1826, and had come to America in 1850. The children; Jacob, Lena, Kate and Frank, are still living at home.

Berndt, William

On September 9, 1861, the day he enlisted in Company L of the 2nd New York Heavy Artillery, in the company of his friends John Baumann and Jacob Sutorious, William was a 5'6" farmer with a dark complexion, gray eyes and brown hair.

Born on October 26, 1836 in the German town of Hebersdorf bei Neugirt, he was the son of Samuel Berndt, a master wind miller, and Anna Rosina Kaske. He was baptized August William Berndt on November 3, 1835.

Following the war he married Mary Fermer, born in Pilsner, Austria on April 5, 1846 to Joseph and Katherine Fermer. The wedding took place at St. John's Lutheran Church in College Point on November 8, 1868 with Pastor Ebendick performing the ceremony. Witnesses to the marriage were George Muecke and Christian Stiebeck.

From ca. 1875 on, the family lived in Brooklyn, but returned to College Point in the mid 1880's to live at 231 10th Street, today's 119th Street.

The pension record indicates he was shot in the neck at Pegram Farm near Petersburg, Virginia on September 30, 1864. *"The missile passed from beneath the chin on the right side of the neck, about 2" below the ear."*

The record goes on to say he was left on the field through the day but was picked up during the night and spent several months recuperating at Beverly Hospital in Burlington, New Jersey from October 16, 1864 to January 16, 1865. One official record says he died from that wound, but obviously such was not the case, and Roemer's book, page 253, says only that he was severely wounded.

Over the years he and Mary were parents to seven children. They were; Annie, born September 28, 1870, Mary, August 19, 1871, Charles, October 6, 1872, Josephine, April 5, year unknown, William, July 18, year unknown, Hannah, April 19, 1882 and Henry, October 20, year unknown.

William appears in the 1900 and 1910 College Point Census records where it is indicated that his arrival in America took place in 1860.

A member of the GAR in College Point, William died on July 22, 1917 at the age of 84, and is buried in Flushing Cemetery along with Mary, who died on December 9, 1919. The daughter Hannah, who had married a man named Steiner, took care of her widowed mother following William's death.

Bertschinger, Gustav

GAR member Gustav Bertschinger served in Company E, 2nd Battalion of U.S. Engineers and applied for his pension using the name August Berger, a name that was also used on the original GAR Charter Application.

August or Gustav, from Switzerland, was 38 in the 1880 Census of College Point on page 309B. His wife Rosa was also 38 and from Switzerland. They had three children; Hy, 6, Ed, 5 and Rosa, 3, all born in New York. Other than his membership in the GAR, nothing else is known.

Beyerly, Peter

Peter is enumerated in the 1860 Flushing Census on page 741. He is 34, a machinist from Bavaria, married to 27 year-old Marie, also from Bavaria. Anna Bihn, a 51 year-old midwife, lives with the family. John, 6 and William, 1, are their two children; both born in New York.

Peter is among those included on the 1863 Provost Marshall's list. He is also named in Munsell's *History of Queens County* as having served in the 15th New York Heavy Artillery, actually the 15th Regiment of New York State Militia, a thirty-day unit called out to garrison Fort Richmond in New York Harbor from June 6 to July 7, 1864.

He appears in the 1880 Census of College Point on page 298C where he is 54, still married to Marie and working as a machinist. The aforementioned Anna Bihn is identified as Peter's mother-in-law, and no children other than John and William, are enumerated.

John Beyerly lives in College Point in 1920, but there are no further records for his father, Peter.

Bisky, Louis

Friedrich Ludwig Bisky was born in Berlin in 1817 and on February 26, 1859 married Henriette Friedericke Kurtz, born in Muhlhausen, Germany ca. 1837. The marriage took place at the Philadelphia City Hall in the Mayor's Office. James B. Kenney, an Alderman, performed the ceremony.

Bisky enlisted in Company C of the 45th New York on September 1, 1861 and on that day he is described as being 43, a goldsmith standing 5'11" having a fair complexion, blue eyes and brown hair. During his distinguished career he served as Ordinance Officer of his Brigade.

Louis was killed at the Battle of Chancellorsville on May 2, 1863. His body was never recovered from the field, but his named is etched on the Flushing Memorial to Civil War casualties.

Two children were born; Julius, October 16, 1860, and Emma, December 5, 1863. Pastor August Ebendick baptized both children at St. John's Lutheran Church in College Point. Emma married Hamilton Roe.

He and his wife appear in the 1860 Census in New York City. Louis *Brisky*, as his named is spelled, is a gilder. Fredricka, as her named is spelled, claims birth in France. Living with the couple is a man named Frederic Kuhltz, a 49 year-old silver plater from Bavaria and Catherine, his 40 year old, French-born wife.

His widowed wife, Henriette Friedericke, and the two children, appear in the 1880 Census of College Point on page 243A. Julius dies in 1887 at the age of 27 and is buried in Flushing Cemetery. Henriette died at her Amity Street home in Flushing on May 20, 1923, and is buried with her son. Interred with them is an unidentified Louis Bisky who died in 1912.

On October 24, 1986 Dr. Kurt Wernicke, then of the Museum for German History in what was East Berlin, gave a photographic print of a portrait of Louis Bisky drawn by Salomon Levy in 1849, to the National Archives. It is reproduced in the pages of this book.

Bockler, Chrisostomus

A 35 year-old comb-maker named Chrisostomus appears on page 701 of the 1860 Census of Flushing. Born in Prussia, the surname appears as *"Dibler"*, but he is very likely the man who on enlistment day, October 4, 1861, stood 5'9" had a dark complexion, dark hair and gray eyes. In his pension application he claims that he *"suffered a hernia while building a corduroy road in Alabama while carrying large timbers."*

Following his October 22, 1864 discharge from the 58th New York Infantry, he lived in College Point and, according to his pension application, worked as a mechanic. In the 1880 Census of College Point on page 313B, he lives with the family of Maurice Roessler and works in the rubber factory.

Eventually he makes his way to the Soldier's Home in Hampton, Virginia where he died on February 28, 1885. It appears he never married.

Bracken, John

John Bracken, whose name appears in the *Flushing Journal* list of College Point volunteers spelled *Paschen,* was born in Westmeath, Ireland in 1826 and on October 1, 1861, the day he enlisted in Company L of the 2nd New York Heavy Artillery, he was a 24 year-old blacksmith standing 5'6" with a light complexion, blue eyes and dark hair.

His military record indicates John was wounded at Fort Hill near Petersburg in Virginia on July 10, 1864 and sent to the 3rd Division Hospital to recover. A 30-day furlough was granted from Fairfax Seminary Hospital early in August and he was reported as a deserter as of December 31st of that year. The report was deemed *"improperly made"* and removed at the time of his widow Mary's application for widow's benefits.

Bracken is named in Roemer's book as having transferred from the 2nd New York Heavy Artillery on August 18, 1862 and then deserting as noted above.

On August 17, 1864, while on his 30-day furlough, Bracken married Mary Frances Hayes in a Catholic ceremony conducted by Rev. John Brady at St. Anthony's Church in the Green Point section of Brooklyn. They had one daughter there named Mary, born on January 5, 1876.

According to the pension record, John lived in Long Island City where he shoed horses for a living. Both Jacob Roemer and Dennis Illerd wrote letters in support of the pension application.

Bracken, a blacksmith all his life, died on May 24, 1885 and is buried in Calvary Cemetery in Woodside, Queens.

On November 1, 1887 Mary married a man named Patrick Johnson and moved to Bridgeport, Connecticut. Patrick died in Fairfield on July 22, 1907 and Mary died eleven years later on April 13, 1918 at the home of her daughter Mary.

Brill, Christian, Sr.

Christian was born on November 30, 1846 in the town of Lembeck in Germany. He enlisted in Company L of the 2nd New York Heavy Artillery on September 1, 1861. At the time he stood 5'7", had a light complexion, brown hair and brown eyes.

In the 1860 Census of Flushing there appears on page 701 a 23 year-old shoemaker by this name, but there is neither a way to confirm his identity, nor to connect him to the Christian Brill, Jr. who follows.

He was discharged on November 19, 1863 whereupon, the pension record indicates, he married Caroline Beatty on December 3, 1866 in the town of Bethel in Sullivan County, New York. Rev. Walter S. Brown, a minister of the Gospel, performed the ceremony.

One week after the wedding the couple returned to College Point where he worked as a clerk in a shoe store. As his health deteriorated, Christian began to repair shoes at his home, but by July of 1867 the couple decided to return to Bethel where on January 22, 1868 he died of consumption.

Caroline remarried on January 4, 1871 in White Lock, another town in Sullivan County. She filed for widow's pension benefits under her new married name, Beatty, and at the time of her application on May 15, 1911, she was living at 54 Leroy Street in Binghamton, New York. The application was rejected, as his death was determined not to have been caused by anything having to do with his military service.

Brill, Christian, Jr.

The Brill men are the source of much confusion with Sr. being born in 1846 and Jr. in 1842, along with the unavailability of Jr.'s pension record. Here is what is known from available sources.

At the time of enlistment, also October 1, 1861, Jr. was an 18 year-old tinsmith, standing 5'4", with a dark complexion, brown eyes and black hair. He was discharged on April 3, 1864 and applied for a pension on September 13, 1880. His widow Mary Ann, applied for her widow's benefits on May 13, 1911. Christian had passed away on February 18, 1910.

His service record indicates he became a prisoner of war on October 30, 1863 following the Battle of Knoxville in Tennessee. College Pointer David Schultz would lose his life during this same battle.

Christian was admitted to a hospital at Danville, Virginia on January 2, 1864 suffering from Small Pox, and again on April 23rd as a result of diarrhea. After his release on December 11, 1864 he was admitted to the hospital at Camp Parole in Annapolis, Maryland on December 16, 1864 and eventually discharged in New York City.

In 1880 he is living in Newark, New Jersey, married to Mary, born in England, with three children; Annie, 11, Alfred, 2 and Elizabeth, 6 months, all born in New York. That he lived in New Jersey at this time is mentioned in the pension application of Daniel S. Johnston, Jr. with whom he was imprisoned.

Briody, Richard Henry

Richard Briody was born in New York City on June 1, 1841 to Henry or Nicholas Briody, the record is unclear, and his wife Mary Madden, both from Ireland, and baptized on the same day at St. Mary's Church at the corner of Grand Avenue and Ridge Street in Lower Manhattan on the East side.

Having a light complexion and blue eyes, Richard stood 5'8" and in 1861 was a comb-maker in College Point when he entered the service. He was taken prisoner at the First Battle of Bull Run, July 21, 1861, less than two months after enlisting, and held as a prisoner. The record does not indicate when he was released, but Richard was mustered out on May 24th of the following year in Washington, DC.

Less than a year later on March 17, 1863, Father Joseph Huber married Richard to Elizabeth Larkin at Saint Fidelis Church. Her large family lived in College Point and can found on page 720 of the 1860 Flushing Census. They were neighbors of the Dockendorf family, the author's ancestors.

Following the ceremony they lived at 79 Perry Street in Manhattan, then moved to New Jersey, then relocated again in Brooklyn, ca. 1870.

Richard died on March 23, 1912 and is buried in Calvary Cemetery in Woodside. At the time of his death the couple was living in Brooklyn near Sheepshead Bay at 2660 East 21st Street.

Broid, J.

While this individual appears in the August 23, 1862 *Flushing Journal* list of volunteers from College Point, there is no one by this name who served in the 79th New York Infantry, or in any other unit. The roster of soldiers in the 79th lists Robert and William Boyd and one William Bloyd who deserted.

J. Broid along with Z. Baumeister, supposedly of the same unit, will for now, remain a mystery.

Buckley, John

There are two people by this name cited in the 1860 Census of Flushing. One appears on page 701, an unmarried 22-year-old comb-maker from Ireland.

The other, on page 744, is an 18 year-old, New York-born son of an Irish day laborer also named John Buckley, 43, and his wife, 51 year-old Mary, also from Ireland. Young John has three younger siblings; William, 10, Mary, 9, Charles, 5 and James 3.

Records indicate that John Buckley, one of these two, died at Charleston Harbor on November 5, 1863 while serving in the Navy.

His name appears in the list of casualties that appeared in the July 21, 1866 edition of the *Flushing Journal* and his name is etched on the Flushing Memorial to Civil War casualties.

To date this is what is known of this person, whichever of the two he is.

Buhl, Peter

Peter appears in the 1860 Census of Flushing on page 717 with his named spelled *Puhl*. He is 45, a laborer from Wurtemburg and married to Pauline. Charles, 11, Julius, 9, and William, 1, are their children.

His name appears in a *Flushing Journal* article dated November 6, 1861 indicating his service in the 15th Regiment of New York State Militia.

While he probably never went to war, he is listed as the Orderly of the unit. In the article he authorized the burial of another member of the unit, George Naumann, whose brief biography appears further on in this book.

Peter appears in the 1870 Census of Flushing on page 212 married to Paulena. They have three children; Charles, 21, Julius, 19, and William, 10. None of these individuals appear in the 1880 Census and nothing else is known of Peter Buhl.

Buser, Charles

GAR member Charles Buser was born on September 7, 1843 in the village of Buchten in the Canton of Basel, Switzerland, to Johan Jacob Buser and his wife, the former Elizabeth Schatzmann.

Buser came to America in 1859 and on September 1, 1861, the day he enlisted in Company B of the 15th New York Heavy Artillery, he stood 5'9", had a fair complexion, blue eyes and brown hair. Why he enlisted in Philadelphia is unknown, but after the war he lived in New York City, West Point, and ultimately in College Point, where he worked in one of the silk mills.

Charles married M. Lisette Kirscher on February 5, 1870 in Highland Falls, New York and in 1880 he and his wife live in New York City with the children; Mary, born October 10, 1870, Rose, March 2, 1872 and Charles who is 10 months old. His wife's name is written as Elizabeth. The names of three more children are in the pension record, Henry, born August 27, 1883, Herman, September 7, 1885 and George, May 29, 1888.

The 1900 Census indicates the family still lives in College Point on 17th Street. Charles is an engineer.

In 1920 Charles is a widow and lives at 226 17th Street in College Point with his daughter Rose now married to John Delemont, a cousin named Anna Eble, and his unmarried daughter Mary, called Mamie. He lives here until his death on June 26, 1923. His son Herman lives in College Point and Henry lives in the Winfield section of Queens.

Coffin, Lowell

GAR member Lowell Coffin is a Massachusetts native who served in the 46th Infantry from that state, and was an original member of the GAR in College Point. Beyond that, little else is known.

Colvin, John

GAR member John Colvin is the son of Thomas Colvin, a 31 year-old boot-maker from England, who appears with his wife Mary, nee Haley, 24 also from England, and his family, in the 1850 Census of New York City. John, born December 28, 1845, is the eldest of four children. He has three sisters; Sarah, born ca. 1846, Margaret, born ca. 1847 and Emma, who is three months old.

In the 1860 Census of New York City, Jennette is listed, born ca. 1855, and Susan, ca. 1859. A three year-old boy named Edward is also enumerated in the 1860 Census. There is no listing for either Margaret or Emma so they probably died, plus another son named Charles would be born after 1860.

Following his July 28, 1865 discharge from the First Connecticut Heavy Artillery, John returned to marry Catherine Bradley in Flushing in 1868. According to information in the pension record provided by his brother Charles, three children were born; John, ca. 1871, Annie, ca. 1873 and Peter, ca. 1875.

Following the death of Catherine on December 28, 1878, coincidentally John's 33rd birthday, John had enlisted the aid of a young woman named Mary Murphy to take care of the children.

On October 31, 1880 John married Mary Murphy at St. Michael's Catholic Church in Flushing with Father John McKenna performing the ceremony. A few months later, without explanation, Mary left. There was no divorce.

Five years later on February 3, 1885, with no apparent mention of the marriage to and eventual departure of Mary Murphy, John married once again this time to Susan Hunt Carpenter. The ceremony took place at St. George Protestant Church in Hempstead, Long Island. According to the pension record, seven children were born, but only five are listed; Mary Ann, born on November 30, 1885, Eleanor, September 10, 1888, Thomas, February 22, 1890, Arthur, June 1, 1893 and Susan, November 21, 1897.

Susan applied for benefits from Providence, Rhode Island where she had moved as a result, she claimed, of John's drinking habits. The pension was denied, the reason being John's marriage to Mary Murphy had never been dissolved.

According to the Census, John is renting a room at 152 Washington Street in Flushing in 1920, and is listed as being an unemployed widower. He died two years later on May 3, 1922 and is buried in Mt. St. Mary's Cemetery.

Connors, Thomas

Thomas Connors was born in Port Arlington, the Capital of County Laois, Ireland ca. 1842 and appears in the 1860 Census of Flushing on page 696, an 18 year-old laborer from Ireland. He is the son of Margaret Egan, a widow who in 1860 lived in New York City. Her husband, first name unknown, had died in Ireland in the mid 1850's and she then emigrated to the United States. Why her surname is Egan is not spelled out.

Thomas enlisted in Company K of the 61st New York Infantry on September 8, 1862. His military record says that on that day he was a laborer, age 22, stood 5'10" with a light complexion, blue eyes and light hair.

Less than a year later, on July 2, 1863, the first day of the three-day Battle of Gettysburg, Thomas lost his life. Colonel Nelson A. Miles, who would be awarded the Congressional Medal of Honor for gallantry at Chancellorsville and later gain fame both as an Indian fighter and for the capture of Geronimo, Chief of the Apache Indians, certified his death.

On September 15th, just before departing for the seat of war, Thomas married Johanna Bowden at St. Michael's Catholic Church in Flushing. Rev. James O'Beirne performed the ceremony and on June 28, 1863, a daughter, Margaret, was born. Her father Thomas died four days later.

On April 11, 1875 Johanna married Patrick Carroll, a widower himself, in a Catholic ceremony at St. Fidelis Church in College Point. Father Joseph Huber performed the ceremony. In 1880 Patrick and Johanna appear on page 260B of the Flushing Census with Patrick's two sons, Dennis, 17 and William, 14.

In the same 1880 Census on page 326D there is an 18 year-old servant, New York born female named Maggie Conners living with the family of Robert S. Tucker. She could be or appears to be the child Margaret, born in 1863.

On September 4, 1879 Thomas' mother wrote a letter to the Pension Board seeking benefits claiming she had not heard from Johanna in 12 years and was in need of financial support. I don't believe she received any.

The name Thomas Conner *(sic)* is etched on the Flushing Memorial to Civil War casualties.

Cooper, William

Swiss-born William Cooper married Eleonora Cuppers from Germany, in New York City on September 13, 1858 in a ceremony performed by Rev. S. W. Gaisenheimer.

He joined Company L of the 2nd New York Heavy Artillery on August 28, 1861, and in a little over a year, 2nd Lieutenant Cooper was discharged on a Surgeon's Certificate of Disability by special order #284 dated October 8th. According to Col. Jacob Roemer, he had suffered a serious hernia.

Following William's military service he, his wife Eleanora and two daughters; Margaret, born September 8, 1863 and Eleonora, January 2, 1869, are found in College Point in 1870 on page 237 of the Flushing Census. The couple is also enumerated in the 1880 Census of College Point on page 315A with their daughters and a son, Gustav, who was born October 21, 1872.

William works at the rubber factory, lives on until he dies on March 14, 1903, and is laid to rest in Flushing Cemetery.

Cordier, Daniel

Daniel Cordier is listed on page 191 in the 1850 Census living in the 15th Ward of New York City.

In 1860 he is listed on page 720 of the Flushing Census as being a 30 year-old, German-born florist living with Elizabeth, his 28 year-old wife, and another female named Elizabeth who is 20. There is no indication of the relationship.

Daniel is listed in Munsell's *History of Queens County* as having served in the 15th New York Heavy Artillery, but it was actually a 30-day enlistment in the 15th New York Regiment of National Guard Infantry from June 6, 1864 through July 7, 1864.

While there are numerous persons named Cordier living in College Point in 1880 and beyond, there are none named Daniel.

Cornell, James C.

GAR member James C. Cornell was born in Flushing on January 11, 1844, to Benjamin Cornell and his wife Mary. The family appears in the 1850 Census of Flushing on page 300. Benjamin is a painter and, curiously, only Ellen, his sister, is enumerated. James and Isaac are not.

In 1860 Benjamin is 40 years old and a New York-born laborer. Mary is 39, also born in New York, and in addition to 16 year-old James, there is 14 year-old Isaac and the daughter Ellen, who is 10.

On enlistment day, August 6, 1861, James was 18, a sash and blind-maker standing 5'7" with a light complexion, blue eyes and brown hair. It is known that he was wounded at the Second Battle of Bull Run on August 30, 1862 in Virginia, and that he is mentioned on page 220 of Jacob Roemer's book on the 34th New York Light Artillery. He was discharged on June 21, 1865 at Hart's Island in New York Harbor.

What came to light upon reviewing his Military Record at the National Archives was significant in that on February 21, 1865 he was recommended for the Medal of Honor by Major General John G. Parke, Commander of the 9th Army Corps for conspicuous gallantry, to wit: *"for his proficiency as gunner, he rendered great service at the Battle of the Wilderness, Spotsylvania, North Anna, Cold Harbor, and before Petersburg, June 17th. At the latter place he succeeded in exploding two of the enemy's caissons which brought fourth a huzza from the whole line and caused the enemy to withdraw from their position."*

It appears the Medal of Honor was never awarded, as Cornell's name is not included among the acknowledged 1,195 recipients from the Civil War.

Did he know he was recommended for the honor? There is no way to know; but that his valor in the face of the enemy was recognized by Major General Parke surely puts him in the ranks of Carl Ludwig, John Starkins and Joseph Hibson.

In the 1870 Flushing Census on page 44 James, 26, works as a carpenter on the railroad and a woman named Doty *(sic)*, 22, keeps house. Isaac, 24, his brother and a brakeman on the railroad, also lives with him. No relationships are noted, but it is possible that Doty may have been Isaac's wife.

A copy of the Marriage Certificate found in the pension file indicates that on May 26, 1880, James married Sarah Harpell, 12 years his junior, in Whitestone. Rev. William F. Dickinson conducted the ceremony at Grace Church with William Schilling and Arabella Harpell serving as witnesses.

Sarah Harpell is the daughter of Seth Harpell, a stonemason whose family appears in the 1860 Census of Flushing on page 763. Seth served in Co. C of the 74th New York Infantry and was killed at the Battle of Gettysburg on July 2, 1863, the same day as Thomas Conners. He had enlisted on September 3, 1862 and is buried at Gettysburg National Cemetery in the New York Plot, Gravesite G-37. His name is etched on the Flushing Memorial to Civil War casualties.

The couple appears in the 1880 Census of Whitestone living with the William Schilling who is married to Annie, Sarah's younger sister. No children have been born, but there was at least one daughter named Rosalie, who reported her mother's death in Roosevelt, New York on June 11, 1941.

In the same census, Isaac lives in Newtown and is a baggage-master married to a woman named Vienna who was born in Connecticut. While it is not definite that this Isaac is brother to James, it is a probability as Vienna is 32 and may be the *"Doty"* from the 1870 Census who was 22 at the time.

James C. Cornell, who had worked as an assistant surveyor, died at Roosevelt, Long Island on April 6, 1916 so Sarah outlived her husband by 25 years.

Denno, Tuffeil

GAR member Tuffeil Denno was born in Montreal, Canada on July 4, 1845 and then moved to Vermont with his parents, Theodore and Mary, who are listed in the 1850 and 1860 Vermont Census records. By 1860 Tuffeil is no longer enumerated with his parents and is not found elsewhere in that census year.

On enlistment day, August 22, 1864 he stood 5'6", had a fair complexion, blue eyes, brown hair and listed his occupation as farmer. In March of 1865 just before the war's end, he contracted measles and recuperated at a field hospital near Point of Rocks, Virginia. He was mustered out of Company C of the 9th Vermont Infantry the following June 13th.

His marriage to Leah, whose surname appears as *Filiatraulh*, took place at the Congregational Church in Fairhaven, Connecticut on June 22, 1875. Two children were born; Edith, June 2, 1879 and Frederick, August 11, 1884. After the marriage the family lived both in Brewster, New York and on Long Island before finally settling in Whitestone in January of 1885 where he lived at 83 South 11th Street.

In 1903 he worked for the highway department. He died in Jackson Heights on March 27, 1929, the actual last member of Adam Wirth Post No. 451 to die. His son Frederick lives in Elmhurst in 1920 married to Alice and father to two sons.

Dietrich, George

GAR member George Dietrich was a 19 year-old cigar-maker on the day he enlisted and stood 5'6" with a dark complexion, blue eyes and brown hair. His military record confirms he was confined for a time at a convalescent camp in Alexandria, Virginia from which he received a disability discharge due to the loss of the big toe of his right foot.

There is a record on file indicating George did apply for a pension, but for reasons unknown, it could not be found at the National Archives.

He moved to College Point following discharge on February 13, 1863, and appears on page 240C in College Point's 1880 Census married to Caroline. He is a 35 year-old, German-born *"cegar"* maker and Caroline, also from Germany, is 24. They have a one month-old son named George.

Twenty years later the 1900 College Point Census has Caroline enumerated as a widow and employed at the rubber factory. The record further indicates she was born in May 1856 and living with her are son George, 19, born June 1880, and daughter Kate, 13, born May 1886.

George Dietrich died in College Point on December 1, 1886 and is buried in Flushing Cemetery.

Dillman, Henry

Henry appears in the 1860 Census of Flushing on page 715 along with his wife Catherine and family. Both are from Baden, in Germany. He is 32, a peddler, and she is 30. There are three children; Godfrey, 5, Henry, 3, and Mary, 1.

He appears in the 1863 Provost Marshall's list and while the official record says it was the 13th New York National Guard, it is more likely the 15th.

The family appears on page 254 in the 1870 Census of Flushing living in College Point with three additional children; Louis, 10, Frederick, 6 and John, 3. One more child is enumerated on page 306D in the 1880 Census of College Point. The child is named Charles and he is 9.

Dillon, Michael

Michael Dillon appears in the list of College Point volunteers that appeared in the August 23, 1862 edition of the *Flushing Journal*. His military record indicated he was born in New York ca. 1842, stood 5'7", and had a dark complexion, black eyes and dark hair. His service in Company E of the 10th New York Infantry began on October 4, 1861.

According to his military record, Michael suffered a scalp wound on June 24, 1862 at the Battle of Gaines Mill in Virginia. He then deserted at the end of April 1863, and did not apply for a pension. As a result, nothing else is known.

Dockendorf, Francis

There were three members of the family of Matthias and Catharine Dockendorf who served during the Civil War. Francis or Frank, as he was known, was the youngest of the trio, and the last to enlist. No College Point family sent more sons to the seat of war.

Born in Kaiserslautern, Germany on February 14, 1847, Frank arrived in the United States with his mother and five of his siblings on September 7, 1858 aboard the ship *"Zurich"*. Mathias, his father, had left Germany early in the 1850's followed by his brothers, Frederick and Joseph in 1857.

In 1860 the entire Dockendorf family appears on page 720 of the Flushing Census. Enumerated are Frederick, 17, Joseph, 15, Francis, 13, Henry, 11, Catherine, 9, Charles, 3, the author's great grandfather, and finally John who is one year old.

Francis enlisted in Wilmington as a substitute for George R. Swain from a town called Cedar Creek One Hundred in Sussex County, Delaware on December 29, 1864. The record says he was 21 at the time and a manufacturer. In truth, he was actually only 17, 5'6" with gray eyes, a fair complexion and light hair. A note indicated his enlistment was for but one year, not three, and that, for reasons unknown, he was not entitled to a bounty.

George R. Swain was a 41 year-old farmer who in 1860 lived with a 20 year-old female, named Leah, a 1 year-old female named Ida, and a four-month old male child named Frank.

It does not appear that Francis ever filed for a pension and, in fact, only his military file survives to prove his service. Nevertheless, he returned to College Point and married a woman named Kate whose surname is unknown.

In the 1870 Census of Flushing he is enumerated on page 211 living in College Point and working in a tin factory. There is one child, William, who is one month old.

On page 242C of the 1880 Census of College Point, he is a laborer and there are two children enumerated, Charles, 5 and Lena who is 3. It appears baby William did not survive.

In 1900 the family appears living on Second Avenue. There is another daughter listed by the name of Emma, born in 1887.

Kate died on December 29, 1904 of appendicitis and Frank, suffering from nephritis, died two years later on November 21st. Both are buried in Flushing Cemetery.

Dockendorf, Frederick

Frederick was born on February 28, 1843 in the little village of Homburg, Germany, to Matthias Dockendorf and Catharina Roth. As noted previously, Mathias left Germany without his family, and came to America early in the 1850's. Two other members of that family joined him on April 15, 1857 when the bark *Sarah Park* docked in New York Harbor after a journey from Havre in France.

On board were two of his sons, Frederick Dockendorf, age 14, and a Joseph, age 8, according to the ship notation. Joseph was really closer to twelve. Catharine and the rest of the Dockendorf family would join them in 1858.

Frederick appears with his family on page 720 in the 1860 Flushing Census. Mathias, his father, was born on January 11, 1818 in Kaiserslautern, Germany and married Catharina Roth there on November 30, 1843 at St. Martin's Catholic Church.

In May 1861 Frederick, by now a rubber worker for Conrad Poppenhusen, enlisted to serve in Company I of the 20th New York Infantry. He was 5'4" with blue eyes and blond hair and before his tour of duty would end, he, along with other members of Company I, would be subject to Court Martial on the charge of mutiny and misbehavior before the enemy.

On April 29, 1863 shortly before the Battle of Chancellorsville, a number of men from the 20th, rightly believing that the terms of their enlistments had been met, had stacked their arms. As the battle began, many of these Germans in the regiment refused to fight, and as a result the Court Martial took place in the field.

He and about 200 other men were found guilty, sentenced to forfeit all pay, bounties and allowances possibly due, and to be dishonorably dismissed from the service. They were then to be confined at hard labor for the remainder of the war.

The Court Martial took place and the sentence approved and promulgated in General Order No. 24 dated May 6, 1863.

It was called a *"mutiny"* by the Turners, a sobriquet the Regiment had earned as a result of its large German population, Turners being a German Fraternal Organization founded in Berlin in 1811 to promote patriotism and nationalism through gymnastics.

There was a *"Turn Hall"* in College Point, a gymnasium so to speak, and a great furor arose in support of the *"mutineers"* in this German-American community as well as in others, so much so that President Lincoln got involved resulting in an August 10, 1863 pardon.

Frederick received his bounty, but the controversy did not go away until February 27, 1905 when Congress passed the Acts for the Relief of Certain Enlisted Men of the Twentieth Regiment of New York Volunteer Infantry. This action removed the conviction from the records of the soldiers who had been originally accused and found guilty.

It had taken 42 years, but Frederick and the others finally won their justly deserved, Honorable Discharges.

Returning to College Point, Frederick married Wilhelmina Menk on December 27, 1867 at Saint John's Lutheran Church. Pastor August Ebendick performed the ceremony and over the next sixteen years six children would be born to the couple; William, November 9, 1870, Joseph, April 14, 1873, Christine, July 3, 1875, Frederick, January 9, 1878, Louis, January 26, 1881 and Amalia, March 7, 1883. Baby Frederick would die on July 25, 1878.

By the time of the 1870 Census, the Dockendorfs are expecting their first child and Frederick is working at the rubber factory where he will be employed for the rest of his days. They appear on page 249 of the Flushing Census.

The family is again listed on page 314D in the 1880 Census of College Point. William, Joseph and Christine have been born.

Fritz, as he was called, was there in 1884 when the Adam Wirth Post No. 451 had its beginnings in College Point and, happily, a photograph of him in his GAR uniform appears in this book.

Serving in many capacities, Frederick's name appears on many letters written in support of soldiers' applications for their pensions. He was also a member of the Marvin Lodge, Number 252, of the International Order of Odd Fellows, and of the Deutsche Rhein Lodge, Number 287.

Frederick and Mina appear in the 1900 Census of College Point living at 235 15th Street with four of their children.

Wilhelmina passed away on December 26, 1905 and in 1910 Frederick lives with Louise Heilmann, his sister-in-law.

He was living at 104 10th Street (119th Street) when he died at the age of 74 on January 14, 1917. Pastor Mottram, who followed Pastor Ebendick at St. John's Lutheran Church, celebrated his funeral liturgy and he is buried in Flushing Cemetery with his wife Wilhelmina.

Dockendorf, Joseph

Joseph, the younger brother of Frederick, was born December 30, 1844 in Kaiserslautern, Germany. He was baptized there at St. Martin's Catholic Church and accompanied his brother in 1857 on the journey to America, joining their father who had emigrated a few years earlier.

He is there at age 15 along with Frederick on page 720 in the 1860 Flushing Census working as a laborer at the India Hard Rubber Company. A year earlier in 1859 he had lost the index finger on his left hand as a result of an accident.

On September 3, 1861 he enlisted in Company G of the 46th New York Infantry, claiming to be 18 years old and working in College Point as a barkeeper. He is a small man, 5'3" with blue eyes and light hair. It appears that he passed his time in the service somewhat uneventfully as the pension record contains no medical records or other information. He was discharged in Washington, DC on July 28, 1865.

A year after his discharge on September 30, 1866, Pastor Ebendick married Joseph to Elizabeth Boller at St. John's Lutheran Church. They became parents to nine children, of which five survived to adulthood; Joseph, born March 27, 1867, Margaret, May 30, 1870, Johanna, June 18, 1875, Louise, April 17, 1878 and Henry, August 5, 1880.

Oddly, baby Joseph is baptized at St. Fidelis Catholic Church and his sponsors are Uncle Frank Dockendorf and his wife Catherine.

In 1880 he is working in the rubber factory and the baby, Johannah, is in kindergarten, probably the one begun by Conrad Poppenhusen, the first free kindergarten to be established in the United States.

In 1884 he became an original member of Adam Wirth Post No. 451 of the GAR and submitted many affidavits in support of pension applications for his fellow veterans. A curiosity, he always signed his name with two f's, as in Dockendorff.

In 1900 Joseph is a hotelkeeper in one of the many such establishments in College Point at the time.

He died of malarial fever and heart failure on January 3, 1911 and Elizabeth outlives him by another nineteen years, dying on October 4, 1930. They are buried together at Flushing Cemetery.

Of their children, Joseph marries Minnie Mueller and they have eight children; Margaret marries Herman Bornemann; Johannah marries Alfred Eisenhart; Louisa marries Edward Grundy, and Henry marries Grace Seitz.

Dockendorf roots go deep in College Point and their descendants are many, including the author of this work.

Doherty, Bernard

A Bernard Doherty appears on page 701 of the 1860 Flushing Census living with a James Doherty, 19, who is probably a brother. Bernard is a 17 year-old laborer from Ireland. This name also appears in the August 23, 1862 list of College Point volunteers published in the *Flushing Journal*.

Bernard enlisted in Company B of the 1st New York Cavalry on September 19, 1861. It does not appear that he filed for a pension so what is known is only that he was captured and held prisoner at Martinsburg, West Virginia on July 3, 1864, and paroled on March 1, 1865. He was then discharged at Alexandria, Virginia the following June 27th.

Dougherty, John

John Dougherty, also spelled Doherty, is the son of James, who died in May of 1853, and Ann, his wife. They had married in Ireland on May 25, 1837.

The family appears in the 1860 Flushing Census on page 734. Ann is 50, John, 23, Patrick, 19, Mary, 17, Thomas, 14, James, 10. Living with them is 27 year-old Mary Donohue, a seamstress.

Prior to his enlistment in Company F of the 63rd New York Infantry on April 3, 1862 at the age of 23, John worked as a mechanic in a button factory, very likely the comb factory of Conrad Poppenhusen. He stood 5'7", had a fair complexion, blue eyes and brown hair. Five months later on September 17th, he lost his life in the Battle of Antietam.

There are three original letters in his mother's application for pension benefits filed from College Point. In one written to his mother on September 4th, he describes what it is like to be an Army on the march, how very special it is to be a member of the Irish Brigade with their laughter, jokes, and singing and finally this sentence:

"Those articles that you mention in one of your letters, I have them yet and wear them all the time, indeed they give me a feeling of safety in the time of danger when the shells were bursting over us and the bullets flying thick around I felt perfectly safe."

In this letter he also mentions Patrick and Tom Egan whose stories follow, as well as a sister named Mary whose recent *"letter of the 27th gives more Strattonport news than all I got since I left."*

The other letters mention a visit by President Lincoln to camp and a hearty *"three cheers"* given by General McClellan for the Irish Brigade. He also requests that his mother buy a dress for herself and for an aunt with the $25 he had recently sent.

His mother and brother James are in the 1870 Census of Flushing on page 67 in College Point. Living with them are Thomas Egan, his wife Mary and a daughter named Annie, who is six months old.

In 1880 Ann lives with her son Patrick and his family in College Point.

Drakert, Frank

GAR member Frank Drakert was born in Hesse-Darmstadt, Germany on July 19, 1841 and came to America in 1858.

On the day he enlisted in Company F of the 6th New York Infantry, also known as the Wilson Zouaves, he stood 5'5", had gray eyes and black hair. He was a butcher by trade.

During his service he had a bout with dysentery in New Orleans from May 15, 1863 through June 10th. The pension record says he lived in New York City until 1865, whereupon he moved to College Point with his wife Margaret and family.

Three children are named in the pension application; Frank Joseph, born February 10, 1868, George, January 20, 1870 and Caroline, September 25, 1871, however the 1880 Census in College Point, page 304D, enumerates two additional children; Margaret, 4 and Elizabeth, 2. Frank's surname inexplicably appears as *Freges*.

Margaret died on April 18, 1893 and Frank continued to live in College Point.

In the 1900 Census of College Point he owns his own home, works at the comb factory and his son Frank lives with him.

Twenty years later father and son still live together at 207 16th Street. The Civil War veteran died on February 13, 1921.

Duer, Franz

GAR member Franz or Frank Duer came to America in 1859 according to the 1900 Census of College Point, and very likely moved to the village following his wartime service.

Tall for the time, he stood 5'10" on April 23, 1861 when he enlisted Company B of the 8th New York Infantry. His military career was eventful. He was wounded on June 18, 1862, not only in his left hand resulting in the loss of two fingertips during the Battle of Cross Keys in Virginia, but also on his right side where *"the ball lodged in his abdomen"*. He was also captured and spent time in an unspecified Confederate prison in Richmond until his release on September 13, 1862.

Following his discharge on April 23, 1863, he came or returned to College Point, where in June 1864 he married Apolonia Froelich and became father to George, born in June, 1865, Theresa, August, 1867, Frank, June, 1874 and Katherine, February, 1876. It is likely that Apolonia is the 19 year-old sister of George Fralich who appears on page 734 of the 1860 Census of Flushing and that would seem to indicate that Franz was in College Point before the war. She is a *"factory girl"*.

In 1880, according to information on page 303B of the College Point Census, Frank owns a saloon in College Point. It appears Theresa may have died as she is not listed, and August is enumerated as Horace, possibly a census-taker's error. His son George became an active member of the Sons of Union Veterans.

Franz, now widowed, appeared in the 1900 Census working as a barkeeper in the hotel owned by Otto Muelenbrink, and died later in the year on November 11th at 309 11th Street, the home of his son Herman.

Egan, Patrick

Born in 1840 in Ireland, Patrick worked in the rubber industry, but, surprisingly, not for Conrad Poppenhusen, rather for the New York City-based Horn Rubber Novelty Products Company.

He enlisted in Company H or the 10th New York Infantry on April 30, 1861 and was discharged on May 7, 1863.

Following the war, his company sent him to Germany where on December 7, 1866 he married Phillipina Kramer (possibly Mannheim), at Karlsruhe. George Kettel, the U.S. Consul in Germany at the time, officiated at the wedding.

Sometime following the marriage, the couple returned to New York where on April 23, 1868 a son named John was born and then baptized at St. Boniface Church in Brooklyn on June 8, 1868.

The pension application states that Patrick had contracted a very bad cold at the Battle of Shepherdstown Ford which in latter days set in as consumption resulting in his death on September 4, 1870. He was buried in a cemetery at St. Fidelis Church, but when Mt. St. Mary's Cemetery was opened in Flushing, his remains were moved there.

On November 30, 1873 Phillipina married Jeremiah O'Neill himself a veteran, and together they had five children; Francis, September 10, 1874, Edward, August 3, 1876, Phillipina, November 13, 1877, Mary, April 3, 1882 and Charles, July 13, 1893. The family lives in New York City in 1880.

Egan, Thomas

The record says that Thomas Egan was 17 on the day he enlisted in 1862, joining Patrick, probably his brother, who had enlisted in the 10th New York Infantry in early April 1861. Both are named in the letter written by John Dougherty described previously, and in 1870 Thomas lives with John's mother in College Point.

The military file indicates that Thomas had actually been detailed as a Provost Guard at his Division Headquarters, but it also says he deserted as early as February 13, 1863. There is no pension application made at any time thereafter, but it appears he returned to College Point as in the 1870 Census of Flushing he is enumerated on page 105 married to Mary, and working as a coachman.

By 1880, still living in College Point, he works in the rubber factory and has five children; Ana, 9, Marsala, 8, *(sic)* Mary, John, 3 and Jane, 1.

The family lives on 15th Street in 1900 and Thomas, a rubber worker, says he was born in January 1844 and had come to America sometime ca. 1850.

A widower working at the rubber mill, Thomas is there in 1910 along with his daughter Marcella *(sic)* and a son named Eugene, born in 1883 and another daughter named Elizabeth born in 1887. This census asks if the individual is a Civil War veteran. Thomas indicates in the negative, perhaps because of the desertion, or perhaps because this is an entirely different individual.

Thomas, Elizabeth and Eugene are also enumerated in the 1920 Census where Eugene indicates he works for the New York City Fire Department.

Ehm, Jacob

Jacob Ehm is enumerated in the 1860 Census of Flushing on page 733, a 36 year-old basket maker from Bavaria married to Susannah, 32, with two children, Catherine 9 and Mary 7.

Jacob is listed in Munsell's *History of Queens County* as having served in the 15th New York Heavy Artillery, but it was actually a 30-day enlistment in the 15th New York Regiment of National Guard Infantry from June 6, 1864 through July 7, 1864.

He is a chair-maker in 1870 according to information on page 230 in the Flushing Census. There are two additional children; Dora, 3 and Henry, 1.

The family also appears in College Point in the Census of 1880 and again in 1900 when only Jacob and Susannah are enumerated. He is still a maker of chairs.

Emmerich, John

John Emmerich appears on page 699 in the 1860 Census of Flushing, the 18 year-old son of George, a 48 year-old laborer from Hesse, in Germany and Christina, 50, from the same area. John has four siblings; George, 21, Margaretta, 16, Peter, 14 and Philip, 11.

The record indicates he was a landsman in the Navy, had enlisted at the Brooklyn Navy Yard on August 24, 1863, and was discharged from there a year later.

He appears on page 35 in the 1870 Census of Flushing living in College Point, working in the comb factory and married to Bertha, origins unknown, is 23. A three year-old daughter named Minnie is also enumerated.

The family appears in the 1880 Census of College Point on page 238C. John, still married to *"Berda"* works as a peddler and Minnie, now 13, works in the rubber factory. There are two additional daughters, Julia, 10 and Kate, 5.

Engelhardt, Charles

Charles Engelhardt was born in Weissenburg, Germany, ca. 1823. When he came to America is unknown.

Prior to the Civil War on June 30, 1850 he married Elizabeth DeCamp in Bridgeport, Connecticut where the couple is enumerated in the Census of that year. He is a 28 year-old confectioner and she is 29. In 1852 or thereabouts, a son named Morris is born.

He enlisted on August 20, 1862 and while serving in the 14th Connecticut Infantry, the record indicates that Charles *"suffered a hernia at the Battle of Antietam caused by a skull concussion,"*.

As a result of the injury he received a disability discharge on February 8, 1863 and following the war he worked for two years at the Rubber Company along with veterans Charles Weiss and John Hoelle. At different times he worked as a lamplighter in College Point, as an express agent for the Long Island Rail Road, and in both the Funke and Rhenania Silk Factories.

He, Elizabeth and son Morris appear in the 1870 Census of Flushing on page 223, where Morris is employed as an apprentice engineer.

In 1880 Charles is working as an express agent and lives with Elizabeth in College Point. They are found on page 299A of the Census. Morris has married Christina Semon and lives with her family in College Point. Morris becomes an active member of the Sons of Union Veterans in College Point and in 1920 lives in Great Neck.

As of September 14, 1888 Charles is listed as living at the Fitch Home for Soldiers in Noroton Heights, Connecticut. He died on June 26, 1891.

Erling, Charles

Hamburg-born Charles Erling enlisted in Boston on August 13, 1863 as a substitute for a man named William J. Osborne. Erling was 36; stood 5'7" with a light complexion, blue eyes and light hair.

His military career in Company D of the 11th Massachusetts Infantry lasted less than a year, as he was wounded at the Battle of the Wilderness on May 5, 1864, and died two days later. He left behind a widow, Julia, whom he had married on September 6, 1856 in a Dutch Reformed Church ceremony conducted by Rev. F. M. Schneeweise in New Brunswick, NJ.

There were two children born before he left for war; Julius, in Connecticut in 1859, and Charles, in New York, probably College Point, in 1862.

The pension record says Julia was living in College Point on June 7, 1865 when the application was filed, and by 1880 she had returned to New Brunswick to live there with her children, of which two more are listed, a sons George born in 1868, and William born in 1873. They carry the surname *Earling* as it appears in the record, but the children could not be sons of Charles.

No information other than the fact that Julia is a widow, perhaps twice, is given. The pension, filed in 1865, offered no clue.

I suspect, based on the birth of Charles, Jr. in 1862, that the family had moved to College Point after the 1860 Census and that Charles, Sr. had gone to work at the rubber factory. Why he enlisted in Boston is a mystery.

Fahner, Jacob

According to the record, Jacob Fahner actually enlisted in College Point in 1861, and while he was a member of Company I of the 20th New York, he did not lay down his arms before the Battle of Chancellorsville early in May, 1863. He also did not apply for a pension.

On page 230 of the 1870 Flushing Census, he is 37, a Baden-born carpenter married to Mary, 29, born in Saxony. There are four children at the time; Mina, 5, *Charley*, 4, George, 3 and Catherine, 1.

By 1880, on page 300C of the College Point Census, Mina is working in a silk factory and a son named Jacob, 4, has been born.

Jacob died on March 1, 1881 and is buried in Flushing Cemetery. Marie, Charles and George appear in the 1910 Census in College Point where the record indicates Marie is a widow and has her own income. The record also indicates she has had seven children of which five are alive. Charles and George are ribbon weavers.

She appears again in 1920. Her unmarried son Charles lives with her. Son Jacob lives next door married to Harriet, no surname known, with three children; Hazel, 16, George, 13 and Lester, 7.

Farrell, Henry

GAR member Henry Farrell lived in College Point when Post No. 451 was formed. The information in his military record indicates he was born in New York, but enlisted in Ohio on October 29, 1862, for reasons unknown. He was 18 and stood 5'6" with a light complexion, blue eyes and brown hair.

His military record indicates further that he was mustered out at Camp Cleveland, Ohio on July 13, 1865.

In the 1880 Census of Whitestone on page 228 D, a 30 year-old, Irish-born soldier by the name of Henry Farrell is listed and he is very likely the Civil war veteran. Other than his service in the 20th Ohio Light Artillery, and a photograph in his GAR days, nothing else is known about him.

Feuerbacher, August Frederick

Gray eyed August, at 5'6", was already a married man and father on the Tuesday in September 1861 when he enlisted in Company C of the 45th New York Infantry. He had married Catherine Deuschle in the town of Konigen, Wurtemberg, in Germany on October 18, 1849. They had at least four children; Charles, born in 1857, Phillipina, ca. 1861, Frederick, 1864 and August, late 1869 or early 1870. The family as it existed, is enumerated on page 706 in the 1860 Census of Flushing.

At Gettysburg on July 1, 1863, the pension data tells us, August claimed to have been shot in the left arm. He was sent to Cuyler Hospital in Germantown Pennsylvania to recuperate, but was reported as having deserted on August 2nd. Twelve days later he returned to the hospital and on September 2nd went back to his unit to finish out the war.

He was subjected to a Regimental Court Martial convened in the field near Stafford Court House in Virginia to consider a charge of desertion. While he was found to be not guilty of that offense, August was, nevertheless, convicted of being absent without leave, and sentenced to pay for his rifle and accoutrements that he had lost. He was also required to make up for the time he was absent and thus he was not discharged along with the rest of the regiment.

August is employed as a cutter and lives in the 19th Ward in Brooklyn in the 1870 Census, appearing on page 404. No additional children have been born and the surname is spelled *Feurbach*.

At the time of the pension application in 1873 he was living at 650 Flushing Avenue in Brooklyn.

August died in 1877 and his widow, Catherine, spelled *Tiather*, a variation or misspelling of Catherine perhaps, appears in the 1880 Census of Kings County with Frederick and August. The son named Charles, appears in the same Census also. Phillipina, I suspect, is married.

Fink, John

John Fink appears in the 1860 Census of Flushing on page 719. He is 34, a laborer from Baden, married to Catherine. They have five children; Jacob, 7, born in Baden, followed by Barbara, 6, Catherine, 4, John, 3 and Abalonia, 2, all born in New York.

John is listed in Munsell's *History of Queens County* as having served in the 15th New York Artillery called out to garrison Fort Richmond in New York Harbor. His was a 30-day enlistment in the 15th New York Regiment of National Guard Infantry from June 6, 1864 through July 7, 1864.

On page 218 of the 1870 Census of Flushing, John, working at the comb factory, and his family are enumerated. Children listed include; Jacob, 19, Barbara, 17, Cattren, *(sic)* 14, John, 13, Abalonia, 12, Rachel, 10, Caroline, 8, Martin, 7, Kate, 5, Louisa, 3 and Mathias, 1.

The family is in College Point in 1880 and is found on page 309B of the Census. John Sr. works at the rubber factory, which was in 1870, known as the comb factory. Neither Catherine nor Jacob are enumerated, but the rest of the children are; Barbara, 25, and her brother John, 22, work in the rubber factory. Also listed are: Regina, (Rachel) 19, Carol, 18, Martin, 16, Margaret, (probably the Kate who was 5 in 1870), 14, Louis, 12 and Matthew, 11. Carol works in one of the College Point silk factories, while Martin is an apprentice plumber.

John died on May 16, 1883 and is buried in Flushing Cemetery. By 1920 only sons Matthew and John remain in College Point.

Fisher, John

GAR member John Fisher was born in Germany on November 2, 1837. According to his pension file on enlistment day, May 9, 1861, he was a farmer and stood 5'6", with a light complexion, blue eyes and light hair.

He was mustered in at Willets Point and served in the 15th New York Engineers as a *wagoneer*. I suspect he drove a wagon.

Between December 1862 and March 1863 he was reported as being an *"absent teamster on a pontoon train"*. He was mustered out on June 25, 1863 and after the war, lived in both Bayside and Westchester County.

Fisher died on September 20, 1911 at the National Home for Disabled Volunteer Soldiers in Virginia.

Foster, Samuel Jr.

Samuel Foster was born in New York on August 30, 1843. His parents were Samuel Foster Sr., a ship-builder born in New York City in 1816, and Alice Quackenbush Foster, born in Middletown, New Jersey in 1820.

In 1860 he appears on page 751 of the Flushing Census living with his parents and siblings; Mary, 21, William, 19, Alonzo, 12, Albert, 6, Sarah, 5, and Henry, 3. One more brother, Frederick, will be born in 1865. Sarah will marry a man named Philips and be widowed by 1880.

In 1861 on October 1st he enlisted in Company L of the 2nd New York Heavy Artillery at Little Neck, NY. On May 14, 1864 he was promoted to the rank of 2nd Lieutenant and served as an orderly to General Samuel Davis Sturgis. On the same day he was commissioned into the 4th New York Light Artillery, but there is no information on his date of discharge.

Following on his service, Samuel was married for a brief time to Emma or Emily Meigs who died in late 1865 or early 1866. They had been married but three or four months and living in a little village near Bergen Point, New Jersey where Samuel was working. She is buried in Brooklyn's Green-Wood Cemetery.

He married Susan C. Bragg on January 18, 1869, the ceremony being performed by Rev. L. B. Wilkes at 6th Street in Brooklyn. There were three children born; Alice, October 31, 1870, Louis, March 11, 1872 and Grace, June 13, 1875.

In 1880 Samuel, Sr. and Alice are still alive and living in Brooklyn. Daughter Sarah, who is living with them, has a 9 month-old daughter named Jennie.

Samuel Foster died at Covington, Kentucky on April 14, 1917 and is buried at Spring Grove Cemetery there. At the time of the pension application, Susan was living in Covington at 2208 Sterritt Avenue. She was granted the widow's pension benefits.

Fowler, Cornelius

GAR member Cornelius Fowler is a native of Flushing who, according to his pension record, had at least one sibling, John, who is three years older.

The 1850 Census of Flushing, page 303, lists one Cornelius Fowler, age 17, a laborer, born ca. 1833. He also appears in the 1860 Census of Flushing on page 655.

On enlistment day, November 17, 1862, Cornelius was a 28 year-old sailor standing 5'8" with blue eyes, brown hair and a dark complexion.

He suffered a gunshot wound to his left leg at Petersburg, Virginia on June 19, 1864. The ball that went through his thigh resulted in his being discharged on a certificate of disability on May 27, 1865.

After his May 27, 1865 discharge from the 61st New York Infantry, he married Mary Kiested in Jamaica in Queens, at the home of David Van Sicklen. Rev. Mr. Walsh officiated. Mary's birth date was December 19, 1846.

In 1870 the family resides in Flushing and is enumerated on page 207 of the Census. Cornelius is a stonemason and there are two children; Thomas, 8 and Elizabeth, 1. For reasons unexplained, Elizabeth, not Mary, is the name given for the adult female in the family. She is 30 in the Census record.

In 1880 the family is still in Flushing enumerated on page 275C. Cornelius, 45, is listed as Cornelia, and the sex indicated is female, an obvious error. Thomas still lives at home joined by Frank, born ca. 1868, George, ca. 1871, and Patience A., ca. 1876. She will be called Anna. There is no mention of the daughter named Elizabeth and she may have died. The birth year for Frank may be incorrect in this census record, as he does not appear in the 1870 Census. No occupation is listed for Cornelius, but over the years he will be employed as a bridge tender.

Cornelius died on July 7, 1902 at his home in Bayside and is buried in Flushing Cemetery, but there is no mention of when Mary died.

Fowler, George Oscar

GAR member George Fowler was born in Flushing on September 1, 1841 and the 1850 Census of Flushing enumerates the family of Saul Fowler with a 9 year-old son named George. Saul is 47, a New York-born painter married to Elizabeth, 42 and also born in New York. George has six siblings, Theodore, 18, Caroline, 16, Frances, 11, Mary, 6, Henrietta, 4, and David, 1.

Fowler enlisted in Company F of the 6th New York Infantry in Astoria, and was an original member of Post No. 451 in College Point. On enlistment day he was a painter and stood 5'10" with a light complexion, dark eyes and hair. He received a disability discharge on February 4, 1863 from a Virginia convalescent camp.

In 1880 George lives in Whitestone married to Margaret and is working as a house painter. There are three children; Oscar, 9, Elizabeth, 7 and Edward, 2.

The family next appears in 1900, still in Whitestone. Oscar, Edward and another daughter named Jesse, born in January 1880, are enumerated. George is an auctioneer, Margaret says she was born in New York in January 1848 and Oscar is a soldier.

George Fowler died in Whitestone on February 5, 1918 and Oscar continues living in Whitestone in 1920. There is no indication as to when or where his wife Margaret died.

Frank, Lewis

Louis (*sic*) a 27 year-old shoemaker from Hesse, Germany, appears in the 1860 Census of Flushing on page 705 married to Ann, 28, from Ireland. They have four children, Michael, 5, John, 3, Elizabeth, 4 and William, 1.

His name appears in the list of volunteers from College Point that appeared in the August 23, 1862 *Flushing Journal*.

His military record indicates that he enlisted in Company L of the 2nd New York Heavy Artillery on October 1, 1861. Furthermore, he spent almost four months in Camp Park Convalescent Hospital at Crab Orchard, KY, from September 5, 1863 to January 4, 1865. He was transferred to the Veteran's Corps on September 15, 1863, but there was no record of his final discharge.

While he did file for a pension, it could not be located at the National Archives. He died at the National Home in Wisconsin on January 23, 1926 and is probably buried there. There is no information as to where or when Ann passed away.

Franke, Anton

Anton Franke was born in Germany in August 1835 and came to America in 1860. His name appears on the Provost Marshall's list of 1863 as living in Strattonport. He joined the 58th New York Infantry at the age of 25 in 1861, but apparently never filed for a pension.

He appears in the 1870 Census of Flushing on page 236 married to Kate and working in the rubber factory. There are three children listed, Anton, 11, Annie, 5 and Philipena, 1, born in November 1868.

In 1880 Anton is a carpenter living in College Point and found on page 303B of the Census. His son and namesake Anton, is married and living in New York City, while the two daughters remain at home.

In 1900, Anton, a widower, lives in College Point with his daughter Philipena. He is a silk weaver. It is not known when Anton passed away.

Freund, Edward

Edward was born in Dessau, Saxony, Germany ca. 1837, emigrated to the United States, and at age 23, enlisted in College Point on May 20, 1861.

He was taken prisoner during the Battle of Chancellorsville on May 4, 1863 along with Friedrich Behring. It was at this precise time that about 200 soldiers of the 20th New York Infantry had lain down their arms in the belief that their enlistments had come to an end. Edward chose not to participate in that event and that made all the difference. He was paroled 11 days after his capture and discharged two weeks later on May 1st in New York City.

Pastor August Ebendick performed the marriage of Edward to Christine Behring at St. John's Church on November 6, 1864. She is the daughter of Civil War veteran Frederick Behring who appears on page 719 of the 1860 Census.

Christine, born in Oberhein, Germany on September 25, 1843, is the sister of Amelia Behring, who married another veteran, Julius Steinbeck. Her brother Paul is a witness to the marriage as is her brother in law, Julius Steinbeck.

In 1870 the family lives in College Point and is found on page 216 of the Flushing Census where Edward works at the comb factory. Three children have been born; Lena (Caroline), born ca. 1865, Adeline, ca. 1867 and Edward, ca. 1868.

Ten years later, Edward works at the rubber factory, but the child Edward is not enumerated. Four more children have been born; Louisa, ca. 1871, Bertha, ca. 1873, Carl, ca. 1875 and another son, also named Edward, born September 6, 1877. Three more children will be born following the census; Emilie, November 7, 1880, Katherine, October 24, 1883, and Henry, September 15, 1887. The pension record tells us that Amelia Steinbeck was the attending nurse at the births of the final four children.

Edward died on December 30, 1892 and is buried in Flushing Cemetery. Christine appears in the 1900 Census with the children, again in 1910 and in 1920 is still living in College Point with her sons Charles and Edward who have not married.

Christine passed away on July 23, 1926, and is buried with her husband in Flushing Cemetery.

Frey, Joseph

Joseph Frey, a brush maker from Baden, Germany, was a veteran of the Mexican War having enlisted in Company H of the 5th Regiment of Infantry on November 3, 1846 at the age of 23.

He was wounded in the left wrist and the inside of his left leg above the knee at the Battle of Churubusco that took place near Mexico City on August 19, 1847.

Three months later he was discharged, returned to Williamsburgh in Brooklyn and began receiving his pension. Two years later on March 11, 1849 he married Elizabeth Horn at St. John's Lutheran Church. Rev. Baissel performed the ceremony.

In the 1850 Census taken August 17th he and Elizabeth have an eight-month old son named Edward, born December 22, 1849. Edward died eight days after the census was recorded and over the years the following children were born; Frederick, May 21, 1851, Margaret, August 10, 1853, Wilhelm, April 13, 1856, Theodore, March 10, 1858, twins, Edward and Edmond, July 9, 1860, Augusta, August 27, 1865 and Emil, born March 8, 1869 and baptized by Pastor Ebendick at St. John's.

When the call to duty goes out again in 1861, Joseph enlists again on October 1st, this time in the 2nd New York Heavy Artillery, and serves until his discharge on June 21, 1865.

The family appears in College Point in the 1870 Census of Flushing on page 253. Margaret is a domestic and Frederick works at the rubber factory. Joseph's annual brush-maker's income is $3000.

At some point he moves to San Francisco in search of a milder climate for his rheumatism, but his situation does not improve. He is unable to work, has very little money, and eventually returns to the East Coast where on April 18, 1876 he enters the Barnes Hospital Soldiers Home in Washington, DC. Col. Roemer writes a number of letters in support of his pension application and on February 22, 1877, he passed away at the Soldiers' Home.

Biographies

Elizabeth, widowed, and the family live in Newark, New Jersey in the 1880 Census, and are found in Essex County on page 368D. William, Theodore, and the twins Edward and Edmond all are employed in the Celluloid Works. Margaret lives at home, along with Augusta and Emil, who attend school.

Elizabeth passed away in Atlantic Highlands, New Jersey on June 20, 1914, outliving her husband by 37 years.

Freygang, Charles J.

There is a Charles J. Freygang named in Munsell's *History of Queens County* as having served in the 15th New York State Militia, the 30-day unit called out to garrison Fort Richmond in New York Harbor.

The family is enumerated in 1870 in College Point on page 262 of the Flushing Census. They have three children; Hermania, 10, Hugo, 5, Paulina, 1. Charles is 39 and a hotelkeeper from Prussia married to Maria, 35 from Bavaria.

In the 1880 Census of College Point, page 241B, there is a 50 year-old saloonkeeper, now using his middle name, Julius, Freygang. Two more children are enumerated; Charles, 10 and Henry, 8.

It is not known when Charles, Sr. died but the family is prominent in 1900 with Charles Jr. running a hotel.

In 1920 the same Charles Jr. lives in Whitestone and works in the street-cleaning department, probably for the City of New York.

Fritz, Louis

Louis appears in the 1860 Census of Flushing on page 740, an unmarried 19 year-old painter. This record indicates he was born in New York, but subsequent records indicate he was born in Baden, Germany. Living in the same location are two other young men who will also serve in the military; William Schneider and Hiram Warner.

On June 5, 1861 he enlists in Company K of the 6th New York Infantry.

Then on October 9, 1861 while on picket duty during the Battle of Santa Rosa Island, (Pensacola Bay) in Florida, Louis was struck in the left arm by a rebel minie ball. He was one of 27 casualties suffered by the 6th New York Infantry, also known as Wilson's Zouaves, as a result of a surprise, early morning raid by the Confederates.

He survived the wound, was discharged on June 25, 1863, and returned to College Point to marry Mary Jockers, a sister of veteran Adam Jockers, at St. Fidelis Catholic Church. Father Joseph Huber performed the ceremony on December 26, 1863 with Adam serving as one of the witnesses.

The pension record indicates that Louis suffered from many illnesses following the war, among them *"tongue fever"*, malarial fever, dropsy and rheumatism.

He and Mary were parents to nine children; Wilhelmina, born September 19, 1864, Henry William, February 14, 1866, Therese, August 14, 1867, Edward John, November 18, 1871, William Frederick, January 1, 1874, Emma Catherine, March 5, 1876, Louis, November 12, 1877 and Edward Frederick, August 7, 1880, all born in College Point.

By 1880, Louis is a saloonkeeper living in College Point, still married to Mary, and the two oldest children work in the rubber factory. The family is on page 311B of the Census.

In 1884 Louis will join the GAR and his son Henry becomes an active member of the Sons of Union Veterans. Two years later on January 26, 1886 Louis dies as a result of liver disease and rheumatism and is buried in Flushing Cemetery.

Gardner, Rufus C.

The Gardner brothers, Rufus and Savillian, are both sons of Aaron Gardner and his wife Mariah. Their family roots go back at least to 1840 in Orange County, New York in the town of Newburg, where Aaron is enumerated.

In 1850, still in Newburg, Aaron is a 38 year-old farmer with five children; Chauncy, 14, Anna, 11, Savillian, 10, Rufus, 8, and Mary, 4 months. Mary Gardner, 79 and probably Aaron's mother, is also in the family.

The family is enumerated in the 1860 Census of Flushing on page 723 indicating Aaron and Rufus are comb-makers and Savillian's name is written as what appears to be *Sarah*, an obvious error.

Both brothers entered the service on the same day, August 12, 1861, and joined the same unit, the 48th New York Infantry. Their names appeared in the list of College Point volunteers that was published in the *Flushing Journal* on August 23, 1862.

It is likely they were both employed in the rubber factory in 1861 when the war broke out. Rufus enlisted and in less than a year, received a disability discharge on July 29, 1862.

It is also likely that he returned to Newburg as City Directories for 1891 and 1892 indicate that Rufus C. Gardner is employed in a meat market and that he lives in a boarding house.

Why he did not apply for pension benefits following his disability discharge is unknown. His father and mother along with two additional brothers; Irwin, born ca. 1855 and Albert ca. 1860, are enumerated in the 1870 Census of Newburg as is Chauncy, his wife Anna, and son Willard.

Both Aaron and Maria, parents of Rufus and Savillian, are still alive in 1880 living alone in Newburg.

Gardner, Savillian

Unlike his brother Rufus, Savillian did apply for a pension and it indicates he was born in 1841, was 5'6" with a light complexion, dark hair and dark eyes when he enlisted on August 12, 1861.

Savillian's name is listed as William in the *Flushing Journal* list published on August 23, 1862.

He suffered a shell wound in his right hip at Chester Heights near Petersburg, Virginia in early September of 1864. Following his discharge on September 16th, he lived in New York City where in the 1869 Directory his address is given as 107 West 49th Street and he deals in liquors. Another address, 837 8th Avenue also is given in the pension file.

Nothing else is known of either of the Gardner brothers.

Gear, Samuel

According to a Bible record, GAR member Samuel Washington Gear was born in Meriden, Connecticut on January 18, 1839 to Samuel and Delia Norton Gear. Her name is also written Adeline *Naughton*.

He enlisted in Company F of the 1st Connecticut Infantry on April 22, 1861 and was discharged in New Haven the following July 31st. Following his three-months service he married Hanna Marie Bates on November 26, 1861. On July 1, 1863 a son named Samuel is born.

The family lives in Massachusetts in 1880 where war veteran Samuel is a tinsmith. They live in Cambridge and appear on page 237D of the Census of Middlesex County.

In 1900 the family lives on 20th Street, today's 129th Street, and the record says Samuel was born in 1840 not 1839, and that Hanna Marie, 57, had given birth to two children of which only one was alive.

Hanna Marie Gear died on August 13, 1910 and four years later Samuel married a second time to Sarah Ann Bennett, born in Epwell, England. Rev. Forman performed the ceremony at the Methodist Episcopal Church, probably in Whitestone.

Sam and Sarah, under the name Marie, appear in the 1910 Census living on 20th Street indicating Sam is a watchman and again in the 1920 Census where Samuel is described as being a retired veteran. He died on September 17, 1922.

Gelbart, Theodore

GAR member Theodore Gelbart was born in Gernsbach in Baden, Germany on November 3, 1839 and is the son of Jacob Gelbart who appears in the 1860 Census in New York City along with a second son named Charles. Both are tailors, while Theodore is an engraver.

On enlistment day, May 6, 1861, he was an engraver living at 20 Christian Street in New York City and stood 5'5" with blue eyes and dark hair. He served in Company B of the 20th New York Infantry.

At the Battle of Antietam, September 17, 1862, he lost his left arm and was eventually fitted with an artificial limb.

Following his disability discharge in Baltimore, Maryland on May 3, 1863, he married Ida Florence Edgerton on April 27, 1870 in Meriden, Connecticut in a Lutheran ceremony. Rev. Mr. Graeber performed the ceremony at the German Lutheran Church there.

The family appears on page 372D in the 1880 Census of New Haven, Connecticut living in the town of Meriden. Theodore is yet an engraver and the couple has a daughter named Harriet, called Hattie, born on July 11, 1871. She married a man named Reynolds and remained in the Connecticut area.

At some point Theodore moved to College Point where he joined Post No. 451 of the GAR.

Ida died on October 25, 1911. Theodore spent a short time in a Veterans Hospital in 1920 and eventually died on December 21, 1924 in Hartford. He is buried there in Cedar Hill Cemetery.

Gentner, Nicholas

The brewing of beer was one of the most important business enterprises in College Point in the middle of the 19th Century and among the first breweries to be established in the town was that belonging to Nicholas Gentner, a German from Baden who had come to the area from Newark, New Jersey in 1854. His place stood on Sixth Avenue between 14th and 15th Streets, today's 22nd Avenue between 123rd and 124th Streets. Short-lived, the place closed in 1856.

In 1860 Nicholas and family are enumerated on page 742 of the Flushing Census. He says he is 39, from Baden, and married to Margaret, 42, also from Baden. There are six children; William, 16, Barbara, 14, Michael, 13, Ferdinand, 7 Margaret 5, and Andrew, 1.

Nicholas became a member of the 15th New York National Guard unit that saw duty for thirty days commencing June 6, 1864 through July 7, 1864. As his service was for such a short time, he was not permitted to apply for a pension. Nevertheless, he and his family became a part of the fabric of life in College Point.

The 1870 Census of Flushing, where they appear on page 252, the record incorrectly says he is 38, and Margaret, 35. Nicholas is now working at the rubber factory. Michael, Frederick (Ferdinand) and Andrew continue to live at home.

In 1880 Nicholas, 60, is still at the rubber factory and appear on page 293A of the Census. Margaret and Andrew, also at the factory, are still in College Point as is Ferdinand, now a deputy sheriff, who will become an active member of the Sons of Union Veterans organization.

Glaeser, Charles

Charles Glaeser appears on page 706 in the 1860 Census of Flushing. He is 31 and a laborer from Baden married to Mary, 29, also from Baden. They have four children; Mary, 7, Louis, 5, Charles, 3 and William, 1. Joseph Bookman, a 40 year-old laborer from Switzerland, lives with them.

Charles is listed in Munsell's *History of Queens County* as having served in the 15th New York Heavy Artillery, but it was actually a 30-day enlistment in the 15th New York Regiment of National Guard Infantry from June 6, 1864 through July 7, 1864. The unit was called out to garrison Fort Richmond in New York Harbor.

Charles and parts of the family live in College Point in 1870 and appear on page 230 of the Flushing Census. The daughter Mary is listed as keeping the house, neither Louis nor Charles Jr. is enumerated and there are three additional children; Ludwig, 6, Emma, 4 and John, 1. Charles works at the rubber factory.

There is no other information available on this individual or his family.

Grant, Fred

GAR member Fred Grant was born in New Orleans, Louisiana, ca. 1847.

On June 10, 1863, he enlists in New Orleans in Company K of the 13th Maine Infantry. His mustered out on August 20, 1865 in Savannah, Georgia.

In 1880 he lives in Whitestone and works as a tinsmith. He is as yet unmarried, but on November 23, 1881 he weds Margaret Doyle at St. Fidelis Church in College Point. Father Joseph Huber performs the ceremony.

Fred is first to die on February 20, 1906 followed by Margaret on January 26, 1914. Both are buried in Mt. St. Mary's Cemetery.

Green, John

There are two men named John Green in the 1860 Census of Flushing appearing on pages 696 and 757. Either or neither could be the soldier who enlisted on September 2, 1861 and who subsequently deserted the 34th New York Light Artillery on March 12, 1864, also in Flushing.

His name appears in the August 23, 1862 edition of the *Flushing Journal* and for obvious reasons, there was no pension application so he will remain a mystery.

His military record indicates he was born in *Monegal*, probably Donegal, Ireland and was a farmer standing 5'8" with a light complexion, brown hair and eyes on the day he enlisted. It indicates further that he was sick on a number of occasions, spent time in various convalescent hospitals in Virginia and Kentucky where he reenlisted in the town of Nicholasville on January 1, 1864. The last notation indicates that from April to November 1864 he was sick and on March 13th was left in Flushing to recuperate.

Nothing else is known of John Green.

Griffin, Albert

GAR member Albert Griffin was born and raised in Flushing. His New York-born father was named Jacob, a grocer, and his mother was Elizabeth. Both appear in the Flushing Census of 1850 along with three children, Hester, 7, Albert, 5, and Sarah, 1.

Ten years later the family appears in the 1860 Census of Flushing on page 772. There is a 10 year-old daughter named Martha who may be Sarah, it is not clear, and three more children; Jacob, 7, Mary F., 5 and Elizabeth, who is 3.

On enlistment day, October 9, 1861, Albert said he was 18, but was actually 16, and stands 5'6". Following discharge from the 34th New York Light Artillery on June 21, 1865, he returned to marry Mary McCracken on January 6, 1869 at the Zion Episcopal Church in Douglaston. Rev. H. M. Beare, who was the third clergyman enumerated in College Point in the 1860 Census, performed the ceremony.

Albert, a farmer, and Mary, keeping house, live with his parents in Flushing in 1880. There are no children, but another son has been born to Jacob and Elizabeth. His name is Frank and he is 15.

The pension record names a son-in-law, Herman Anderson, but gives no name for his wife, who would be Albert's daughter for whom no name is known.

Albert, afflicted by alcoholism, died on February 3, 1898 and is buried in the cemetery of Zion Episcopal Church in Douglaston where he was married. Mary died a few years later on December 28, 1906.

Gunzert, Theodore

From what is known about this man, it can be assumed that he was competent and quiet. Born on March 5, 1830 in Ellsarangen, Germany, he enlisted in 1861 and rose to the rank of Lieutenant, First Class. He became a prisoner of war following the First Battle of Bull Run in Virginia on August 31, 1862.

Following the battle he was sent to a Confederate prison in Richmond, whereupon he was released at Aiken Landing, Virginia on November 8, 1862. He was then sent to Camp Parole near Annapolis, Maryland then on to the General Signal Corp.

After mustering out in October 1865 at Nashville, Tennessee, he went to Philadelphia and on December 22, 1866 was married to Annie Mary Burcher by Alderman William B. Becker.

A photograph of Theodore taken in the middle of the 19th century and obtained from the U.S. Army Military History Institute at Carlisle, Pennsylvania, appears in this book.

Theodore, working in the rubber factory, and Mary, born in Switzerland, are enumerated in the 1870 Census of Flushing on page 232. No children are listed.

In 10 years the couple has left College Point and appears in the 1880 Census living in New York City, Theodore is a porter and his name is spelled *Gunzer*.

In 1897 the last address known for Theodore Gunzert is 15 Thompson Street in New York City. There is no indication that there were ever any children born to this couple.

Harrington, Thomas

Thomas Harrington poses something of a mystery.

The official records list two individuals by this name joining the same unit, the first as a Private into Co. K on May 12, 1861 and the second as a Sergeant into Co. H on the next day. Both mustered out on July 10, 1863; the unit was the 25th New York Infantry.

One of these two, if there actually were two, tells the true story of Thomas Harrington, a College Point veteran who appears on the August 23, 1862 *Flushing Journal* list of volunteers from College Point.

The pension record does little to shed any light and in fact it makes the matter even more confusing.

The applicant stood 5'8", had brown hair and blue eyes when he enlisted at the age of 23, and he may have been working in College Point at the time. There is nothing to substantiate this point however.

Following his service in the Army he enlisted in the Navy and served aboard the *Pensacola* for a short time and was then transferred to the sloop *Monongahela*.

The application stated he had contracted gastritis at Harrison's Landing, Virginia in July 1862 and after leaving the service for good lived at one time in the town of Groton, and at another time in East Pepperell, Massachusetts, where he worked in the paper industry.

Thomas was married twice, the first time to Roxanna Josephine Gilson. The couple is found in the 1870 Census of Pepperell, Middlesex County on page 274.

Roxanna died on October 14, 1872 and the second marriage, to Grace Bell, took place on June 13, 1874. The family is enumerated in the 1880 Census of Pepperell on page 386B. Thomas, a Government Employee at the Paper Mill, is 42 and Grace, keeping house, is 36. There is a child named Lillian, born to Roxanna on September 18, 1870.

Thomas suffered from disease of the stomach and was reported dead on September 16, 1906 in Pepperell.

Harvey, Andrew

GAR member Andrew Harvey was born in England ca. 1835 and served in the U.S, Navy on the ship *Blackhawk* during the Civil War. There is no record that he ever applied for a pension, but the family does appear in the 1880 Census living in Flushing on page 193A. He is married to Ann and they have four children; Elizabeth, 9, Andrew, 7, Lily, 3 and William, 10 months. Andrew, 45, is a cabinet-maker and Ann, 34, keeps the house and was born in England.

Ann lives yet in Flushing in 1920. She is a widow and lives with her daughter Lillian who has married Elijah Nimmo. Her daughter Elizabeth, unmarried, lives with the family as well.

Haubeil, Charles

Charles is the 23 year-old son and namesake of his 45 year-old, Bavarian born father who runs a hotel in College Point in 1860 and appears on page 727 of that Census. His mother's name is Phillipina and he has six siblings; Matthias, born ca. 1846, Wilhelmina, ca. 1850, Elizabeth, ca. 1850, Catherine, ca. 1851, Jacob, ca. 1853 and George, ca. 1856. There is also a 23 year-old servant from Bavaria named Elizabeth Mauran.

His parents also appear in College Point in 1870 on page 101 of the Flushing Census.

He enlists in Company E of the 32nd New York Infantry on June 6, 1861, but there is no record of his having been discharged. Be that as it may, his parents continue to live in College Point on page 292D of the 1880 Census running a livery stable. Charles appears in that Census on page 251D living in New York City, married to Matilda and living with her brothers; Christopher and Thomas Fair, plus a host of other people. Charles is a gas fitter; Matilda, who keeps the house, was born in Ireland.

In his pension application dated July 5, 1892, Charles claims that he was honorably discharged and that he was hospitalized in May of 1862, but he is listed on the rolls as having deserted. He claims further that he left the hospital ship *"Vanderbilt"* on sick leave in July of that same year, nevertheless his application was rejected on the grounds of desertion on October 24, 1892 and the pension was never awarded.

I suspect he was telling the truth.

Haubeil, Martin

Martin, the brother of Charles, is also listed on page 727 of the 1860 Flushing Census. On July 7, 1861 he enlists in Company C of the 74th New York Infantry and receives a disability discharge on February 17, 1863.

He then re-enlists in Company M of the 15th New York Heavy Artillery on March 4, 1864 and is mustered out on August 22, 1865.

Martin, also known as Mathias, appears in the 1870 Flushing Census on page 88. Living with him is a 22 year-old female named Elena who may be his wife, but she is listed as a servant, and a one year-old child named Charles. Perhaps it exists, but no 1880 Census record was found for him anywhere.

Hebel, Jacob

Jacob Hebel is enumerated in the 1860 Census of Flushing on page 706. A 49 year-old shoemaker from Hesse, he is married to Elizabeth, 45, also from Hesse, and they have two children; Jacob, 10 and Sarah, 4, both born in New York.

Jacob served in the 15th New York Heavy Artillery, but it was actually a 30-day enlistment in the 15th New York Regiment of National Guard Infantry from June 6, 1864 through July 7, 1864. The unit had been organized to garrison Fort Richmond in New York Harbor.

Jacob, Elizabeth and the two children appear on page 254 in the 1870 Census of Flushing living in College Point. His annual shoemaker's income is $3000 and he has $500 worth of personal property.

Jacob Sr. and Elizabeth are also still in College Point in 1880 and are found in the Census on page 307A. He is still working at his trade; shoemaker. In the same Census, Jacob Jr. is married to Susan and has his own son Jacob.

There is no indication of when either Jacob or Elizabeth passed away, but the family name remains in College Point for years to come.

Hefermehl, John

John, born in Hesse, Germany, appears in the 1860 Census of Flushing on page 734, the 14 year-old son of Augustus, a 39-year-old carpenter and his wife, Christiana, 36, from Frankfurt. John has three siblings; a sister Augusta, 9, and two brothers, Rudolph, 3 and Adolph, 1.

His military career in Company D of the 15th New York heavy Artillery, began on the day after Christmas 1863, and he received a $62 enlistment bounty. His military record says he was 19, a blacksmith, standing 5'1" with a dark complexion, brown eyes and hair. He was actually 17 and according to his military record, less than three months later, the following March 10th, he died of disease and inflammation of the lungs in the hospital at Fort Lyon.

His name appears on a June 23, 1866 list of fallen soldiers from College Point that appeared in the *Flushing Journal*. It is also etched on the Flushing Memorial to Civil War casualties. Regrettably, his family did not apply for pension benefits. The Hefermehl family appears in College Point on page 230 of the 1870 Flushing Census.

By 1880 his mother Christiana has passed away and his father Augustus now lives in New York City with daughter Augusta. No other information is known about this individual.

Heilmann, John P.

John is called Peter Heilmann and appears on page 740 in the 1860 Census of Flushing. He is a 32 year-old mason from Hesse married to 31-year-old Emily from Saxony in Germany. They have three children; John, 7, Louisa, 5 and Henry, 2, all born in New York.

After enlisting on September 17, 1861, the record indicates he deserted the 34th New York Light Artillery on June 29, 1862, however he returned to the unit and was reinstated without punishment, due to the intervention of his new Captain, Captain Jacob Roemer.

The family lives in College Point in 1870 and is found on page 250 of the Flushing Census. Peter, the name he was known by, remains a stonemason and son John works on the railroad. This record indicates that Henry and Louisa are both 11 and apparently twins, something not supported by the 1860 data. There are three additional children, Emma, 9, Emilia, 4, and Julius, inexplicably called Louisa, 1. The sex indicated is M obviously for male.

In 1880, the last year of his life, Peter and Emily still live in College Point and are enumerated on page 308D of the Census. He dies on October 10th and is buried in Flushing Cemetery.

Sons John and Henry work at the rubber factory. Daughter Emilia and son Julius, who will become an active member of the Sons of Union Veterans organization, continue to live at home.

Helfreich, Valentine

Born in Bavaria ca. 1825, Valentine, a laborer, married Kunigunda Noeth, a tailor, on April 22, 1850. The family is listed on page 722 in the Flushing Census in College Point in 1860 with their 8 year-old son George. They would have another son, John, born on January 26, 1861.

Valentine stood 5'8", had a light complexion, gray eyes, and dark hair and worked as a cooper, or barrel-maker, during his one year of soldiering in Company C of the 58th New York Infantry that began on October 4, 1861. His military record says he was *"left sick in Sperryville, Virginia"* where he died of consumption and dysentery on August 11, 1862 at the military hospital there.

His name is etched on the Flushing Memorial to Civil War casualties.

Information in the pension files indicates that Kunigunda lived at 463 Greenwich Street in New York City on September 3, 1863. A year later in 1864, Father Joseph Huber married Kunigunda to Anthony Eisenberger at Saint Fidelis Church.

The couple moved to Brooklyn and is found on page 256A in the 1880 Census. Four sons are enumerated; Joseph, born ca. 1867, Christian, ca. 1870, Henry, ca. 1874 and William, ca. 1876. According to the Census, Anton also worked as a cooper and Kunigunda continued to work on coats.

Hemminger, Charles

Charles Hemminger has no connection to College Point other than the fact that his son, Charles, was a member of the Sons of Union Veterans organization. His name appears in the article, source and date unknown, describing the presentation of a flag to the mother of David Schultz after whom the Post was named.

For the record, Charles Hemminger was born in Germany ca. 1838 and enlisted in Company D of the 139th New York Infantry on September 9, 1862. On that day he was a butcher by trade and stood 5'9", with a light complexion, blue eyes and light hair.

Following his discharge on June 19, 1865 he married Mary, surname unknown, and four children are named in the 1880 Census of Great Neck. They are; Charles, 11, Hulda, 8, Fred, 5 and Kate, 2.

Nothing else is known of this veteran. He never lived in College Point, but for a period of time his son Charles lived there and was a part of the fabric of the town. For that reason his name is included in this book.

Herbig, Hieronymus

According to letters and affidavits in his pension file, Hieronymus Herbig lived in College Point from 1856 through September 1857 and worked as a comb-maker. He moved then to New York City and lived there through 1859, and then to South Orange, New Jersey where he worked for a *Mr. Düttenhoefer*.

Hieronymus was born on September 29, 1831 in Brückenau, Germany. On enlistment day, May 27, 1861, he was 31, stood 5'6", and had a light complexion, red hair and gray eyes. He served in Company F of the 31st New York Infantry and did have some health problems during his two years service. According to his own affidavit, he said:

"I became sick I believe it was the 15th day of April 1862 at Chibbing Point in the campaign of Yorktown on diarrhea. On the 7th day of May after the Battle of West Point, I was sent in the hospital at White House Landing where I had the whole body full of red spots, my gums were swollen and became decayed so that nobody could see my teeth and I had inflated lips where the blood run out, the lips were a kind of black. I was treaded until the camp was broken then I was transferred to Philadelphia and treaded in the U.S. Hospital a Broad Street. I was not very well, but I asked the doctor to let me go back to my regiment. He said that there weren't many who longed to go back to their regiment, but said that I don't look well and promised that by the next transport to let me go. At the Battle of Chancellorsville on the 4th day of May 1863, I was taken prisoner and the next day on our march to Richmond we had a heavy shower we marched through ponds which were so deep that the water would cover our shoulders. We were wet through and it had rained for three days and (we) had lain in the water. I believe that caused my diseases. I stood at Belle Island and then was transported to Annapolis, Md., from there to new York City and was discharged on the 4th day of June. After my discharge I had sore eyes and Dr. Joseph Strauch of College Point treated me.

The affidavit continues with his medical history, and the pension was approved.

After discharge he married Wilhelmina Dietz on April 14, 1867. Rev. Foersch performed the ceremony at 67 Stanton Street in New York City, and the couple went on to have at least nine children. The were; Caroline, born January 24, 1868, Otto, ca. 1869, Elizabeth, September 15, 1871, Leopoldine, July 7, 1873, Richard, ca. 1875, Frank, June 25, 1877, Minnie, August 24, 1880, John, September 26, 1882, Jerome, January 5, 1884 and George, February 6, 1886.

In the 1880 Census of College Point the family is enumerated on page 237B with Hieronymus working at the rubber factory. Within the year on August 1st Hieronymus moves the family to Flushing where he started a restaurant that failed by October 6th due to his frequent illness and eye problems.

In the early 1890's through at least 1894 he was the postmaster in College Point, but a document indicates one of his unnamed daughters did most of the work.

Herbig passed away on May 5, 1907 and only John and George are enumerated in the 1920 Census in Queens, though not in College Point.

Heyne, Lewis

Gottfried Ludwig Heyne was born in Germany ca. 1825, but stopped using the name Gottfried or Gottlieb after his August 31, 1851 marriage to Anna Maria Johanna Wenk from the town of Oldenburg in Germany. Rev. G. A. Reichert performed the ceremony in the German Evangelical Lutheran Church located at 7th and Franklin Streets in Philadelphia, Pennsylvania.

The pension record gives no indication as to why Lewis moved to College Point, but on enlistment day, May 9, 1861, he stood 5'11", had a light complexion, gray eyes, light hair and claimed to be a machinist. He served in Company F of the 15th New York Engineers.

During his service he was run over by a wagon and suffered a gunshot wound in his left ankle.

Following his discharge on June 25, 1863, he and Anna Marie returned to Philadelphia. They had five children and all were born in Philadelphia. They were William; born August 15, 1853, Frank, August 12, 1858, Louis, June 26, 1866, Amelia, October 29, 1868 and Joseph, March 7, 1870. Amelia would marry Harry Reed and support her father in his quest for a pension.

Lewis and Anna Marie are found on page 320C in the 1880 Census of Philadelphia living in the 1st Ward of District 21.

Lewis died on January 30, 1901 and is buried in Philadelphia's New Cathedral Cemetery.

Hibson, Joseph

GAR member Joseph Hibson was born in England on August 3, 1843 to Charles Hibson and Esther Lowe.

He had enlisted in Company A of the 48th New York Infantry on August 21, 1861 and his wartime record was distinguished by virtue of his becoming the third area veteran to be awarded the Congressional Medal of Honor on October 23, 1897. The citation reads:

"While voluntarily performing picket duty under fire on July 13, 1863 near Fort Wagner in South Carolina, he was attacked and his surrender demanded, but he killed his assailant. The day following he responded to a call for a volunteer to reconnoiter the enemy's position, and went within the enemy's lines under fire and was exposed to great danger. On July 18th he voluntarily exposed himself with great gallantry during an assault, and received 3 wounds, one of them a gunshot wound to the left elbow, permanently disabled him for active service and caused the loss of use of his left arm.

On July 1, 1868 he married Margaret McCluskey at St. Francis Church on 31st Street in New York City. Father Flynn performed the ceremony. Over the years there would be at least four children; Esther, born July 7, 1868, Charles, August 19, 1870, Ann, ca. 1873, and Margaret, ca. 1877.

The family lives in New York City in the 1880 Census and is found on page 68A in the 21st Ward of District 10. Joseph is employed at the Post Office and Margaret keeps the house. All of the children are listed and living with the family is Margaret's sister Ellen, 30, whose surname is spelled *McCosker*.

He died at Flushing Hospital on April 14, 1911 and is buried in Cypress Hills Cemetery also in Flushing. Margaret lives on until November 11, 1920 and is buried at Amityville, NY.

Hickman, Richard

GAR member from Whitestone, Richard Hickman enlisted under the name John T. Richey because, as it said in the pension file, *"he did not want his people to know that had had enlisted."* Perhaps this was because he was born in Maryland, a border state during the Civil War, and his family may not have supported the Union cause. Efforts to identify his parents were not successful.

Born on June 3, 1847, Richard Thomas Hickman was 5'7" with blue eyes and brown hair when he enlisted in 1864. Serving in the 210th Pennsylvania, he was wounded in the left knee at the Battle of Five Forks.

He had a tattoo on his right forearm that had a shield and the letters S.H-T.H-J.H, but there is no indication of its meaning, but the H could be a reference to his last name.

Following his discharge on May 30, 1865, for reasons unexplained he reenlisted in Battery C of the U.S. Engineers on August 9, 1871 and served until August 9, 1876.

At some time, probably ca. 1868, he married Mary who was also from Maryland and whose surname is unknown. They appear in the 1880 Census of Whitestone on page 233A. Richard, 34, runs a saloon, and Mary, 28, keeps house. The children are; William, 12, Andrew, 11, Thomas, 5 and Charles, 2. Sister-in-law, Emma Atkins, 18 and Ida Bowers, 12, also a sister-in-law, live with them. Mary's maiden name is either Atkins or Bowers; the record is not clear.

The pension record offers no more information.

Hobson, Josh

GAR member Josh Hobson served in Company C of the New Jersey Volunteers. While there is a Joseph Hobson who served in the 1st New Jersey Infantry, his pension record indicates he spent his entire life in New Jersey. Beyond that nothing is known of this individual.

Hoelle, John

John, born ca. 1838, was a native of Baden, Germany, the son of John Hoelle and Frances Klein.

At the time of his enlistment in the 11th Connecticut, joining along with Wyllis Tyrrell, John was 5'6", had a light complexion with blue eyes and auburn hair.

His name was spelled incorrectly as Haley and his pension application states, *"he was wounded at Petersburg by a piece of shell that exploded 10 feet away from where he was standing, hitting his arm and the inside of his right knee."* He was hospitalized at Harrison Landing, Virginia for a few days.

Following his November 15, 1864 discharge at Varina, Virginia, John returned to College Point and on May 30, 1871, married Maria Hansel. The ceremony took place in New York City at 67 Stanton Street. Rev. John A. Foersch performed the ceremony.

Maria, born in Germany, was the widow of John Hansel who had died on March 18, 1870, and the record adds that her parents were Anthony Buck and Maria Steger.

By 1872 John had given up the painter's trade and gone into saloon keeping, a business he runs in College Point in 1880. Mary's 3 children by John Hansel, and here the name is spelled Hauser, are enumerated. They are John, born ca. 1863, Anna, ca. 1866 and Felix, ca. 1868. There is also a daughter named Julia born in 1874, the child of John and Maria.

John Hoelle, an original member of Adam Wirth Post No. 451, died on March 29, 1897. He is buried in Flushing Cemetery, presumably with Maria, who died at the age of 58 on March 3, 1908.

Hoenig, William

At enlistment August 13, 1862, William Hoenig, a laborer born on March 11, 1843 in Lambsheim, Germany, stood 5'6", had a dark complexion, gray eyes and black hair.

His name appears in a *Flushing Journal* article dated August 16, 1862 where he was described as having enlisted after a large and enthusiastic war meeting in Strattonport.

He married his first wife, Ellen Kennally, at St. Fidelis Catholic Church following the war. Children born from this union were; John, December 1, 1868, Mary, October 4, 1870, Katherine, March 11, 1872, Elizabeth, December 25, 1872, William, January 17, 1875 and George, May 12, 1877.

Ellen died on July 26, 1879 and sometime after her death William married a second time to Anna Marie Mangler, herself a widow, whose maiden name was Veit. A Justice of the Peace performed the ceremony, but William was unable to recall the date in 1915 when he was responding to pension-related questions from the Department of the Interior.

Anna Marie had been married to Peter Mangler, a 39 year-old grocer, and lived in Brooklyn at the time of the 1860 Census. She was 36 and there were three daughters; Minnie, 11, Addie, 9, and Annie, 7.

There was also a John Mangler and family living in College Point in both 1870 and 1880 and from his age, 42 and 52, it can be deduced that John could be Peter's brother. Anna Marie died on March 26, 1911.

In 1880 the widowed William, his mother Christena living with him, is a constable in College Point. He is enumerated in the 1900 Census, a laborer, with his wife Anna Marie, called Mary, and children William, Lizzie and George.

William lived on until January 24, 1917 dying at his home, 31 11th. He is buried in Flushing Cemetery. His unmarried daughter Mary attended to him as did his daughter Katherine whose married name was Sperling.

Hollweg, August

August was born in Wald Solingen in Prussia and christened in the Lutheran church there on August 8, 1839.

It is not known when his family emigrated, but he does appear on page 713 of the 1860 Census of Flushing, the 20 year-old son of Dorothy Hollweg from Prussia. August has an 18 year-old sister named Augusta; his father's name was Hermann, and his mother's maiden name was Boeddinghaus.

While his name appears on no other list, the spelling is unique to both the 1860 Census and the military record. It does not appear that he ever applied for a pension, but it is reasonable to conclude that he is the individual found in the 1860 Census and thus a veteran from College Point.

Horn, Michael

Michael Horn appears in the 1860 Census of Flushing on page 719, the 19 year-old son of Philip and Eva Horn, 45 and 46, from Hesse in Germany where he was born. He has four siblings; Margaretta, 22, Adam, 9, Charles, 5 and Henry who is 2.

He has the distinction of having served for possibly the shortest time of any man from College Point, having enlisted at the age of 20 in Company I of the 20th New York Infantry on May 3, 1861, and then being discharged three days later by order of Col. M. Weber, Commander. No reason is given, but since he enlisted, he is included in this work.

Michael stayed in College Point, became a baker, and is enumerated in 1870 living with his wife Wilhelmina and their two children; Eddie, 3 and Annie, 2. Living with the family is a 52-year old woman named Christina, possibly Wilhelmina's mother. The family is found on page 249 of the Flushing Census.

The family appears again in 1880 on Page 245A of the Census with the same two children. Brother Henry, a *huckster*, lives with his widowed mother.

Horstman, Charles

Charles Horstman is named in both the 1863 Provost Marshall's List where he lives on Nichols Avenue in College Point, and in Munsell's *History of Queens County*, where he is said to have enlisted in the 133rd New York Infantry.

The individual who enlisted in this unit, Charles Hoffmann, *(sic)* lived in the Williamsburgh section of Brooklyn from 1859 until he enlisted in New York City in 1862 under this name at the supposed age of 27. He was 5'7", had a light complexion, light hair, blue eyes and worked in the rubber factory.

He was in a Frederick, Maryland hospital in the months of July and August 1864 suffering from an unspecified lung disease. Following the war, he moved to the Philadelphia area where he pursued his occupation of tailor.

On November 29, 1868 he married Mary Meyer in Somerset County, Pennsylvania and they were parents to at least four children; Harry, born April 15, 1877, Josephine, September 1, 1879, Jennie, June 5, 1885 and Oscar, September 5, 1886.

The family, still in Somerset County, appears on page 476A of the 1880 Census. Charles is working as a tailor.

He died on March 23, 1890 from the lung disease that plagued him following the war. Mary lived on until March 23, 1928 where she died in Jennerstown, Pennsylvania.

Houser, John

GAR member John Houser, also spelled Hauser, was born in Germany ca. 1835 and joined the 5th Regiment of New York Heavy Artillery on August 16, 1862. He was 5'9" with a light complexion, black hair and gray eyes.

According to his pension application he suffered a gunshot wound to his left arm between the elbow and the shoulder on September 16, 1864 during the Battle of Winchester. He spent four days in a Brigade hospital and three months at Haddington Hospital in Philadelphia. His discharge took place at Harper's Ferry, Virginia on June 22, 1865.

The first of his three wives was Elizabeth Scales. No date or place is given for the marriage, but they had at least two children; John, born in December 1862 and Henry, on May 20, 1866.

The record says Elizabeth was an inmate at the Buffalo State Insane Asylum from ca. 1898 until her death on May 29, 1902. She is buried there in St. Matthew's Cemetery.

John appears in the 1880 Census living in Great Neck with sons John and Henry. He is a laborer working at a hotel run by Stephen Ninesling and it appears the couple was not living together.

There is no record of a divorce from Elizabeth, nevertheless John married his second wife, Cornelia Smith, from Whitestone on June 20, 1887, and she died three years later on March 9, 1890 in Great Neck.

Mary Dombroski from Russia became wife number three on July 1, 1890 and the couple lived in the Woodhaven section of Queens at 305 Chichester Avenue.

Her application for pension benefits was denied because John had never divorced Elizabeth. While a Justice of the Peace had performed their marriage, the Board did not recognize it as being valid.

John died on April 16, 1904 at age 69 at Nassau Hospital in Mineola.

Howard, William, J.

William, a native of Ireland, appears on page 711 in the 1860 Census of Flushing married to Elizabeth, surname unknown, who was born in England. He is a laborer and they have six children.

The pension record tells us that William and Elizabeth Thomas were married at Oxfordshire in England on November 9, 1847 by Rev. Mr. Rushton of the Protestant Episcopal Church, the Church of England.

Their children born in England included; Frank born December 3, 1847 and Thomas, December 11, 1849. Those born in New York were; Joseph, March 25, 1852, Elizabeth, January 7, 1855, Louisa, October 22, 1857 and Mary August 14, 1860.

William Howard's name is mentioned a number of times in Roemer's book on the 34th New York Light Artillery. Called *"Billy"* by Roemer, he is the cook of the Officer's Mess and one time at Fredericksburg, was asked by the Colonel to make *"three kettles full of good, hot coffee for soldiers who had marched a great distance in a cold soaking rain."*

In 1870 William has returned from the war and the family lives in College Point enumerated on page 253 of the Flushing Census. While there is no occupation listed for him, we can assume he worked at the rubber factory. His income known from Census data, is $2000 per year, and living with them is a 73 year-old woman named Mary Lockwood. Born in England, it is likely she is Elizabeth's mother.

In 1880 William works in the rubber factory. Theresa, more likely Elizabeth, keeps the house and the son named Thomas, a carpenter, is still at home along with Louise, whose married name is Henderson, but whose husband is not enumerated. The family is found on page 292C of the Census in College Point.

William died in College Point on January 13, 1892 at the age of 69 and is buried in Flushing Cemetery. Elizabeth died shortly thereafter on May 6, 1893 and is buried with him.

Illerd, Dennis

One of the more mysterious stories in this collection of veterans' stories, 5'10" Dennis is the son of Dennis Mahon of Ireland and his wife Margaret Caley. His parents' names were cited on his 1881 New York City Marriage Certificate.

It is difficult to discern if his parents were in the United States in 1860 and even more difficult to figure out why he would enlist under the name of Illerd or Ellard instead of his family name, be it Mahon or Mahoney, but he did.

Dennis was born in Ireland somewhere between 1839 and 1842, the discrepancy being the result of conflicting ages appearing in various pension-related documents. He enlisted in Co. L of the 2nd New York Heavy Artillery on October 1, 1861 and was discharged on June 21, 1865.

There is some indication that he was a widower, and that he had been married in St. Michael's Church in Flushing prior to his October 29, 1881 marriage, again in Flushing, to Carrie Kristine Vogel.

At the time she was already married, but not divorced from Jacob or Carl Greutzinger, whom she had had arrested for assault and threatening to kill her. This information is a part of the pension application and was, in fact, a primary reason why the pension was denied. Her parents were Christopher Vogel and Barbara Dyne.

Carrie had contracted a legitimate marriage to William Allen on March 17, 1862 while he was home from the Army on furlough. He returned to his post in Company G of the 42nd New York Infantry and was subsequently killed at the battle of Antietam six months to the day on September 17th.

In October Carrie applied for and drew a widow's benefits long after her March 11, 1866 marriage to Carl or Jacob Greutzinger.

Some years in the future, ca. 1877, she threw him out as a result of the abuse she experienced, and, while good for her, she never divorced him and her claim in the application for Dennis's pension that the marriage was over as a result of Carl's being absent for over five years, was denied.

In his pension application Dennis claimed to have been wounded in the area of the right knee at the Second Battle of Bull Run, August 30, 1862, but the application was rejected on the grounds of there being no disability from the alleged wound. A subsequent application in February of 1891 initially had a more positive result, but that too was rejected late in April of the same year.

Dennis and Carrie lived together until February 12, 1889 when he entered the State Soldiers and Sailors Home in Bath, New York located in Steuben County. He virtually made that institution his home until his discharge on October 17, 1902. He subsequently died, exact date unknown, in College Point at the home of his unmarried sister Mary, who died, herself, in 1906.

Such a mysterious story: one that started out as a mystery and certainly ended in the same fashion.

Jockers, Adam

Adam was born in New York City on February 9, 1842 and while his father's name, Michael, is provided, his mother is unidentified. On enlistment day, May 3, 1861, he is an 18 year-old clerk in the 1860 Census of Flushing, 5'7", with a dark complexion, gray eyes and brown hair. He served in Company D of the 20th New York Infantry.

The pension application tells us that prior to the war he was an active member of the Gymnasium Society of College Point and at the time of his enlistment in 1861 he worked at the comb factory.

On September 10, 1862 he suffered a rupture at Sugarloaf Mountain in Maryland. He also suffered a wound to his right arm during General Hooker's Retreat from Fredericksburg, Virginia ca. May 14, 1863. The wound necessitated a 24-hour stay in a field hospital.

Surviving the rupture and the wound he returned to College Point where on January 24, 1864 he married Caroline Becker in St. Paul's Episcopal Chapel. Rev. Augustine W. Cornell performed the ceremony.

Working at the rubber factory, Adam and wife Caroline appear on page 216 in the 1870 Census of Flushing with three children; William, born on February 10, 1866, Edward, June 12, 1867, and Amelia, June 8, 1869.

By 1880 Adam is yet working at the rubber factory and eight more children have been born; George, March 20, 1871, Emilie, June 8, 1869, Lillie, July 7, 1872, Hubert, January 25, 1877, Harry, March 21, 1881, Frank, August 14, 1883, Frederick, January 11, 1883 and Benjamin Harrison, September 10, 1889. The family is found on page 295B of the Census.

The 1900 Census finds him in College Point, a comb-cutter, living with Caroline and seven of the children; Harry, Frank, Fred, Benjamin, William, and Lillie.

An original member of Post No. 451, Adam wrote many letters in support of pension applications made by his fellow veterans. He died on January 29, 1908 and Caroline died on February 19, 1914. Both are buried in Flushing Cemetery.

Johann, Matthew

Matthew Johann served in Company I of the 5th New York Regiment of National Guard, a 30-day unit sent to Pennsylvania to do guard duty during a critical point of the war, the Gettysburg Campaign. Most certainly, had it been necessary, the unit would have been called up to fight in the three-day battle early in July. They did not take part, and the unit was mustered out on July 17th.

Matthew's son William became an active member of the Sons of Union Veterans in College Point.

In 1880 Matthew lives in College Point and the Census record, page 302D, indicates that he is from Prussia, 42, married to Catherine, 34, and earns his living as an undertaker. Catherine is the daughter of William Becker, one of two undertakers in College Point in 1860.

On page 240 of the 1870 Census of Flushing, William Becker and his wife Susannah live in College Point with their married daughter Catherine. Her husband's name is written as *Martin*, but it was actually Matthew. The surname is spelled *Johim* and Matthew works as a cabinet-maker. Three children have been born; William, 4, Susan, 3, and Peter, 1.

In 1880 Matthew and Catherine continue living in College Point and have seven children. In addition to William, 14, Susan, 12, and Peter, 11, there are; Josephine, 8, Catherine, 6, Anna, 4, and Jacob, 1. Living with him is his widowed father-in-law, William.

It is logical to conclude that Matthew arrived in New York after the Census was taken and married Catherine sometime prior to 1866. The record does not indicate when either Matthew or Catherine passed away.

The Johann Funeral Home continues to this day in College Point.

Johnston, Jr. Daniel S.

GAR member Daniel S. Johnston, Jr. born in Glenwood, Long Island, is the third son and namesake of his father who also served in the war.

The Johnston family has the distinction of sending four members to the Army and they all enlisted in the same unit, the 34th New York Light Artillery. They were; Daniel, Sr. and Jr., John J. and William E. who died of chronic diarrhea on August 28, 1863. His name is etched on the Flushing Memorial to Civil War casualties.

In 1860 the Johnston family lives in North Hempstead and appears on page 378 of the Census. From Scotland, Daniel Sr. is a dealer. John, 20, William, 18 and Daniel, 14, all born in New York, are boatmen.

Daniel was born on April 7, 1844 and in 1861 lived in Manhasset. At 5'6" with blue eyes and brown hair, he enlisted on October 5, 1861 alongside his brothers and father. The pension record indicates that he was absent, deserted actually, for a period of six months and twenty-four days. When he applied for his pension, that time was deducted from his pensionable service time.

The record says that during the war he was taken prisoner on October 30, 1863 during the Battle of Knoxville at Lenoir Station, Tennessee and sent to Andersonville Prison in Georgia as was Christian Brill, Jr. and another soldier named James Kiernan.

Johnston was paroled at Wilmington, North Carolina on February 27, 1865 and returned to service at Camp Parole near Annapolis, Maryland on March 2, 1865. There is no record of Daniel's imprisonment, but it probably occurred. Daniel is also mentioned in Roemer's book as having saved an artillery piece at Cedar Mountain in August of 1862.

He moved to College Point following the war and married Elizabeth Deakin in April of 1872. They had four children; Charles Edgar, born June 13, 1873, Daniel Sanford, January 20, 1876, William Hall, May 23, 1878, and Nellie Kathleen, September 19, 1885.

In the 1880 Census of College Point, page 314D, all but Nellie are enumerated. Daniel is a painter and Lina Freund, 15 year-old daughter of veteran Edward Freund, is a servant in the home.

Elizabeth died on September 25, 1892 and three years later Daniel married Mary E. Brill at the First Reformed Church in College Point. Rev. Bannister performed the ceremony. Mary was a widow and had been married to one Francis Buckley. She may have been a sister to Christian Brill, but that cannot be confirmed.

Mary lived with Daniel for a period of but three months *"on account of cruel treatment, obtained a separation from him"* according to a note in the pension file.

She applied for pension benefits from West Orange, New Jersey in 1913 where she lived, claiming she had not seen Daniel for the previous seventeen years.

He died on December 10, 1920 in Rockaway Beach where at age 75, he was retired and living alone.

Kabisch, Franz

Franz Herman Kabisch was born on May 5, 1835 in the village of Seitz in Germany and came to America in 1855. At the time of his enlistment in Company G of the 7th New York Infantry on April 23, 1861, he was a comb-maker, 5'5", blue eyes, and blond hair with a fair complexion. In his pension application he says he was wounded at the Battle of Antietam. He was discharged on May 8, 1863.

The record tells us, but there is no specific documentation of his marriage to Ida Schmidt that took place before 1862. Her full name was Ida Emilie Fredericke Ernestine Schmidt and they had three children; Karl, born December 4, 1862, Rudolph, July 29, 1868 and Elise, October 10, 1869.

In the 1880 Census, Frank and his family live in New York City and Elise is not enumerated. Frank is a grocer and son Charles (Karl) is a jeweler's apprentice. Ida passed away on November 12, 1881.

Shortly after Ida's death, on January 26, 1882, he married Marie Sophie Henriette Starberg, herself the widow of one Carl Schultz who had died in Hamburg, Germany on April 22, 1874. The marriage took place in Hoboken, New Jersey and Pastor Leopold Mohr performed the ceremony.

Marie was born in Mecklenburg, Germany on October 9, 1837 and arrived in America in 1880 according to the 1920 Census of Brooklyn where she, Frank and two grandchildren, William, 28 and Carrie, 21 are enumerated.

In 1926, while living in Connecticut with his son Rudolph, Frank died at the age of 91 on December 21, 1926. He is buried in Wonx Spring Cemetery in the town of Southington.

Kanz, John

John was born in Wurtemburg, Germany ca. 1840. It is not known when he emigrated, but on enlistment day, October 7, 1861, he was a 5'7" butcher with a light complexion, blue eyes and light hair. It appears he was listed as both Kanz and Kantz.

His name appears on the August 23, 1862 *Flushing Journal* list of College Point volunteers, and as such he probably worked at the rubber factory.

Kanz suffered a gunshot wound between his 3rd and 4th fingers at the Battle of Cross Keys in Virginia on June 8, 1862. His pension application contained his original Discharge Certificate, unique in that it was the only original certificate found in any pension file reviewed for this book. He was discharged on October 1, 1865.

Following the war, on February 25, 1868, he married Mary Bussart at Saint Martin's Catholic Church in Louisville, Kentucky. Three children were born and also baptized at that church. They were; Ann, born January 27, 1869, Josephine, March 27, 1871 and Agatha, called Maggie, August 19, 1874.

John Kanz fell from a horse in Louisville and died as a result of his injuries on September 26, 1875. His wife, Mary, died shortly thereafter on March 2, 1881. Both were relatively young. At most John was 35 and Mary could not have been much older.

In support of the application for survivor's benefits, Annie wrote a letter from her home at 216 Arthur Street in Louisville and claimed that the children *"were raised as orphans and felt as if they had been neglected."*

All of the children had married at the time the application was processed and their married names were Ann Schellany, Josephine Schindler and Maggie Koch. The pension was denied as John's death was not a result of any injury sustained during the war.

Both John and Mary are buried at St. Michael's Cemetery in Louisville.

Kanz, Robert

R. (for Robert) Kanz appears on the August 23, 1862 list of Civil War volunteers from College Point that appeared in the *Flushing Journal*. While the unit is designated Lincoln Cavalry, it was not the unit in which he served. Rather it was the 52nd New York Infantry that he joined on November 6, 1861.

John Robert Kanz had married Fredericka Kettenacker on November 8, 1859, at the German Dutch Reformed Church in Morrisania, the Bronx, New York. The church is also called the Independent Evangelical Protestant Church in the pension application.

When he enlisted at age 31 just two days before his second wedding anniversary, he was a musician, stood 5'6", had a light complexion, blue eyes and fair hair., His service time would be short.

On June 28, 1862 while on the retreat from Fair Oaks to Harrison's Landing in Virginia, he died in an ambulance wagon of Marasmus, also called camp fever. The medical report indicates he contracted the fever as a result of *"lying on swampy ground and drinking swamp water."*

He and Fredericka had no children together and are not listed in the 1860 Census of Flushing. It is likely that the couple moved to College Point prior to the onset of the war and that Robert probably worked in the rubber factory. It is not known if he was a brother to John Kanz, described previously, but given the unusual surname, that too likely.

Kaufmann, John

John Kaufmann was born in Haningen, Germany ca. 1831. Prior to 1856 he emigrated to America and appears on page 717 of the 1860 Census of Flushing. He is 29 and living with his mother Christina, 59, from Baden, and a 29 year-old female named Catharine. She is probably a sister to John.

From about 1856 he worked at the India Rubber Company in College Point until entering military service on October 1, 1861.

While serving in the 34th New York Light Artillery, John is mentioned on page 171 in Roemer's book where Roemer describes his response to a crisis during the Tennessee Campaign and the Siege of Knoxville when shells they were firing failed to explode requiring some strategic and dangerous action, i.e. boring out the defective shells.

Roemer wrote: *"Sergeant Kaufmann became greatly excited, jumped up and cried out "For God's sake, stop your work; you will have us all blown up if you bore those shells here in the fort."*

Roemer continued boring out the shells and all worked out well in the end.

He also wrote a letter in support of Kaufmann's pension application in which he indicated that because of a severe case of rheumatism contracted at Fredericksburg, Virginia in December 1862, John *"had to be relieved as Sergeant and made Quartermaster Sergeant to make his work lighter."*

After serving in the Army, St. John's Lutheran Church in College Point was the site of his marriage to Friedericke Stark of Hirschberg, Baden, Germany. A son named George was born ca. 1867 followed by a daughter, Elizabeth on November 17, 1874.

On page 250 in the 1870 Census of Flushing, John *Coffman*, as the name is spelled, works as a cooper and living with the family is his 67 year-old mother Christina.

John worked at the rubber factory in 1880 and is listed in Census of College Point on page 306D.

From January 1882 he took up residence at the Soldiers' Home in Steuben, New York and eventually returned to College Point. Sadly, he took his own life on January 14, 1887 at the Tompkinsville Station on Staten Island. Reports in his pension record seem to indicate there were no signs of the action he was to take. His widow reported he had purchased a weapon, but no particular notice was taken of this event. Friedericke died sometime in 1913.

Kelly, Cornelius

Cornelius Kelly was born in Ireland in 1815 and appears on page 724 in the 1860 Census of Flushing with his Irish wife Mary and a 12 year-old daughter named Julia born in England. Three other children are listed; Mary, 7, Johannah, 6 and John, 3, all born in New York City.

The record says he was a day laborer, age 30, but he was much older, at least 45, and had moved to College Point from New York City where he had lived from the early 1850's working as a shoemaker.

He enlisted in Company C of the 15th New York Engineers on September 5, 1862 and the pension file indicates that he had two very unpleasant, wartime experiences; first suffering a crushed index finger while loading timbers for building pontoon bridges at Belle Plaine near Falmouth, Virginia.

The second event took place in August of 1864 when he lost the sight in both of his eyes, but after a time was able to return to light duty. As a result of what the Surgeon termed *"moon blindness"*, Cornelius was only able to work during the day. He was discharged on July 2, 1865.

He works as a laborer in College Point in 1870 and is found on page 223 of the Flushing Census, still married to Mary. Daughters Julia and Mary work in the rubber factory; John still lives at home and there is another daughter, Hattie, who is 9. That he was able to resume his shoemaker trade is in doubt as the pension record clearly indicates his inability to work as a result of the accident to his finger.

When the 1880 Census of College Point is taken, he is a widower living with daughter Julia who is married a man named Lebkey. Her husband is not enumerated. Cornelius' daughters, Hannah and Kate, are still single and living in the family. The Census record appears on page 235A.

Cornelius died early in 1890, but there is no indication of his burial place.

Keppler, Jacob

Jacob Friederich Keppler is son of Jacob and Christiana Burch. He married Christine Louise Adler on November 24, 1844 at the Lutheran Church in Besigheim, Neckarkreis in Germany, and they became parents to three children; Christian Freiderike, born April 2, 1842, Carolina Wilhelmina, February 23, 1844 and Catherine Friederike, May 8, 1851.

The family booked first-class passage aboard the Clipper Ship *"Julia"*, sailing on February 20, 1854 from Mannheim in Germany, to Antwerp then on to New York. The original ship documents are contained in the pension files.

Jacob enlisted in Company K of the 45th Pennsylvania Infantry on October 22, 1861 in Harrisburg. He was 40, a gardener, standing 5'6", with a fair complexion, gray eyes and brown hair.

It is not clear that the family lived in Harrisburg at the time of the enlistment. Within the year Jacob is killed at the Battle of South Mountain and the record says he was 43. There is a letter in the pension file dated September 14, 1862, written from College Point, to document the marriage of Jacob and Christine in Germany.

He may have gone to work at the rubber factory, but that will never be known, nor is there any further record of people by the name of Keppler in College Point. There is a Frederick Keppler, 38, living in Brooklyn in 1880 who could easily be the son born in 1842.

The name John Keppler is etched on the Flushing Memorial to Civil War casualties. Why his first name was not Jacob is not known.

Kiernan, John

John Kiernan, 22 and born in New York, appears in the 1860 Census of Flushing on page 696. He is unmarried and a laborer.

The *Flushing Journal* list of College Point volunteers indicates that a John Kiernan served in the Lincoln Cavalry, but no one by this name served in that unit.

There was however, a 23 year-old John Kiernan who joined the 34th New York Light Artillery and then supposedly deserted on April 3, 1863. The military record says he *"left the battery at the railroad station in Covington, Kentucky"*.

There was no pension application, however a person by this name does live in College Point in 1870 and is found on page 255 of the Flushing Census. He is 33, married to 32 year-old Margaret and they have four children; James, 9, Ella, 4, Bernard, 2, and Henry, 2 months.

The family lives in Flushing in 1880 found on page 264A of the Census. John, 40, works at the gashouse. Wife Margaret, 39, and children; Ella, 13, Henry, 9, and another son named John, 2, are also enumerated.

Nothing else is known about this veteran, if he was a veteran indeed.

Kiernan, Patrick

Patrick was born in New York City in 1845, the third of three sons born to Patrick and Anne, his parents, who had married in New York City on November 15, 1835. His brothers were; Brian, born ca. 1841, James, ca. 1842 and Peter, ca. 1850. The family lived in College Point in 1860 and appear on page 692 of the Flushing Census.

During his tenure in the Army, Patrick spent a lot of time away from his unit and absent without leave. His pension record gives the dates.

The record also states that he was wounded at least twice, once to the hand at Poplar Grove Church on September 30, 1864, and at another time, place unspecified, to the head.

As a soldier, Patrick also suffered from chronic dysentery and eventually died from it on November 5, 1870 in the Charity Hospital in New Orleans, Louisiana. His mother applied for and received his pension.

Koch, Charles

Born at Alsfeld in Hesse-Darmstadt, Germany in 1820, Hartman Carl Koch came to America prior to 1860 and appears in the Flushing Census on page 71. He is 40, a baker, and married to Elizabeth Braun who was born in the town of Romrod, in Hesse Darmstadt in 1821.

They were wed on January 3, 1846 at the German Reformed Protestant Church at 127 Norfolk Street in New York City. Pastor Berkey performed the ceremony. There are two children in 1860; Louisa, 14 and Charles, 10.

Charles enlisted as a Private in the 58th New York Infantry, the Morgan Rifles, on October 4, 1861, and was mustered out on October 22, 1864. His name appears in the August 23, 1862 *Flushing Journal* list of volunteers from College Point.

The pension record indicates that Carl was in the National Soldiers Home in Elizabeth City, Virginia where he died on January 27, 1893. At this time Elizabeth is living in New York City at 301 East 71st Street. She died prior to November 1898 for that is when the pension checks stopped.

Kulle, Albert

Albert Kulle was born in Berlin, Germany on July 26, 1845 to Charles and Fredericke Heinrich Kulle who had four other children; Augusta, Antonia, Bertha and Charles. The record does not provide their respective ages, but the family came to America shortly after Albert's birth and from 1851, until his joining the Army, lived in Valley Stream.

On the day he enlisted in the 158th New York Infantry, August 25, 1862, Albert stood 5'11", had a dark complexion, hazel eyes and brown hair. His pension file indicates nothing out of the ordinary.

On January 28, 1877 Albert married Caroline Schnitzius at St. Mark's Lutheran Church on East 6th Street in New York City. Caroline was born in New York City on October 10, 1856 and the family appears in the 1880 Census of New York City spelled Kalle. Albert is a policeman and there are two children; Albert, 1, and Caroline, 7 months.

By the time the pension application is filed only two children under the age of 16 are listed; Clare, born April 21, 1891 and Alice, October 1, 1892.

In 1895 Albert and family move to College Point and are there in 1910. Albert, a retired policeman, is enumerated with Caroline and two daughters, Clare, 19 and Alice, 17. Both daughters work in the rubber factory and Albert lives off his own income, source unknown. Caroline has given birth to 7 children overall, but Clare and Alice are the only two alive when the 1910 Census is taken.

Albert died at his home at 235 16th Street on August 8, 1924 and is buried in Flushing Cemetery.

Landt, Henry

Henry Landt's name did not make it onto any list of College Point soldiers, but he lived in College Point in 1860 and is on page 712 listed as a 19 year-old clerk.

During his service with the 162nd New York Infantry he was taken prisoner at Deep Bottom, Virginia on July 26, 1864 and given parole the following October 15th.

Following his discharge he returned to New York City and married Philipina Zimmer at the Church of Saint Luke located at 617 West 42nd Street. Three children were born; Caroline, July 7, 1868, William, November 19, 1869 and Matilda, December 16, 1871.

William passed away on December 14 1892 according to the pension record. Matilda married a man named Johnston and lived in Hudson County, New Jersey at least through 1920 where she appears in the Census with three children.

Henry is almost 32 when on July 27, 1872 he dies at 457 West 46th Street and is buried in the Lutheran Cemetery in Queens. Philipina lived on until October 29, 1926 dying at the home of her daughter Caroline married to Henry Jordan and living at 151 Spring Street in Hoboken, New Jersey.

Lane, Charles

GAR member Charles Lane's application for membership indicates he entered the Navy on March 17, 1862 and was discharged on July 7, 1865. He served on the ships *North Carolina* and *Morning Light*.

In 1880 there is a soldier by this name in Whitestone and by his age he could be one and the same. Sadly, nothing else is known of this individual.

Lark, Joseph

GAR member Joseph Lark is on the original roster, but nothing else is known of his life.

Lark, Peter D.

GAR member Peter Lark was born in Highland Falls, New York in 1844 to *Quearan* and Mary Elizabeth DuBerry Lark.

In the 1850 Census of Orange County, New York, the town of Cornwall, his father, whose name in this record is spelled *Quirring*, is a 45 year-old laborer from Germany while his mother Elizabeth is 36 and also from Germany. Peter is 7 , and the third of six children; Mary 11, Joseph, 9, Elizabeth, 5, Louis, 3 and John, 9 months, all born in New York.

Peter enlisted in Battery A of the 6th NY Engineers six months before the war began at the age of 18. From that time until November 24, 1890, he remained in the military.

In 1880 a soldier, age 38, by this name lives in Whitestone, very likely the Civil War veteran. He is married to Catherine, 34, and they have three children; Mary, 9, Eva, 7 and Emma, 1.

The pension record says nothing of a first wife, however on June 15, 1898 he married Dorothea Snell, 29, at St. John's Lutheran Church at 281 Prospect Avenue in Brooklyn.

At the time Peter was a Police Captain at Green-Wood Cemetery and nine months after the marriage, using a pistol, he took his own life. The examining physician indicated that a grippe Peter had contracted was the cause of the suicide, and five months later in August, his daughter, Mildred Belle Lark, was born.

Dorothea lives at 311 19th Street in Brooklyn in 1920 where she works as a matron at Green-Wood Cemetery. Peter is buried there.

Lasche, Robert

Ernst Robert Lasche, born on June 3, 1840 in Rosswein in the Saxony area of Germany, and baptized there five days later, came to America around 1854 with his parents according to his pension record. He apparently never used his original first name, choosing to be known as Robert for his entire lifetime.

On enlistment day, May 3, 1861, he was working as a clerk, stood 5'5" with a fair complexion, gray eyes and black hair. He suffered a wound to his left leg in the Battle of Antietam on September 17, 1862. He was discharged the following year on June 1st only to re-enlist in a Wisconsin unit, Company H of the 35th Infantry, where he became an officer. Lasche was discharged at Nashville, Tennessee in July of 1865.

Following his two enlistments, one in Williamsburgh and the other in Madison, Wisconsin, he married Friedericke Marie Nicolai in Milwaukee on November 4, 1866.

He and his spouse remained in the Madison area to raised the six children; Stephen M.J., born October 4, 1867, Max, December 25, 1869, Bruno, April 8, 1871, Cora Marie, November 29, 1874, Olga Marie, August 6, 1877 and Esme Marie, February 14, 1880.

Of the last three girls born, Cora would marry G.W. Emlesse, Olga; R.W. Pearson and Esme; C.L. Markle.

Robert died in Milwaukee on July 23, 1917.

Leppert, John

John Leppert was 19 on enlistment day, April 30, 1861. His unit was Company E of the 10th New York Infantry and he stood 5'7", had a light complexion, dark hair and blue eyes.

In his original pension application he stated that" *At Norfolk, VA, in Fort Norfolk handling spiked artillery in May 1862 making room for tenting, I was ruptured by heavy lifting and treated by Dr. Doolittle of the Regiment."*

Contained in the original pension file were letters written by Pastor Ebendick, and veterans D.S. Johnston, John Emmerich and Henry Wurtz.

Following his discharge on May 7, 1863, he returned to College Point and took up the life of a farmer. Pastor August Ebendick married John to Katie Dockendorf, sister of the three Dockendorf brothers who had also served in the war. The ceremony was performed at St. John's Lutheran Church on September 24, 1870. Three daughters were born; Mary, December 17, 1873, Katie, January 10, 1877, and Louisa, September 22, 1879.

The family appears in the 1880 Census of College Point on Page 306D. John is employed as a laborer, and the youngest daughter is called Emilia and not Louisa.

John dies the following year on December 21, 1881 and is buried in Flushing Cemetery, but there is a postscript to this story.

Ten years after John's death, his widow had a daughter by a man named Charles Rausch, and subsequently the child died December 18, 1899 at the age of 9. While Katie *"kept company"* with him for three years, she never lived with nor married Rausch, and in fact her affidavit requesting a resumption of pension benefits says, *"After my child was born, he ran away with another woman...an Irish working girl from Flushing. He had promised to marry me and recognized the child as his"*

The daughter had been named Sophia and she carried the name of Leppert, not Rausch. As a result of the child's birth, Katie stopped the pension benefits she had been receiving since John' death in the mistaken belief, as someone had told her, she would *"get into trouble with the government"*. *"In fact, she told the Special Examiner aiding her in her quest for a resumption of the benefits, she was threatened with exposure to the government by some jealous-minded person."*

To support her application, veterans Charles Marx and William Hoenig wrote letters, as did her brother Joseph Dockendorff and his wife, all to no avail. The request was denied on September 24, 1909.

The pension record does not say when Katie Leppert died, but in 1909 she lived at 511 2nd Street, today's 111th Street, in College Point with her daughter Mary who had married a man named Charles Walter. The Walter family appears in the 1910 Census in College Point and only a son named Carl lives in the family. It is likely her mother had died in the months following the rejection of benefits and the taking of the Census.

Mary Walter is a widow in the 1920 Census living at the same home with her unmarried sister, Louise, the one incorrectly called Emilia in 1880.

One final postscript to this story: The Leppert daughter named Katie born in 1873 married John Siegenthal on October 6, 1894. She gave birth to a son named Walter in 1906 and this son married a woman named Elsie Schroeder ca. 1935. A son named Walter was born on February 18, 1938 and he married Ellen Haas, the author's sister, on January 10, 1960. Family lore always held that the Siegenthal and Dockendorf lines had connected at some point. Indeed, they had, over a hundred years ago.

Lindecke, William

GAR member William Lindecke was born in Berlin, Germany and on enlistment day, September 15, 1864 in Michigan, stood 5'4" with blue eyes and black hair.

He lived in Brooklyn following the war and worked as an oiler in a machine shop before moving to Lindenhurst in 1869 where he delivered milk.

He subsequently married Aurora Parthe on January 5, 1873 at Breslau, called Lindenhurst today. Rev. Stoll performed the ceremony.

Five children were born; William, 1875, Edward, possibly called Otto, August 1, 1876, Arthur, 1877, Alvin, December 31, 1881, Aurora, March 29, 1884.

The pension record indicates that William had died before the application was processed in July of 1889.

In 1880 the family lived in Babylon on Long Island where William was working as a farmer.

In 1885 he moved to College Point, worked as a lamplighter and joined the GAR. His pension application said he *"fell off a log while heading for Raleigh."* He got his pension.

William, whose German name was Wilhelm, died on September 3, 1891. Aurora lives with her unmarried son Alvin in Babylon in 1920 and died in Lindenhurst in July 1923.

Louis, Frank

Louis Frank, a 27 year-old shoemaker from Hesse, is found on page 705 of the 1860 Census of Flushing with Ann, 28 from Ireland and their four children; Michael, 5, John, 3, Elizabeth, 4 and William, 1.

His name appears on the list of College Point volunteers that appeared in the August 23, 1862 *Flushing Journal*.

Neither he nor Ann are found anywhere in the 1880 Census, and Louis apparently did not apply for a pension.

Ludwig, Carl

While he and his brother William were fond of saying they were born in Paris, in his brother William's pension file William says he was born in Hot Alteneig, Brachander Fulda in Germany. Their father's name was Jacob and mother's was Caroline.

Carl, 19, and William, 22, described as farmers, arrived in New York Harbor on June 20, 1861 aboard the ship *Germania* that had sailed from Havre in France. Three months later they were both in the Army.

On induction day Carl is described as standing 5'6", almost a foot shorter than brother William, at 6'4". He had brown eyes and hair and says in the record that he was born in Paris.

Carl Ludwig was wounded in the Battle of the Wilderness, May 5-7, 1864, near Spotsylvania Courthouse in Virginia. He was also awarded the Congressional Medal of Honor for bravery during the Battle of Petersburg that took place 37 days later, June 18, 1864.

In making the award, the Assistant Secretary of the Army's citation reads:

"This soldier, as gunner of his piece, inflicted, singly, a great loss upon the enemy, and distinguished himself in the removal of the piece while under a heavy fire."

On December 21, 1861 President Lincoln had signed into law a provision proposed for the Navy for a medal *"to be bestowed upon such petty officers, seamen, landsmen and Marines as shall most distinguish themselves by their gallantry in action and other seamanlike qualities during the present war."*

Shortly thereafter on July 12, 1862, a similar resolution for the Army was signed into law as well, *"to be bestowed upon such noncommissioned officers and privates as shall distinguish themselves by their gallantry in action, and other soldier-like qualities during the present insurrection."*

In the 1890's the Civil War gallantry of many soldiers was recognized and Carl Ludwig's award was given on July 30, 1896 at Washington DC in a letter from Col. F.C. Ainsworth of the Record and Pension Office. In addition to announcing the award, the letter further stated the medal would be sent a few days later.

Ludwig is one of three area men to have this honor bestowed upon him, the others being John Starkins and Joseph Hibson. A fourth man, James C. Cornell, was recommended to receive the honor, but for reasons unknown, the Medal of Honor was never conferred.

Biographies

The pension record also says Carl was wounded in the left hip at Hare House in Virginia on June 22, 1864, but I think this date actually refers to an injury sustained by his brother William.

A year after he returned from the service, Carl married Caroline Emiline Christine Kruse of Hanover, Germany, in New York City. Rev. J.H. Baden performed the ceremony on October 1, 1866 and in the years to come three daughters would be born; Elizabeth on August 16, 1867, Caroline, May 10, 1874 and Lena or Lily, March 27, 1887.

The 1870 Census of Flushing, page 212, says there was another child, a six-month old daughter named Louisa, but she must have died before 1880 where Carl, as does his brother, works at the gashouse.

Carl became an original member of Adam Wirth Post No. 451 and his picture is included in this book.

Carl, Emiline and Lena, a student, appear in the 1900 Census of College Point. He is a rubber worker.

Emiline died on February 18, 1905 and Carl was married a second time on March 25, 1906 to a widow named Marie Kastner. It was she who filed for his pension following his death from liver cancer on May 16, 1913.

Carl is buried in Flushing Cemetery. Marie lives on until January 8, 1939 and dies in Schenectady, New York where she is probably buried.

Ludwig, William

At 6'4" William was a very tall man for the time. He had a light complexion, blue eyes and brown hair and it is in his pension record he says he was born in Paris. It really was Germany.

During his time in the Army he says he was kicked by a horse at Lenoir Station in Virginia on October 28, 1863, wounded at the Battle of Spotsylvania on May 12, 1864, and wounded at Petersburg on June 22, 1864, this time in his left leg.

He survived the horse kick and the wounds and returned from the war to marry Katharina Weissgerber at St. John's Lutheran Church in College Point. Rev. August Ebendick performed the ceremony on March 9, 1866 and the original St. John's Marriage Certificate, in poor condition, is included among his pension papers.

Katharina says she was born on September 10, 1838 in the town of Kusel in Bavaria. Witnesses to the marriage ceremony included Ferdinand Ludwig, an unidentified relative to be sure, and Jacob Hebel.

The family lives in College Point and appears on page 229 in the 1870 Flushing Census. An 8 month-old son named Ferdinand is listed; William is a gardener.

The family lives in College Point in 1880 and William works in the gashouse. Ferdinand has died as he is not listed and there are four children; William, born November 12, 1871, Caroline, March 29, 1874, Charles, September 29, 1876 and Jacob, June 13, 1880. Caroline would marry a man named Young and assist in the preparation of her father's pension application.

Along with Carl, he became an original member of the Adam Wirth Post No. 451, and was one of the twelve signers of the original application.

William appears in the 1900 Census of College Point living with his wife Katharine and son Charles. He passed away on October 6, 1902 and Katharine, who is listed in the 1920 Census living with her daughter Caroline Young, lives on until March 31, 1926. Both William and Katharine are buried in Flushing Cemetery.

Lutters, Ernest

Ernest is 15, a laborer and the second son of Ferdinand and Antonette Lutters in the 1860 Census of Flushing, page 725. Both of his parents are 56 and from Prussia. There are two siblings, Ferdinand, jr., 18 and Emma, a twin to Ernest.

On enlistment day, April 7, 1865, he was a turner and stood 5'8" with a light complexion, blue eyes and brown hair.

Following his three-month's service in the 131st New York, he married Mary Weinz at St. John's Lutheran Church in College Point and they appear there in the 1880 Census. Ernest is a Justice of the Peace, married with four children; George, 8, Lilly, 6, Bertha, 3 and Alfred, 1. At least one more daughter, Maria, is born ca. 1884 and she marries Valentine Zittel.

Mary died after 1880 and Ernest married a second time to Elizabeth Unkelback, born in Worms, Germany. The marriage took place on August 26, 1882 at St. John's Lutheran Church in College Point presided over by Rev. August Ebendick.

The pension file is large and the story it tells is sad.

Elizabeth, his second wife, applied for a widow's pension and among the many documents is an affidavit in which Elizabeth says that Ernest had owned a grocery store in College Point at the time of their marriage. No longer a Justice of the Peace, on September 19, 1889 at 10 in the morning, Ernest told her he was going to New York City to meet a grocery dealer and that was the last she saw of him.

At the time of Elizabeth's application in 1905, the Pension Board conducted a search to see if he was still alive, which indeed he was, in Seattle and then Spokane, Washington.

Apparently he had remarried one Alta Merritt in 1892 and lived in the Washington State area using the alias John Gray. Elizabeth was understandably upset to learn that, not only had he left, but also that he had taken up with another woman... and this was twenty years or more after the fact.

By 1920 Elizabeth lives with her daughter Maria Zittel at 760 7th Avenue in College Point. Elizabeth lives another ten years and died on October 30, 1930.

While the Pension Board tried to learn whether or not Ernest had died, their attempts were not successful and nothing else is known of this individual.

Maher, Patrick

Patrick, age 30, appears on page 692 of the 1860 Census of Flushing married to Johannah who is 26. Both are from Ireland and they have a 2 year-old son named John. It is not known when they emigrated.

At the time of his enlistment on August 21st in 1862 he was 5'9", a laborer with a fair complexion, blue eyes and brown hair.

Within a year he would be at a convalescent camp in Virginia suffering from an advanced case of tuberculosis contracted since his enlistment, so says the Certificate of Disability for Discharge. His name is spelled *Meagher* on the certificate.

A deposition of Johannah taken in 1880 provides a little more information. Father James O'Beirne had married them on July 22, 1855 at St. Michael's Catholic Church in Flushing. Her maiden name was Dempsey and Garret L. Garretson, a prominent nurseryman, employed her as a domestic. Alice Stapleton and Lawrence Maher, probably Patrick's brother, were witnesses.

Prior to his enlistment Patrick had enjoyed good health and was the father of six children all who had died by the time the deposition was taken indicating that the son enumerated in 1860 had passed on.

According to his pension record he returned home following his service and was *"broken down in health and afflicted with consumption"*, the result, he believed, of having coming down with *"a severe cold after a forced march of thirty miles through a rain storm and having to lie on the wet ground in wet clothes when it was so cold as to freeze water."*

He was never able to work and *"gradually failed in strength"* until his death which occurred on the 22nd day of July, 1864, coincidentally his 9th wedding anniversary.

Because of his poverty he was never able to see a physician except once when he went to a New York dispensary and given cod liver oil to drink.

According to Father John MacKenna, Pastor of St. Michael's in 1879, on the first day of August, 1864, shortly after his father death, a son named Patrick, Jr. was born and baptized at the Church.

In 1880, Patrick continues to support his mother who is at this time living in Flushing with her sister Margaret who had married Thomas Fogarty whose family is enumerated on page 327A of the Flushing Census.

Patrick Maher is buried at Mount Saint Mary's Cemetery in Flushing. While he did not die in battle, he was most certainly a casualty of the war and a case could be made for his name to be added to the Flushing Memorial to fallen Soldiers.

Mahlenthal, Emmanuel

GAR member Emmanuel Mahlenthal, who came to America in 1860, was born to Johann Jacob Muhlenthaler, a linen weaver, and Marie Mueller, in the town of Langenbruch, Basel, Switzerland on May 18, 1838.

His surname is not spelled the same way in any record, for example, the report of the New York Adjutant General says his name is G. Manuel Mehlelhuer, but also Muhlenthall.

On the day he enlisted, October 1, 1864, he was a 5'5", chair-maker, with a fair complexion, gray eyes and brown hair.

The pension record indicates he was married to a woman named Fanny, date unknown, prior to his enlistment. In the 1880 Census of New York City the entry reads Manuel Muhlethaler, 43, silk weaver from Switzerland. He is married to Ferina, surname unknown, 42, also from Switzerland. There are four children enumerated; Amos, born May 15, 1864, who works in a piano factory, Sophie, June 22, 1866, who works in a laundry, Philip, 12, at school, and Louisa, born August 29, 1880.

From the same pension record it appears there was another son named Jacob, born November 18, 1876, but that child is not enumerated in 1880. It is likely he had died.

Fanny died on November 13, 1884 in Paterson, New Jersey, and he was married a second time to Christina Buecher, the widow of William Gradenburg. The marriage took place on October 15, 1887. Rev. Henry Beiderbecke performed the ceremony, possibly at his home, 803 East 169th Street in New York City.

In 1900 Emmanuel lives on 12th Street in College Point with his named spelled Muhlenthaler. He is married to Christine, described as the mother of three children, two of which are still living. One of them named Minnie, is living with them.

Christine's first husband William had also been a silk weaver, and in the 1880 Census in New York City, his name spelled Radenburg. Minnie is his child as is another child, Emma, 6. She is not enumerated with her mother in 1900 and it is not known if she is the other living child.

In 1908 Emmanuel lives in Ohio, possibly at the soldier's home. He died on March 25, 1910, but the place is not indicated.

Mahoney, Michael

Michael appears on the August 23, 1862 *Flushing Journal* list of College Point volunteers, however his unit is incorrectly identified as the 29th New York Infantry.

He actually served in the 34th New York Light Artillery and apparently never applied for a pension.

The military record indicates that he received a disability discharge at Camp Barry in Washington, DC on May 29, 1862. He was 37 on enlistment day, September 2, 1861, but that is all that is known.

Mandeville, George

GAR member George Mandeville's name appears on the original application for charter with a line, inexplicably, drawn through it, but it does not appear on the roster that was printed for the Memorial Day Exercises in 1928.

From his pension record it is learned that he was injured on September 17, 1862 at the Battle of Antietam in Maryland *"while jumping over a fence he fell and ruptured himself on the right side."*

Mandeville was born in Brooklyn ca. 1834 and following his wartime service he married Margaret McLaren whose first husband David had died on September 19, 1868 at the age of 35, and is buried in Flushing Cemetery. Rev. J. Carpenter Smith performed the Episcopal ceremony at St. George's Church in Flushing on June 10, 1871.

The family appears on page 238C in the 1880 Census of College Point. George is a carpenter and three children are enumerated; David, a 23 year-old engineer, Margaret, 20 and Katie, 17, all by Margaret's first husband.

In 1890 the family lives at 167 3rd Avenue in College Point and it is at his home that George dies on November 2, 1897. He is buried in Flushing Cemetery.

Marx, Charles

GAR member Charles Marx was born in Baden, Germany on September 18, 1836 and came to America in the mid 1850's.

His marriage to Philipina Brill took place at the First Congregational Church in New York City on January 17, 1858 with the ceremony performed by Rev. Joseph Hanson.

In 1860 he lives in Flushing and appears on page 636 of the Census with Philipina. Charles, a 5'4" tinsmith with dark hair and brown eyes, for some unknown reason, joins and serves in two New Jersey units. His five month military odyssey began on March 11, 1865 and ended at discharge in Newark the following August 23rd.

Following the war he returned to College Point, raised his family and joined the Adam Wirth Post No. 451.

He and Philipina had three children; Ludwig, born July 14, 1867, Louisa, November 3, 1869 and a third child born August 14, 1882, whose name may have been John, but is not readable in the pension record.

Charles and Philipina appear in the 1900 Census of College Point; his son's name is again illegible, but it appears to be John. Living with them is his daughter Louisa and her husband William Fehn who is a plumber.

Charles is a widow in 1910 and lives with William and Louisa, now called Frances. William owns his own plumbing business and in 1920 two sons, Sidney and Frank, work alongside of him.

Ludwig, the son born in 1867, became an active member of the Sons of Union Veterans organization in College Point.

At the time of his death on July 16, 1914, Charles lived at 212 13th Street in College Point.

May, William

GAR member William May was born to Bernhard and Mary Elizabeth Braumuller in the town of Treysa-Cassel in Germany on January 31, 1839.

It is not known when the family emigrated, but on the day of his enlistment, August 30, 1862, William stood 5'6", had a pale complexion, brown eyes and hair, and worked as a clerk. According to his pension record he was taken prisoner after the Battle of Gettysburg in 1863.

Barely a month after his discharge on July 11, 1865, he married Mary Vollkardt at St. George's Chapel in New York City. Dr. Charles Schramm performed the Protestant Episcopal ceremony. The couple moved to College Point on July 2, 1867.

In 1880 there are two children; Anna, 14 and Charlie, 10, enumerated on Page 244C in College Point where he is a laborer. A third child, a daughter named Harriet, is born April 27, 1882. Harriet will marry Jacob Fahner the son of veteran Jacob Fahner, and live in College Point in 1920. Anna marries Edward Michel, who is quite possibly the eldest son of veteran Charles Michel, called Frank in 1880.

Charles and Mary are also enumerated in College Point in 1910 living at 322 13th Street, but the pension record does not indicate when either died.

McClymont, George

GAR member George McClymont was a musician, a drummer actually, during his time in the Army. On July 6, 1861, the day he enlisted in New York City, he indicated he had been born in New York, stood 5'4", had a light complexion, blue eyes and light hair. On January 1, 1864 he re-enlisted at Hilton Head and at the time was charged $1.50 for a damaged drumhead. He was discharged on August 30, 1865 in Washington, DC.

McClymont was welcomed into Post No. 451 on September 8, 1891. While a record of his pension application exists, processed from the District of Columbia on April 29, 1892, the actual file, for reasons unknown, could not be found at the National Archives.

McCormick, Daniel

Daniel at age 25 appears on page 689 in the 1860 Census of Flushing along with 45 year-old James, who is quite possibly his father. Both are laborers from Ireland, but it is not known when they came to America.

His pension record offers scant information other than that his address in 1891 was 471 Myrtle Avenue in Brooklyn, that he apparently never married and that he suffered from disease of the heart and lungs.

In 1870 there is a 44 year-old patient by this name in St. Peter's Hospital in Brooklyn, 6th Ward, page 53. It is difficult to prove that this is the veteran Daniel McCormick as the age, 44, is off by nine years.

McDonald, George

There is a New York-born, 35 year-old, unmarried man by this name on page 749 of the 1860 Flushing Census. He enlisted in Company C of the 63rd New York Infantry on August 23, 1861 and is described in his military record as being a 36 year-old laborer in 1861 standing 5'11" with a florid complexion, blue eyes and dark brown hair.

He was on *"daily duty as the color bearer"* for the 63rd NY and was wounded at the Battle of Antietam on September 17, 1862 in Maryland where he died three days later. There does not appear to have been a widow's pension applied for so it is likely he was unmarried.

A review of all people by the name of George McDonald in the 1860 Census in the New York City area yielded only one at age 35 and that was the one from College Point.

Though his name appears on none of the lists consulted, and acknowledging that his inclusion in this book is purely speculative, it is quite possible that he is an authentic, albeit unrecognized, College Point veteran.

McGowan, William

William McGowan is among those named in the August 23, 1862 *Flushing Journal* list of volunteers from College Point as well as in Munsells' *History of Queens County*. Both records say that he served in the Navy and Munsell adds that he was a landsman on the ship *Wabash*.

There are at least five persons by this name enumerated in the 1880 Census in New York City and Brooklyn, but none live in Queens. Since there does not appear to have been a pension applied for, nothing else is known of this person.

McManus, Robert

GAR member Robert McManus was born in Connecticut in 1840, the son of Mary Mackmanus (*sic*) who appears in the 1850 Census of Hartford. There is no husband enumerated, but the record indicates she is 34 and was born in England. Robert has four siblings, Henry, 12, Ellen, 8, Jane, 6, and Mary, who is 4.

The First Connecticut Infantry was a three-month unit and Robert was in and out very quickly. At some point following his Army tour, he was transferred to the Navy, but nothing is known of that service.

At some point he moved to the New York City area and is enumerated in Brooklyn, married to Ella, in 1880. He is a silver-plater and has one son, Edward, who is an apprentice silver-plater. It is not known when he moved to College Point.

Robert McManus did apply for a pension, but it could not be located at the National Archives. Nothing else is known about this individual.

Metzger, Charles

A man by this name is listed in Munsell's *History of Queens County* as having served in the 15th New York Heavy Artillery, but it was actually a 30-day enlistment in the 15th New York Regiment of National Guard Infantry called out from June 6, 1864 through July 7, 1864 to garrison Fort Richmond in New York Harbor.

Adding a bit of confusion is the fact that in 1860 there are two men by this name living in College Point; one on page 717, age 34, and the other on page 745, age 43. Generally speaking, older men served in this 30-day unit, but I have not been able to confirm which of the two actually did serve.

The older Metzger passes away before the 1880 Census, but his widow Catherine and daughter Adele continue to live in College Point.

Charles Metzger, the younger, an insurance agent in 1880, lives in College Point with his wife Rosina or Rosalie and two sons; John, 21 and Gustav, 13.

Michel, Charles

Charles Michel was born in New Jersey in May 1843 and is found on page 723 of the 1860 Census of Flushing. He is the 17 year-old son of Ann, 41 from Ireland. There is no information about his father, but there is a 3 year-old named Annie and another woman, Margaret Kennedy, living with the family.

Charles is named in a *Flushing Journal* article dated August 16, 1862 as having joined the Navy, but no specific enlistment date is given.

After the war he returned to College Point and is enumerated in the 1880 Census of College Point on page 235B married to Kate, 33, from Ireland. He is a machinist and they have four children; Frank, 11, Charles, 10, Annie, 7 and Henry, 5. Another daughter named Lotta will be born in November 1881.

In 1900 the family lives in Lindenhurst and he is still a machinist living with his wife and son Charles, who is a teamster. Also living with Charles are his married daughter Anna, married to John Shields, son Henry married to Kate, and daughter Lotta married to Frank Schuttinger. Henry and Kate have a son named Allen born in June 1884.

It does not appear there was a pension application made and nothing more is known of Charles Michel. His son Frank marries and is enumerated with his family in the 1920 Census of College Point.

Miller, Frederick

Frederick Miller was born in Germany and is enumerated in the 1860 Census of Flushing on page 712 with his parents; Henry, 50 and Elizabeth 47. The record says he is 12 and has an 18 year-old brother Louis, along with two sisters, Amelia, 16, and Kate, 10. Louis will also serve in the 20th New York Infantry.

On December 29, 1864 Frederick enlisted at Wilmington, Delaware and erroneously claimed to be 21 years old. He stood 5'9", had a light complexion, brown eyes and light hair and was one of three College Point men to serve in the 1st Regiment of Delaware Infantry with the other two being Valentine Piereth and Francis Dockendorf.

Frederick mustered out at Munson Hill in Virginia on July 12, 1865 and two and a half years later on January 23, 1868 married Mary Higginbottom at St. Fidelis Catholic Church in College Point. Father Huber performed the ceremony.

Their children included; William, born November 29, 1868, Elizabeth, June 3, 1870, Frederick, June 30, 1872, Henry, September 12, 1874, Louis, June 19, 1877, Thomas, May 8, 1879, Mary October 1, 1883, Edward, November 22, 1885 and Laura, October 23, 1887. Edward died before the pension application was made.

The 1880 Census of College Point, page 239A, indicates Frederick works in the rubber factory. All the children born prior to the census have survived and living with the family is his mother-in-law, Joanna Higginbottom.

Mary died on May 3, 1892 and is buried in Mt. Saint Mary's Cemetery. Frederick, who works in the rubber factory for his entire life, died on January 10, 1899 and is buried in Flushing Cemetery. It is not known why husband and wife were buried in different cemeteries.

Miller, Lewis

There are two men by this name in the 1860 Census of Flushing, both found on page 712 and both served in the military. Two small bits of information contained in this individual's pension record made it possible to distinguish one from the other; the fact that buried with him is his mother, Elizabeth, and his birth year. He was born in "Obro" or "Ebro", a town in Hesse, Germany, on March 14, 1818.

In 1860, Elizabeth, found at the bottom of page 711, is 54, from Hesse and living with Jacob Warner, 53, from Wurtemburg. There is no indication of the relationship. Louis, as his named is spelled, is at the top of page 712, and earns $1,000 per year as a laborer.

On enlistment day, August 29, 1861, he is described as being a 5'8" blacksmith with a light complexion, blue eyes and brown hair. Serving in the 34th New York Light Artillery, he is mentioned in Roemer's book, and following his November 15 1863 discharge, he returned to College Point. On July 29, 1871, he married Mary McDowell at St. Paul's Chapel. Rev. J.A. Appleton performed the Episcopal ceremony and it appears there were no children ever born to the union.

There is a childless couple, Louis, 54 and Mary Miller, 50 and born in Ireland, living in College Point in 1880. While the age for Louis is off by eight years, and the spelling of his first name is different, I think this is he.

Mary died on September 22, 1904 and four years later, having spent a bit of time at Flushing Hospital, Louis passed away on October 20, 1908.

Both are buried in Flushing Cemetery.

Miller, Louis

The second person by this name was born in Nassau in Germany, the son of Henry and Elizabeth. It is not known when the family emigrated, but in the 1860 Flushing Census, Louis is enumerated on page 712 at the age of 18, along with his father who is 50, and mother, who is 47. He has two sisters and a brother; Amelia, 16, Frederick, 12, and Kate, 10.

It is known that on May 6, 1861 he enlisted in Company I of the 20th New York Infantry, but he did not *"stack his arms"* before the Battle of Chancellorsville early in the month of May, 1863. As such, he was not subject to the court martial that ensued and was discharged on June 1, 1863.

There was no pension application on file for Louis Miller and according to Census records in 1880 there are at least 20 individuals by this name living in the New York City area.

Montgomery, George

There is nothing known of this individual whose name appears on the August 23, 1862 *Flushing Journal* list of College Point Volunteers. He supposedly served in Sickle's Brigade, but no one by this name served in any unit of the Brigade.

Montanye, Washington

GAR member Washington Montanye was born ca. 1830 in New York, exactly when and where is unknown.

When he enlisted in Company A of the 83rd New York Infantry on May 27, 1861 at Riker's Island, his age is given as 26 and he is a 5'7" merchant, with light hair, complexion and blue eyes. His age is not a certainty as he may have been at least 30 on enlistment day. Suffering from chronic diarrhea he received a certificate of disability at Finlay Hospital in Washington, DC dated October 11, 1862.

In 1880 he appears on page 395C of the New York City Census, 16th Ward, District 4, and is employed as a fireman married to Ellen, no last name known, who is 45. The age given for Washington is 33, but it is definite he is older and closer to 50.

Louisa Burgess, 66, is listed as *"mother"*, but it is reasonable to conclude that she is Ellen's mother as her birthplace is England as is Ellen's. Also enumerated is Sarah Hersey, probably Ellen's sister, 25, Lucy Hersey, 7, Sarah's daughter and Ellen's niece, and Katy Williams, a cousin who is 12.

Ellen died on December 2, 1882 in New York City and Washington married Catherine Jane Evans on February 10, 1884 in the Parsonage of Emmanuel Chapel in New York City. Rev. E. Seymour performed the ceremony and a child, Ellen Catherine, is born on August 18, 1886. It is not known where the couple lived.

Washington came to the Whitestone area in 1885 and lives in College Point in 1889. By August 1900 he lives in Sullivan County, New York from where he filed a request for an increase in his pension. Nothing else is known about this veteran.

Motz, Jacob

Jacob Motz served a 30-day enlistment in the 15th New York Regiment of National Guard Infantry from June 6, 1864 through July 7, 1864. The unit was called out to garrison Fort Richmond in New York Harbor.

Jacob, 46, and his wife Elizabeth, maiden name unknown, 44, both from Germany, appear on page 238 in the 1870 Census of Flushing. They live in College Point with their 18 year-old son Jacob, who works with his father in the rubber factory. Three children are enumerated; Margaret, 16, George, 14, and Eddy, 9. The record indicates that the children were born in New York.

Jacob, still working in the rubber factory, Elizabeth, keeping house, and an 18 year-old daughter named Catherine, (not enumerated in 1870) along with an 8 year-old granddaughter named Margaret Knerr appear in the 1880 College Point Census on page 313B in District 7. It is likely she is the daughter of Joseph Knerr who had married the daughter Margaret and are also enumerated in the same Census on page 300D.

While nothing more is known of Jacob and Elizabeth, the Motz family name is present in College Point for many years to come.

Motz, Philip

Born in New York City of French parents on February 12, 1847, on the day of his enlistment in Company D of the 1st US Artillery, January 25, 1865, Philip was 5'3" with gray eyes and auburn hair.

Three years later to the day, he was discharged, only to re-enlist at Fort Hamilton in Brooklyn and serve as a bugler/musician until 1871, being discharged with glowing reports from his commanding officer. While he probably never went to war, he is definitely a Civil War-era soldier to be recognized.

He married Susannah Reindell, the daughter of 38 year-old John, and 42 year-old Anna Reindell who are in College Point in 1860 on page 702 of the Flushing Census. She is 6 at the time, born on March 12, 1855, and has three siblings; John, 12, Frank, 10 and Amelia, 8. Her father is a Wurtemburg-born grocer and her mother was born in Hanover.

The Reindells were travelers as John was born in Pennsylvania before the family moved to New York.

In 1880 Philip and Susannah have two children; Alfred, 3 and Mamie, 10. Susan's widowed mother Anna, 61, and son John, 31, live in the same house along with her other son Frank, 29, his wife Lewisa, 25, and two daughters; Lewisa, 3 and Irene, 1. All are enumerated in College Point on page 234D of the Census.

In 1880 Philip is also a member of the Martin Lodge No. 252 of the International Order of Odd Fellows and becomes an original member of Adam Wirth Post No. 451 in 1884.

His pension was filed on behalf of a minor child named Frederick in 1901 so there was at least one more child born to Philip and Susan.

Philip died on March 21, 1900 and Susan lived on until November 10, 1905.

Muecke, Englebert

Englebert was born ca. 1842 in Prussia and came to the United States sometime before 1854. His mother Johannah, apparently a widow of at least two years, appears in the 1860 Census of Flushing on page 716 living in College Point with Engelbert, 18, his brother Francis, 14, and two sisters, Amalia, 4 and Huldah, 2.

Englebert makes $3,000 a year as a laborer in 1860, and in less than a year on May 3, 1861, he enlists in Company I of the 20th New York Infantry. He is one of the soldiers who lays down his arms before the Battle of Chancellorsville and subsequently subjected to Court Martial in the field. Following his discharge on June 1, 1863, he returned to College Point.

Before the war Englebert had been a friend to veterans Frederick Dockendorf, Charles Marx and Henry Straube, but their letters of support were not enough to convince the government to award his pension to his mother. She applied at least two times and at least once from California, but both applications were rejected on the basis that Englebert's February 16, 1867 death was not war-related. The cause of death was listed as brain fever and he is buried in Flushing Cemetery.

Mutz, Gustav

Gustav Mutz was christened in the Lutheran Church in Solingen, Germany on May 17, 1832. His parents were William Mutz and Anna Maria Kreuzenbach.

It is not know when the family emigrated to America, but Gustav enlisted in Company E of the 29th New York Infantry on June 4, 1861 and was discharged in New York City on June 20, 1863.

On March 21, 1865 Gustav married Justine Gerhardt Schreiner, herself a widow of one Reinhart Schreiner, at the Dutch Reformed Church on Forsyth Street in New York City. Rev. Foersch was identified as the Pastor. They had at least one daughter named Ida, birth year unknown, who in the years to come married a man with the surname Seeley.

On page 249D in the 1880 Census of Monroe County, City of Rochester, there is a 46 year-old, German-born person named Gustav *Matg* married to a 47 year-old woman named Justine. He is an optician, not an iron-polisher, but he could be Gustav Mutz. In the same Census on page 231C, there is a 28 year-old Ida Seeley married to a physician, Dr. J. Edwin Seeley. They have an 11 year-old daughter named Mae.

According to Justine's application, after they married, Gustav had enlisted for three months in a Pennsylvania regiment, but had never applied for a pension for this service. She also wrote that Gustav had run away from Germany so he wouldn't have to serve as a soldier there.

In 1870 the couple purchased property in Rochester, New York, where Gustav worked as an iron polisher. At some point the family did come back to New York City where on February 28, 1884, out of work and in despair, Gustav committed suicide. His remains were taken back to Rochester where he is buried in Mt. Hope Cemetery.

Six years later in 1890, the widowed Justine lives in Jersey City. Her name appears in the New Jersey Veteran's Census, one of the few Census records from this year that survived a massive fire that took place on January 10, 1921 at the Commerce Building in Washington, DC. The census schedules were housed at this site and almost all were lost.

Nau, Michael

In October 1863, while covering the retreat from Lenoir Station, Tennessee to Campbell Station, Tennessee, and Michael came across an ammunition wagon pulled by two horses. It got stuck in mud and he attempted to move it with a fence post. General Burnside ordered him to lighten the load and save the wagon, as the ammunition was very much needed by the troops. A Captain came by and challenged his action, whereupon Michael tried once again to save the wagon and in so doing suffered what Roemer called a *"dangerous rupture"*.

24 year-old Michael Nau enlisted in 1861, and at 5'8", having a light complexion and blue eyes, he served as both a carpenter and a baker in the 34th New York Light Artillery.

He is mentioned specifically in Roemer's book on page 180 when describing a food-related issue, Roemer says,

"Michael Nau, a miller by trade, and another of the Battery's boys, took charge of grinding of corn. It had a happy outcome."

He was married three times. Katharine Baumann, sister of Civil War veteran William Baumann, was his first wife. Rev. August Heidmiller performed the ceremony at the German Lutheran Church in College Point in March of 1861.

They had five children; Mary, born ca. 1861, Emelia, March 22, 1866, Catharine, ca. 1869, Adam, November 5, 1871 and Michael, Jr. ca. 1874. Katharine died October 27, 1879 and is buried in Flushing Cemetery.

Judge Lawrence performed his second marriage in September of 1880 in Flushing. His new wife's name was Elizabeth Bauer. She died in January, 1891 and is buried in Flushing Cemetery also.

He married a third time to Charlotte Wetz, date unknown, who left him in 1894 *"when I was suffering from rheumatism"*, the pension document indicates.

He appears in the 1900 Census in College Point living with a woman named Sarah identified as his wife. This record indicates that Michael was born on June 8, 1836 and that he emigrated to the United States from Germany in 1858.

Michael is an original member of Adam Wirth Post No. 451, and his son Adam became active in the Sons of Union Veterans.

At some time between 1895 and 1896, Michael moves to White Plains. There is no indication of the date of his death or where it took place, presumably in White Plains.

Naumann, George

George Naumann is enumerated on page 706 in the 1860 Census of Flushing. He is 38, from Hesse and married to 38 year-old Louisa who is from the same area in Germany. Four children are listed; Louisa, 9, Emma, 7, Ann, 5 and William, 1.

While he never went to war, he was in the 15th New York State Militia and would have been involved somehow had he lived. His death was reported in the *Flushing Journal* on November 2, 1861.

Nothing else is known of the family.

Newman, Edward

In the 1860 Census of Flushing the name is spelled *Niman* and Edward is the 22 year-old son of Augustus, a 53 year-old comb-maker from Prussia and Amelia, 47, also from Prussia. Edward has two siblings, Amelia, 20 and Velsha, 17. Leon Koch, a 25-year old day laborer from Holland, lives with the family.

Edward was born in Tapiau Province of East Prussia, Germany on December 2, 1838, but it is not known when either he or his family emigrated to the United States.

On May 23, 1861, just eight days after he enlisted in the 121st New York Infantry, he married Lina Eberhard in Flushing. Sam Willett, Justice of the Peace, performed the ceremony.

On June 4th he was in the Army and on that day stood 5'2", had blue eyes, a dark complexion and was working as a machinist. He was reported as having deserted on October 15, 1862 but that turned out not to be the case. After service in the 29th, 65th and 121st New York Infantry units, Edward was discharged on July 17, 1865, and he returned to College Point.

Over the years he and Lina, from Germany, became parents to; Toska, born December 14, 1861, who would marry Mr. Fred Wieland. Edwin A., born May 29, 1865, Alfred W., August 6, 1867 and Emiline, born June 28, 1869, would follow her.

On page 212 of the 1870 Census of Flushing, Edward, working as a machinist, lives in College Point with Lina and the children along with a domestic named Mary Kolzner.

The Newman family appears also in College Point in the 1880 Census on page 246C. According to the record, Toska and Edwin work at a silk factory and Emil is at school.

They continue to live in College Point until August 5th, 1895 whereupon they move to Morrisville, Pennsylvania in Bucks County.

Over the next five years the residence alternates between Trenton, New Jersey and Morrisville for reasons unexplained. Edward was employed as a machinist and die maker.

Lina Newman died on January 14, 1918. Three years later on March 18, 1921, while living with his son Alfred, Edward died in Mercer Hospital in Trenton. Both Edward and Lina are buried at Morrisville Cemetery.

Newman, George

George Newman's name appears on the August 23, 1862 *Flushing Journal* list of volunteers from College Point. He had a very interesting military career, but his pension application sheds no light on anything other than that part of his life.

He began his service in Co. E of the 73rd New York Infantry, Sickle's Brigade, on January 22, 1862 at the age of 22.

He suffered wounds to his arm and shoulder on May 5, 1862 at the Battle of Williamsburg in Virginia and was treated at McKim's Mansion General Hospital in Baltimore from May 10th to the 12th.

From Baltimore he was sent to the Ladies Home General Hospital in New York City from which, so the record says, he deserted on June 25, 1862. Another pension document indicates he later enlisted on June 17, 1863 in the 69th New York for a period of 30 days and was discharged on July 25th.

The roll call of Co. E, 73rd New York for November/December 1863 reports him absent under arrest at Governor's Island for desertion, having been arrested on December 12, 1863 and delivered to Fort Columbus in New York. From here he was sent to Virginia and discharged on a surgeon's certificate.

The record further indicates he was in the Navy for a year from August 17, 1864 until August 16, 1865 serving on the *Vermont*, the *New Hampshire* and the *Rome*.

In 1885 when he first applied for his pension, he lived at 46 West 45th Street in New York City, but his application was denied.

He subsequently wrote a letter refuting the denial of benefits saying: *"Wenn I was wounded I was sent to new york (sic) hospital and was never recovered enough to go back. I tried to get back by going out with the 69th Regiment for 30 days but failed."*

The letter was written from his home at 336 Rivington Street in New York City on June 1 of 1898. While the man never received any pension benefits, it certainly appears he earned them. Alas, nothing else is known of this veteran.

Niemier, Andrew

GAR member Andrew Niemier, born August 4, 1843, was a 5'7" farmer with a light complexion, blue eyes and light hair on August 12, 1862, the day he enlisted in Company C of the 74th New York Infantry.

There is nothing exceptional indicated in his pension file and he appears on page 219B in the 1880 Census living in Whitestone married to Arabella Munson whom he had wed at Grace Episcopal Church in Whitestone on May 15, 1870.

He is 35, from Prussia and Arabella, also 35, was born in New York. There are six children; Martha, 16, Benjamin, 15, Robert, 14, George, 6, Mary, 4 and John, 2.

Another son named Harry is born on March 23, 1881 according to information in the pension file.

In the 1900 Census of Whitestone, Andrew and Arabella live on 23rd Street, today's 132nd Street. According to the record, Arabella was born in New York in 1843 and Andrew is a wood salesman. Son George, 26, is a grocery salesman and John, 21, a soldier. Harry, 18, is a fish salesman and Mary, 24, now known by her middle name Ethel, has no occupation listed. Arabella has given birth to 9 children and 7 are alive at the time of the Census.

Andrew Niemier died in the Woodhaven section of Queens, on September 22, 1919 and in 1920 George lives in Whitestone, as does John.

Noss, Adam

Adam's name appears on the August 23, 1862 *Flushing Journal* list of volunteers from College Point. According to a letter in his pension file written by George Ilch, a baker in College Point, Adam had worked for him prior to his enlistment. Born in Wurtemburg, Germany ca. 1833, there is no indication of when Adam emigrated to the United States.

On January 4, 1864, the day he enlisted in Company K of the 39th New York Infantry, Adam stood 5'8", was a baker with a fair complexion, gray eyes and dark hair.

Returning to College Point following his July 1, 1865 discharge July 4, 1865, the record indicates he had suffered from *"frozen feet"*, probably frostbite, at Prentice Station, Virginia in February 1863.

Noss is enumerated on page 300D in the 1880 Census of College Point. He is a 50 year-old laborer from Wurtemburg, Germany, married to Elizabeth, who was also born in Germany. No children are enumerated.

In 1898, according to the pension record, he is a widower. Adam died on May 27, 1911.

Otto, Herman

Born in Germany around 1824, Hermann Otto, a widower before the war, married Katherine Scherer, herself a war widow, on August 30, 1866. The marriage took place at 67 Stanton Street in Manhattan where another College Point veteran, John Hoelle, would marry five years later. Rev. John Foersch, who performed the ceremony, lived at 62 Stanton Street and is listed in a New York City Directory in 1869. Katherine was born in Weisbach, Germany, the daughter of Philip Ochs and Sophie Weber.

Katherine had been married to Peter Scherer, a soldier in Company E of the 119th New York Infantry who mustered out on June 28, 1865 in Washington, DC and died shortly thereafter on July 12th.

Herman is a listed in the 1860 Census of Flushing on page 744, but there is no indication that he is a widower, and no children are enumerated. We know that he had been married because Joseph Dockendorff attested to it during the pension application proceedings, but no date of death for his wife is cited.

On page 231 of the 1870 Census of Flushing, Herman, working in the rubber factory, and Catherine, keeping house, appear in College Point with the children; Kate, 9, Peter, 7, Maggie 5, and Frederick, 1.

There are four children on page 311B in the 1880 Census of College Point; Peter, 17, Margaret, 14, Frieda, 9, (probably the child identified as Frederick in 1870), plus a new daughter Emilia, 6.

According to Herman's pension application, he had contracted typhoid fever at Covington, Kentucky in July 1863.

Herman Otto died in College Point on December 10, 1895 and is buried in Flushing Cemetery. Katherine died on May 5, 1906.

Palmer, Samuel

Samuel, a comb-maker born in Scotland in 1813, lived in College Point in 1860 and appears on page 613 of the Flushing Census. He is married to Alice, born on July 12, 1825, whom he had married in Belfast, Ireland on November 18, 1842. Her maiden name had been Stewart and the minister's name was Rev. McNeilly. There is no information as to when the couple had emigrated to the United States.

Overall, Sam and Alice had 13 children, of which 5 appear in the 1860 Census. All children were born in Ireland except for the youngest who was born in New York. They are; Hugh, born ca. 1844, Samuel, ca. 1846, James, ca. 1848, Robert, ca. 1850 and Charlotte, ca. 1858.

On October 1, 1861 he enlisted in Company L of the 2nd New York Heavy Artillery and his name appeared in the August 23, 1862 *Flushing Journal* list of volunteers from College Point. Samuel was discharged in Virginia on September 30, 1864, the same day the unit had been engaged in battle at the Pegram Farm.

A sixth child, a daughter, was born in early August, 1861, but her name is not known.

By 1891 only 4 of the 13 are still alive, but we do not know their names. It is very likely that all were living in New York City.

Samuel died in Flushing on June 20, 1867 as a result of chronic diarrhea, and is buried in Flushing Cemetery.

Col. Jacob Roemer, who knew both Samuel and Alice before the war, signed an affidavit dated November 3, 1891 in support of Alice's application for widow' benefits. Supporting her at the time was one Elizabeth Palmer with whom Alice had lived since 1880.

According to information dated July 5, 1892 in the pension record, Elizabeth, the widow of Robert Palmer, Alice Palmer's son born around 1850, had found it necessary to send her sons out to sell newspapers in order to keep the family together.

Alice died on June 27, 1896 at her residence, 202 East 47th Street in New York City.

Pfortner, Max vonder Holle

Max Pfortner vonder Holle was born on April 25, 1833 in Silesia, Germany in the town of *Schuoolawitz*, as it is spelled. He came to America in 1861 and served in the 68th New York Infantry, known also as the Cameron Rifles or the 2nd German Rifles.

On August 1, 1861, the day he enlisted, he stood 5'11", had a fair complexion, blue eyes and dark hair. Following his discharge on August 31, 1862, he returned to the New York City area where on March 15, 1863 he married Augusta Mueller in Williamsburgh.

The ceremony was performed at 67 Stanton Street in New York City with Rev. John A. Foersch officiating. Max lived in New York City until 1867 whereupon he moved to College Point.

He appears on page 249D in the 1880 Census of College Point at the age of 47 married to Augusta, from Hesse in Germany, who is 39. They have 7 children; Robert, born November 29, 1865, Annie, August 16, 1867, Bertha, April 23, 1869, Wolf, November 15, 1870, Frieda, February 20, 1872, Emmo, September 26, 1875 and Otto, March 2, 1877.

Two additional sons are named in the pension file; Max, born May 16, 1864, and Joseph, born November 28, 1884. Neither was alive when the pension application was processed.

In 1900 he is once again enumerated in College Point and indicates he was born in April, 1833. Augusta says she was born in June, 1841 and only 4 of her 10 children are still alive. They are; Robert, Anna, Emmo and Joseph and they still live at home.

In 1910 Max is a widower. Robert and Annie are enumerated along with a 23 year-old daughter-in-law named Clara. She is a widow and has an 18 month-old daughter named Elise. Clara's husband's name is not indicated, but it is Joseph because he is not listed in 1920.

In 1920 Max is still alive and living with his children, Robert and Anna. Son Emmo lives in College Point also, with his married sister Bertha who has married Thomas Corey. Elise is enumerated with Clara and her new husband named Matthew Brown. It is reasonable to assume that it was Joseph who had had died.

Daughter Annie wrote to the Pension Board from her home at 117 18th Street in College Point to announce her father's death on August 12, 1920.

Piereth, Christian George

Christian was born in 1819 in Germany and on September 21, 1845 he married Catherine Merk in Meinbernheim, Wuertzburg in Germany.

It is not known when the family emigrated, but Christian and Catherine appear in the 1860 Census of Flushing on page 732. There are four children; Valentine, 18, Adeleid, 13, Barbara, 10 and Catherine, 7.

Christian was one of a number of College Point men who on June 6, 1864 were mustered into the 15th Regiment of New York State Militia to garrison Fort Richmond in New York Harbor. The unit mustered out on July 7, 1864.

Catherine died in 1862 and Christian married a woman named Rosalie whose surname is not known. She was born in Germany and in the years to come had five children; Margaret, born ca. 1863, twins Elizabeth and Maxmilia, ca. 1866, Ida, ca. 1868, and Christian, ca. 1873.

Christian is enumerated on page 227 of the 1870 Census of Flushing along with Rosa. Living with the family are; Bertha, 20, Catherine, 17, Adam, 12, Margaret, 7, Elizabeth and Maxmilia, 5, and Ada (Ida), 2. Adam is very likely Rosa's son as his birth took place, not in New York, but in Bavaria. Barbara, now called Bertha, works alongside her father Christian in the rubber factory.

Christian and Rosalie appear on page 296C of the 1880 College Point Census. He continues to work in the rubber factory and his surname is spelled *Pierott*. Six of the children still live at home; Adam, Margaret, twins Elizabeth and Maxmilia, spelled *Masinu'l*, Ida and Christian. The twins work in one of the College Point silk factories while Adam and Margaret toil at the rubber factory.

Christian died in June 1893 and is buried at Flushing Cemetery joining his first wife Catherine who had been buried there since August 5, 1862.

Rosa appears in the 1900 Census in College Point caring for a grandson named Frank, and the Piereth family name continues in College Point for years to come.

Piereth, Valentine

Valentine is the 18 year-old son of Christian and what we know of him is limited. He was born in New York City in 1842 and was working as a laborer in College Point when the 1860 Census of Flushing was taken.

According to his military file, he enlisted on December 16, 1861 at Dover, in Company C of the 1st Delaware Infantry. The record says that he was 20 years of age, 5'4" with blue eyes, brown hair, a light complexion and, by occupation, a basket maker.

He was wounded on June 26, 1863 just before the Battle of Gettysburg and was discharged from Hammond Hospital at Point Lookout, Maryland the following July 4th with the notation he displayed *"good character"* while in the hospital. He was officially returned to duty in October, but no reason is giver for the three-month break.

The record also says *"he deserted while on the March to Gettysburg,"* but it was only after the fact that the record was amended to reflect his having been wounded before the battle had even taken place.

Valentine was discharged at Petersburg on September 30, 1864, but he appears in no subsequent census records and is definitely not buried in Flushing Cemetery.

College Point men Francis Dockendorf and Frederick Miller served in this Delaware unit as well.

Plitt, George

On page 274 of the 1850 Census of Flushing, George Plitt, 27, a shoemaker from Germany, is married to Roseanne. Her surname is unknown as is the date George arrived in the United States. The family lives next door to Jacob Roemer who will lead the 34th New York Light Artillery throughout the war.

At some point George and the family moved to College Point and in a November 6, 1861 *Flushing Journal* article, he is described as serving as secretary in the Hamilton Light Artillery, 15th Regiment of State Militia. While he never went to war, he is an authentic College Point veteran.

George and Roseanne appear in 1870 on page 228 of the Flushing Census. They have 5 children; George, 18, Amelia, 16, Emiline, 14, Ernest, 10, and Louisa, 8.

On page 307B in the 1880 Census of Flushing, George is a widower, still a shoemaker, and lives in College Point with Emilia and Ernest who is also a shoemaker.

It is not known when George died, but the Plitt family name continues in College Point for years to come.

Pluemacher, Charles

Charles was born in Cologne, Germany ca. 1838 and came to America in 1857.

On July 20, 1861 he enlisted in Company I of the 20th New York Infantry and was discharged on June 1, 1863.

His name is among those in the August 23, 1862 *Flushing Journal* list of volunteers from College Point.

Charles was very active in the GAR and wrote numerous letters in support of veterans' pension applications on his company stationery, a company that manufactured and sold acoustical equipment for use by scientists and in schools.

While he did himself apply for pension benefits, the file could not be located at the National Archives. His military record confirms that he was 24 when he enlisted and also his experience as a prisoner of war at Richmond, Virginia after being captured at Savage Station on June 30, 1862.

He was released at Aiken's Landing, South Carolina on August 5, 1862 and then rejoined his unit ten days later.

On page 472A of the 1880 Census of Montgomery County, Pennsylvania, he is living in the 4th Ward of Norristown and works as a *cutler*. It is not known what a *"cutler"* does. Charles is married to Augusta, surname unknown, who, at 50, is 7 years older than he is. Three children are enumerated; Charles F., 15, Frederick W., 12, and Margaret J., 14.

It is not known when the family moved to College Point, but at age 82, Charles is enumerated in 1920, married to 56 year-old Elizabeth. Augusta is not listed as his wife, so she must have passed away. The address is 8 11th Street, today the corner of 120th Street and 23rd Avenue. He is still manufacturing and selling acoustical equipment. The Census record also tells us he was born in Cologne, Germany in 1838, and came to America in 1857.

His pension file contained no notation of the date of his death.

Propfer, Augustus

On page 736 of the 1860 Census of Flushing, Augustus, 37, from Hanover in Germany, appears with his 47 year-old wife Barbara from Bohemia, which can be interpreted as Austria. There are no children listed, but they may have married and moved on by this time.

Augustus appeared in the 1863 Provost Marshall's list of possible draftees and subsequently served in the 15th New York Heavy Artillery. His was a 30-day enlistment in the 15th New York Regiment of New York State Militia called out to garrison Fort Richmond in New York Harbor from June 6, 1864 through July 7, 1864.

He next appears in the 1870 Census of Flushing on page 46 where the record indicates he was born in Prussia, is 46, and works on the railroad. He is married to Barbara, born in Austria and she is 55.

Barbara, a widow appears in the 1880 Census of College Point, page 297A, living with a daughter named Eva married to John Leder.

Nothing else is known of Augustus.

Quaid, T.

This name appears on the August 23, 1862 *Flushing Journal* list of volunteers from College Point. Supposedly Quaid served in Sickle's Brigade, but there was no one by this name in that esteemed unit, or in any other unit that saw service during the war.

Rausch, Peter

There was very little information in the pension application for this veteran. He was born on January 22, 1839 at Hesse-Darmstadt in Germany, but when he emigrated to the United States is unknown. At the time of his enlistment, May 6, 1861, he stood 5'5", was a tinker and had a light complexion, blue eyes and dark hair.

He was one of the soldiers from the 20th New York Infantry involved in the Court Martial proceedings in the field and as a result had his pension revoked on May 5, 1895. It should and may have been reinstated as was the pension of Fred Dockendorf and other members of the unit. A son named Peter is mentioned in the pension documents.

The veteran was living at 93 South 16th Street in East Orange, New Jersey on the day he died, February 16, 1914.

Rausmuller, Charles

GAR member Charles Rausmuller was born in Germany in December 1837, and came to America aboard the ship *Germania* that had sailed from Havre in France, and docked in New York Harbor on October 11, 1861. Five days later, at age 24, he enlisted in the 54th New York Infantry.

There is no description of him in the pension file, but it is known that in 1880 he lived in McKeesport, Pennsylvania with his first wife, Johanna Louise Sauer, born in Frankenthal, Germany, and their three children; Charles, born in New York City on August 29, 1869, Thekla, born in McKeesport on October 8, 1873 and Paul, born there as well on October 21, 1877. Charles was a rail inspector.

Louise, the wife of Charles, died on November 9, 1883 and he married a second time, ca. 1893, a widow Margaret Schmitz, whose maiden name had been Knab. The marriage took place in Braddock, Pennsylvania. Margaret was born on March 22, 1844 in the village of Bruch Muehlback, Germany. She had at least one son, named Frank, born in 1880 before the death of her first husband.

At some point Charles and Margaret moved to College Point and appear in the 1900 Census. There is a 22 year-old son named Paul born in 1877 and the record indicates she had given birth to two children.

On November 21, 1904, Charles died and is buried in Flushing Cemetery. Margaret lived at the home of her son Frank and his family at 406 11th Street where she died on March 26, 1926.

Reinhard, Andrew

Andrew or Andreas Reinhard, appears on page 721 of the 1860 Census of Flushing, the 13 year-old son of Veit Rhinehardt, a 38 year-old shoemaker from Bavaria and his 32 year-old wife, Margaret. Andrew has five siblings; Cunigunda, 14, Mary, 11, George, 8, John, 4, and Francis, 1. When the family arrived from Germany is unknown.

On January 11, 1864, the day he enlisted in Company B of the 11th New York Cavalry, Andrew was living on High Street, today's 127th Street in College Point, and working in the factory.

His time in the military lasted but ten months as he died of chronic diarrhea on October 4, 1864 at University Hospital in New Orleans.

His mother filed for benefits and the file contains three letters to her from Andrew, all written in German, prior to his death. Another letter in support of her application written by Father Joseph Huber, Pastor of St. Fidelis Catholic Church, is also contained in the file.

For a short period Margaret moved to a section of Queens called Foster's Meadow, but returned to College Point ca. 1870 where she died almost twenty years later on November 20, 1899.

Reinheimer, Daniel

Daniel Reinheimer was born in Horsbach, Reinfalls, Germany, on September 5, 1826.

Exactly when he came to America is unknown, but Daniel stood 5'8" on September 2, 1861 when he enlisted in Company L of the 2nd New York Heavy Artillery.

Eleven years earlier he had married Hanover-born Caroline Tappe on March 29, 1850, the ceremony being performed by Pastor Busch of the Dutch Reformed Church on Forsyth Street in New York City.

He appears in the 1860 Census of Flushing on page 716 married to Caroline and works as a tailor.

A year later he is a mechanic in the Army and in May 1862, while traveling by train near Baltimore, he suffers a rupture in a fall between a railroad car and a station platform while changing cars.

Treated at the Patent Office Hospital in DC, he was discharged on June 10, 1862 by General Wadsworth on order # 83.

Col. Roemer wrote a letter on August 8, 1893 in support of his pension application and Daniel received his pension. At the time Reinheimer was living at 329 15th Street, today's 124th Street in College Point.

In the 1870, 1880 and 1900 Census records, Daniel remains at his tailoring trade in College Point. In 1900 he lives on 14th Street and is a widower. Daniel died on March 18, 1918.

Rhein, Moritz

This name appears in the list of College Point volunteers that appeared in the *Flushing Journal* on August 23, 1862.

His service in the 7th New York Infantry began on April 29, 1861 at age 40. Enlisting as a Private, he was one of the few men from College Point to attain officer's rank, which he did on March 21, 1862 when he was promoted to Captain.

On May 8, 1863, he was discharged in New York City and it does not appear that he applied for a pension. He is not enumerated in any Census between 1850 and 1880, and nothing else is known of this individual.

Richard, George

George Richard's birth took place in St. Francis, Island of Orleans in Quebec, Canada on November 12, 1828 with his surname being spelled *Dique*.

When he entered the United States is unknown, but in the 1860 Census of Flushing he appears on page 705. His age is given as 24, but he is actually 31, and his occupation is shoemaker.

A year later he enlisted using the surname Richard in order that his mother not know of his action. He was 5'1", with a light complexion, blue eyes and light hair.

In August 1870 he married Caroline Gannon, the widow of John Gannon who had died in 1868. The wedding took place in Newtown, Queens, and her maiden name had been Rierson.

On page 280A of the 1880 Census of Flushing one George Richards, a 40 year-old laborer, lives with James Van Wyck, 40, and his housekeeper Emma, 16. Also in the listing is 41 year-old Emma Caroline from England. The census record also indicates that George has a French heritage. While his age is off by 10 years, it is quite possible this is veteran George Richard and Caroline is actually his wife.

George died on November 14, 1908.

Richter, Franz

There are a number of people by this name in the 1860 New York Census, but none are definitively the Franz or Francis Richter whose name is etched on the Flushing Monument to Civil War casualties.

It is known that the soldier was born in Friestadt, Germany ca. 1820, and that he was married on August 30, 1858 to Julia Radisch, 35, at St. Peter's Church in Brooklyn. Rev. J. Reidenbach performed the ceremony. It is not known when he emigrated to the United States.

Franz had applied for citizenship on November 21, 1860 and on enlistment day, October 15, 1861, was a 41 year-old gardener, standing 5'5" with a dark complexion, gray eyes and dark hair. During his time in the Army he was the company cook according to his military record that also indicated he had re-enlisted as a veteran volunteer on January 1, 1864.

Sadly, he died from the effects of typhoid fever and acute dysentery at the Post Hospital in Bridgeport, Alabama on October 2, 1864. His name is etched on the Flushing Memorial to Civil War casualties.

A few months before Franz enlisted, Julia had given birth to a daughter, Anna Maria Josephine on May 3, 1861. Father Joseph Huber baptized her at St. Fidelis Catholic Church.

The pension application was filed from Germany where perhaps Julia had gone to visit family in her birthplace, the village of Lorenzdorf. Another reference gives an address of 827 Race Street in Philadelphia.

Roessel, Joseph A.

Joseph was the last College Point GAR member to die, doing so on December 30, 1935 at 20-03 120th Street, the home of his brother Elwood.

Born in Hightstown, New Jersey on September 25, 1843, he enlisted in the 29th New Jersey Infantry on September 20, 1862 and mustered out ten months later at Freehold, New Jersey.

Following the war he married his wife Katherine and came to College Point in 1873 where he and Katherine are enumerated on page 303B in the 1880 Census of College Point living with the family of John *Gernhard*. The name is spelled *Roseill* and he is a carpenter, as he will be all his life.

He and Katherine appear in the 1900 Census of College Point living together on 11th Street, today's 120th Street. The record indicates that there were no children.

In the obituary that appeared in the December 30, 1935 edition of the *North Shore Daily Journal* it was written *"he could recall such famous leaders of the period as Lincoln, Grant and Sheridan, all of whom he had seen during his experience as a soldier."*

He was also a friend to Conrad Poppenhusen and E. Platt Stratton and *"having seen the advent of the telephone, electric light and the radio, he hoped to live long enough to see the perfection of television."*

Both he and Katherine are retired in the 1920 Census of College Point and both are buried in Flushing Cemetery, Katherine having predeceased him.

Rooney, Thomas

GAR member Thomas Rooney was actually a Flushing resident, but he was also an original member of Adam Wirth Post No. 451. Born ca. 1843 in Ireland, he enlisted in the 74th New York Infantry on June 6, 1861. It is not known when he arrived in the United States.

While in the service he was wounded at Williamsburg, Virginia on June 5, 1862. *"The ball imbedded itself in the skull bone, fracturing it whence it was cut out, seriously affecting the sight of his right eye."*

He was taken to Hampton Hospital at Fortress Monroe and then to Central Park Hospital in New York City where he recuperated for two months. He also suffered a slight wound at the Battle of Fair Oaks, Virginia.

Following the war he married Margaret Eustace on February 12, 1866 at St. Michael's Catholic Church in Flushing with Rev. James O'Beirne performing the ceremony.

Thomas and Margaret had four children; John, born December 15, 1866, Ellen, November 25, 1867, Edward, February 10, 1873 and Mary, July 23, 1876.

In the 1880 Census of Flushing on page 260A, he is described as being 37 and a builder of railroad bridges. Also listed are Mary, 38, who keeps house and the four children.

Thomas Rooney passed away on April 3, 1900 and is buried at Mt. St. Mary's Cemetery in Flushing. Margaret died 15 years later on May 3, 1915.

Rubel, Henry

Henry was born in Rheindayn, Germany in April 1834 and on enlistment day, May 15, 1861, stood 5'10", with a light complexion, hazel eyes and dark hair. He served in Company E of the 29th New York Infantry.

In his application for a pension, he claimed that he *"hit the big toe on his right foot against a tree trunk at Sperryville, Virginia, while on picket duty,"* and did, in fact, receive a disability discharge on November 8, 1862 from Harewood Hospital in Washington, DC as a result. He had been there since August 18, 1862.

On October 17th of the following year he married Margaretha Ersh, a widow of one Carl Ersh who, though not a casualty of war, had nevertheless died on May 25, 1863. Her maiden name had been Bernius and Rev. Adolph Berchmann performed the marriage ceremony in New York City.

The original Marriage Certificate is a part of the pension file and two children were born of the union; Catherine, on August 19, 1864 and Henry, on August 5, 1866.

On page 212 of the 1870 Census of Flushing, the record indicates he is married to Margaret and works in the rubber factory. Catherine and August are also enumerated.

Again, in the 1880 Census, page 240D, he is in College Point, still working in the rubber factory with no additional children.

In 1900 his wife's name is listed as Anna, but she is really Margaret. Henry still lives at home and works at the rubber factory. The record indicates that Henry had come to America in 1856.

The son Henry, a single man, lives in College Point at 106 15th Street in 1920. He works in the rubber factory as a polisher. The daughter Catherine marries Christian F. Stender and assists her widowed mother in filing for the pension following Henry Sr.'s death on December 9, 1904. A rubber worker all his life, he is buried in Flushing Cemetery.

Schafer, Nicholas

Nicholas was born in Baden, Germany, ca. 1845, came to America, date unknown, and enlisted in the 34th New York Light Artillery on June 12, 1863 at the age of 19.

After his June 21, 1865 discharge, he married Anne Burns from Ireland, at St. James Catholic Church located at 23 Oliver Street in New York City. Father Farrelly performed the ceremony on February 9, 1869 and the witnesses were Michael and Ellen McCormack.

Eight children were born; Nicholas, November 28, 1869, Rose, April 12, 1871, James, November 26, 1872, John, August 30, 1874, Stephen, January 17, 1878, Mary, August 8, 1881, Charles, September, 13, 1884 and David, February 25, 1887.

In the 1880 Census, Nicholas and Annie appear living with her parents James and Rose Burns in New York City. Curiously, none of the children are listed and Nicholas is a clerk in a broker's office.

Nicholas died on July 8, 1907 and is buried at Calvary Cemetery in Woodside, Queens. A work address for him in an 1899 deposition is given as 15 Wall Street. At the time of her petition for his pension, Annie lived at 65 East 130th Street.

Schaefer, Peter

Peter Abraham Schaefer was born in Nassau, Germany ca. 1818 and married Elizabeth Doringer in Neiderwelz Evangelical Church on December 31, 1851. A copy of the Church Book marriage record translated from the German original says he was a miner.

The couple emigrated to America, exact date unknown, and is found in the 1860 Census living in Allegheny County, Pennsylvania, in the town of Reserve. Peter is a well digger and there are four children enumerated; Christian, 7, Louis, 4, Charles, 2, and William, 6 months.

By 1861 the family has moved to College Point, where on August 28, 1861 Peter enlists in the 34th New York Light Artillery.

His pension application contains affidavits indicating he took sick the following October with rheumatism and other illnesses, but went with the regiment to Washington, DC where he was hospitalized and eventually discharged on March 5, 1862. Two weeks later the pension application was filed and approved.

The family is living in College Point and is enumerated on Page 231 of the 1870 Flushing Census. Peter is a laborer and along with Elizabeth there are eight children; Christian, 17, Louis, 14, twins Benedict and William, 10, Kate, 8, Eleanor, 6, Herman, 2, and Peter, 1. With the exception of Christian, all of the children were born in New York. It is very likely that Charles and the son named William who was 2 in 1860, had died.

Peter passed away on March 10, 1874 and in the 1880 Census of College Point, Elizabeth lives with her children, Louis, Charles, who is not in the 1870 Census, William, Herman, Catherine and Lena who is also not named in 1870.

She appears in the 1900 Census of College Point and the record indicates she was born in July 1830 and has had eleven children of which four are alive. She lives on until March 23, 1911.

Schermerhorn, Louis

His pension record indicates that Louis was born in Whitestone on July 26, 1844 and probably lived on the Whitestone Road connecting him to College Point.

He appears in the 1860 Flushing Census on page 689 and was 5'6, fair with blue eyes and brown hair when he first enlisted in the New York State Militia as a student on April 30, 1861 for three months. He did so again on May 25, 1862.

He married Hannah Rickey at St. James Church on Madison Avenue and 71st Street in New York City in a ceremony performed by Rev. Cornelius Smith. A daughter named Addie Prentiss, probably Adelaide, was born on May 26, 1871 followed by Carlotta Egmont on September 27, 1880. Both girls marry; Addie to Horatio Burt Williams and Carlotta to Charles Horatio Pattengill.

By 1880 he is a retired merchant living in Flushing with his wife Hannah and daughter Adelaide, called Addie. The family is enumerated on page 175A of that Census. At the time of the pension application in 1920, Louis is still there living in Flushing at 179 Washington Street.

Schierlitz, Paul

In the 1860 Census of Flushing on page 636 there is a person living with Charles Marx and his wife Philipina. He is a 22 year-old laborer from Germany. His name looks very much like it could be Paul Schierlitz, and the age is right on.

On June 4, 1861 he enlisted in Company E of the 29th New York Infantry. According to his pension record, Paul, who was born ca. 1838, was severely wounded in the right knee by a rifle ball at the Battle of Chancellorsville and captured by the enemy.

On May 2, 1863 he was taken to a Rebel Field Hospital until the 15th whereupon he was exchanged on parole and taken to the 11th Corps U.S. Field Hospital at Stafford Court House, Virginia.

After his discharge in June 1863, there is no further record for Paul anywhere.

Schneemann, Joseph

GAR member Joseph Schneemann was born on July 12, 1839 in Rustenfelde, Germany, but when he came to America is not known.

When he enlisted on May 6, 1861 in Company D of the 20th New York Infantry, he was 22, stood 5'6", worked as a *joiner*, that is to say a carpenter. He had a fair complexion, blue eyes and blond hair. His address on that day was in downtown Manhattan at 161 Chrystie Street.

Following his discharge on June 1, 1863, he continued to live in New York City and moved to Whitestone ca. 1884 where he became a member of the GAR Post No. 451. His address was 136 South 11th Street.

His wife was named Wilhelmina Schiedweiler, born in New Jersey of German parents, and Rev. G. Scheibel married the couple on January 8, 1865.

Over the years they had twelve children; Margaret, born September 21, 1865, Frederick, September 4, 1867, Emma, June 8, 1870, Frank Joseph, July 11, 1873, Emily Augusta, June 16, 1877, Katherine, April 24, 1879, Charles Edward, June 15, 1881, Conrad Albert, October 27, 1883, Caroline, August 18, 1885, Philip Albert, August 6, 1887, Frederica, December 9, 1889 and Walter Roemer, March 29, 1891.

It is interesting that the middle name of his last son was Roemer, also the surname of the commanding officer of the 34th New York Light Artillery, Jacob Roemer. Is there a connection? Joseph served in the 20th New York Infantry, hard to say.

Margaret's married name was Beadle; Caroline's was Hamilton.

Joseph died on November 25, 1916, but when Wilhelmina died was not noted in the pension file. Son Conrad lives in College Point in 1920 married to Margaret. There are no children enumerated.

Schrader, Otto

Otto appears in the 1860 Census of Flushing on page 737, a 36 year-old laborer from Wurtemburg married to 41 year-old Mary from Bavaria. It is not known when he emigrated to the United States, but the couple has a 14 year-old son named Henry who was born in New York.

He enlisted in Company E of the 29th New York Infantry on May 6, 1861, but apparently did not apply for a pension, perhaps because of his age. His name appears on the August 23, 1862 *Flushing Journal* list of volunteers from College Point.

Otto is enumerated on page 220 of the 1870 Census of Flushing living in College Point. He is a 50 year-old carpenter with an annual income of $3000. A woman named Bertha, 50, now keeps house, but there is no way to determine if Mary and Bertha are one and the same. With the age difference, Mary may have died and Otto remarried.

By 1880 there is a Henry Schroeder living in Jamaica who could easily be Otto's son, but beyond that nothing else is known of Otto Schroeder.

Schubert, Emil

On June 6, 1861, the day he enlisted in Company A of the 41st New York Infantry, Emil stood 6'. His name is among those listed in the August 23, 1862 edition of the *Flushing Journal*. He also has the distinction of being named as a casualty of war from College Point, thus having his name etched forever in marble on the Flushing Memorial to Civil War casualties. Only thing is he didn't die in the war, rather his left leg was broken just above the ankle in Washington, DC in April 1862, and the injury was treated at the Patent Office Indian Hospital until the end of May of that year. Emil rejoined his unit ca. July 8th.

His injury report reads: *"Schubert was at the time 1st Lieutenant of the Battery and while riding up on the North side of the Capitol, on return to camp, saw three rowdies knock down a soldier without provocation. He endeavored to arrest them and seized one of them by the collar, but his horse shied and fell. His left leg was caught between his sword scabbard and body of the horse and was broken as above set forth."*

Nothing much is known of Emil other than the facts of his military service. From his pension application it is learned that he cohabitated with one Kunigunde Becker in Washington DC from ca. 1870 and recognized her as his wife without benefit of a formal wedding.

According to a deposition taken on March 3, 1882 on behalf of Kunigunde's application for a widow's benefits, Emil *"never believed in any matrimonial ceremonies regarding the rites of a church and was one of the school of Robert G. Ingersoll"*, a lawyer and former Colonel of the 11th Illinois Cavalry who was a noted agnostic lecturer who attacked popular Christian beliefs. He was also the Attorney General of Illinois from 1867 to 1869.

His military file has him placed under arrest by order of Colonel L.O. Morris of the 7th New York Artillery from June 6, 1863 through October, but no reason is given.

On January 20, 1880 Schubert lived at 1328 G Street in the District of Columbia, but he does not appear in the Census. It is known only that he died on January 24, 1882.

Schultz, Franklin

The August 16, 1862 edition of the *Flushing Journal* reports that he, name listed as *Frederick Schuelzgover*, along with William Hoenig, had enlisted in the Metropolitan Guard, the 133rd New York Infantry. The initial enlistment took place on August 13th and he was mustered into Company C the following September 24th.

Franklin could be Benjamin, the brother of David Schultz who follows, but there is nothing to corroborate that. It is known that he was mustered out on June 6, 1865 in Washington, DC, but apparently did not file for a pension. He is also not listed in the 1880 Census in the New York City area.

Schultz, David L.

David is found in the 1850 Census of Williamsburgh Village in Brooklyn, 11 years old and the second child of Godfrey and Catherine. His father, 49, was born in Prussia and is a maker of combs. Catherine, his mother, is 38 and claims birth in Connecticut. He has an older sister named Mary, 14, a younger brother Benjamin, 7, and two younger sisters, Sarah, 3 and Teresa, 4 months.

The family is found again in the 1860 Census of Flushing on page 739. Godfrey and Catherine are still alive as is brother Benjamin, now 17. Both young men share their father's occupation, comb-maker. Mary Dun, 26, from Ireland is listed as a servant. It appears that older sister Mary has married and the two younger sisters have died, as neither would have been old enough to marry.

D. Schultz is named in the August 23, 1862 edition of the *Flushing Journal*. His unit, the 79th New York Infantry, fought on the 29th of November in 1863 at Knoxville, Tennessee, a battle that took the life of David Schultz. His mother filed for a pension on July 11, 1878 that of course, was granted.

The Sons of Union Veterans Post Number 29 was named in his honor and an article appeared, probably in the *Flushing Journal*, describing the event. Mention is made of a son-in-law named James Hallahan, probably the man Mary married.

Catherine, widowed and working as a school janitor, appears in the 1880 Census in College Point while Benjamin now resides in Brooklyn and is married to Jane E. Schultz. They have three daughters.

Schultz, George

A person by this name is included in the August 23, 1862 *Flushing Journal* list of College Point volunteers. He is said to have enlisted in the Navy, but no more information is forthcoming, and there were very many individuals by this name in the 1880 Census.

Schultz, Henry

Henry appears on page 705 of the 1860 Census of Flushing. He is 26, a carpenter from Bavaria married to 33 year-old Magdaline from Baden. Emigration information is unknown, but the couple has two sons; Charles 6, and August, 3, both born in New York.

Henry enlisted in the 15th New York Heavy Artillery, actually a 30-day enlistment in the 15th New York Regiment of National Guard Infantry, called out to garrison Fort Richmond in New York Harbor from June 6, 1864 through July 7, 1864.

His name also appears in *Munsell's History of Queens County* as having served in the 15th New York Heavy Artillery, but the unit was actually the 15th New York State Militia called out to garrison Fort Richmond in New York Harbor from June 6, 1864 through July 7th of the same year.

While there are a number of individuals by this name in 1880, it is not possible to confirm if any is this veteran.

Schumacker, Frederick

Johann Friedrich Schumacker was born March 28, 1828 in the village of Altburg in Neuenmberg, Germany. His father George Friedrich was an innkeeper. His mother was Margaretha Louise Schulz.

Emigration data is unknown, but he appears in 1860 in the Flushing Census in College Point on page 700 married to Eva with two children; Martin, 17 and Mary, 13. Both were born in Germany.

He served as a bugler until the end of the war and following discharge, returned to Germany where on October 31, 1869, he married Marie Elizabeth Barth. Through 1886 they had seven children.

It is not known what happened to Eva and the two children, but it is likely she died and the two children returned to Germany with their father. There is no mention of them in the pension application.

Frederick died in Neuenberg on October 31, 1882.

Schumacher, Henry

For whatever reasons, Henry Schumacher, whose name appeared in the August 23, 1862 *Flushing Journal* list of College Point volunteers, did not file for a pension. He had enlisted on May 6, 1861, and was also an original member of the GAR Post No. 451 in College Point.

While he was a member of Company I of the 20th New York, he was not among the men who laid down their arms before the Battle of Chancellorsville, and so was not subject to the Court Martial that ensued. He was mustered out on June 1, 1863.

No one with this surname lives in College Point in 1880, but one Henry Schumacher does live in Newtown, Queens, a 44 year-old hotelkeeper married to Catherina, 38. Both are from Wurtemburg and there are five children; Matilda, 23, Bertha, 21, Theodore, 17, Olga, 16, and Martha, 5.

Nothing else is known of this individual.

Sennewald, Theodore

Theodore was born in the village of Allendorf, Saxony, Germany ca. 1843. When he emigrated is not known, but on June 3, 1861, the day he enlisted in the 20th New York Infantry, he stood 5'6" with brown hair and eyes. He was a butcher by trade, but he also spent many years working in the swamps of Louisiana.

The story of Theodore Sennewald *aka* Charles Ritter, is quite interesting in that he is one soldier who is definitively from College Point as his enlistment documents say it was from this town that he enlisted in Company I of the 20th New York on May 3, 1861.

On that same day in New York City, the real Charles Ritter enlisted in the same unit, the 20th New York, but in Company B. I suspect they met and became fast friends.

On September 17, 1862 Ritter was killed at the Battle of Antietam and two months later Sennewald was discharged with the rank of Full Bugle Major.

Perhaps they had made plans to go into business together following the war, but, of course, that will never be known. Whatever the truth, Sennewald took on the name Charles Ritter and was known by that name for his entire life in Louisiana through two marriages.

His pension record, under both names, is thick and contains letters from numerous individuals claiming to have known him in Louisiana, always as Charles Ritter. That stood to reason for following the war he removed himself to the area, started work in the swamp, and married Malinda Cottreux. They had a daughter in 1867. The family appears in the 1870 Census living in Iberville Parish, Ward 6, in the town of Plaquemine.

Malinda passed away on February 10, 1877 and Charles married a woman named Alena, she who would file for his pension on October 4, 1895.

Charles is still a swamp-laborer when the family appears in the 1880 Census in the 2nd Ward of St. Martin Parish on page 46A. There are three children; a daughter Arina, 5, a son Edwin, 3. Malinda is very likely their birth mother and she may have died giving birth to Edwin. There is also a 6-month old son named Charles.

Nothing else is known of Theodore Sennewald *aka* Charles Ritter.

Skinnon, Thomas

Thomas was the son of James and Mary, born in Ballymorrow, County Leitrim in Ireland where his father had died on March 17, 1847 or 1848. The record is unclear.

On April 30, 1861 he enlisted in Company E of the 10th New York Infantry, all of 21, according to pension documents.

When his mother applied for pension benefits following the death of her unmarried son on June 27, 1862 at Gaines Mill, Virginia, she indicated he had *"labored in a gutta percha factory for six years prior to enlistment"*, probably the comb factory in College Point. The named appears to be spelled *Scunnion* and its actual spelling is a matter of much dispute.

It is known only that Mary lived both in Belleville, New Jersey in 1862 and at 209 East 35th Street in New York City in 1864. Information in the pension application indicated that Thomas had given his mother some financial support prior to his military service. There were no other children.

His name, spelled *Skinyon*, appeared in the August 23, 1862 *Flushing Journal*, but it was not included on the Flushing Memorial to Civil War casualties, perhaps because his mother lived in New York City.

It should have been.

Smith, James R.

Prior to his April 30, 1861 enlistment in Company E of the 10th New York Infantry, (along with Thomas Skinnon), James Robert Smith, born in Pennsylvania, worked at the India Rubber Comb Company in College Point, starting ca. 1854. After being wounded in the knee at Gaines Mill, Virginia, James returned to New York City and lived with his brother-in-law, Travis Kenworthy, who had married Sarah Jane Smith, the sister of James.

On September 2, 1866 he married Jane Elizabeth Riley, born in Northern Ireland ca. 1847, at St. Paul's Chapel in College Point. After the wedding they lived both in New York City and Brooklyn and became parents to five children. Two died in infancy, and the other three are Edward E., Walter and Mary Josephine, a daughter born in Brooklyn on November 20, 1880. James was a manufacturer of jewelry.

Jane Elizabeth Smith died of Peritonitis at her home in Brooklyn at 1344 Dekalb Avenue on January 21, 1884. She is buried there in Green-Wood Cemetery. James died two years later in December of 1886 at his residence, Pulaski Street, in Brooklyn. Presumably he is buried with Jane.

Travis Kenworthy and his wife Sarah Jane assumed responsibility for Mary Josephine and thus gave depositions when applying for the pension benefits due a minor child upon the death of both parents.

Smith, William

There is a 22 year-old William Smith living in College Point enumerated on page 725 in 1860 with his parents, 48 year-old Charles and 49 year-old Henrietta. Also listed there are; Elizabeth, 24, Henry, 18, Morris, 16, Charles, 14, Margaretta, 12 and Jacob, 10. This may be the soldier's family, but the name is extremely common.

As a member of Company I of the 20th New York Infantry, he was one of the men who stacked his arms before the Battle of Chancellorsville in early May of 1863, and was subsequently subject to Court Martial and dishonorable discharge.

His name appeared in the August 23, 1862 *Flushing Journal* list of College Point volunteers and following discharge on June 1, 1863, he returned to College Point and married Katherina Steider. The wedding ceremony, performed by Father Joseph Huber, took place at St. Fidelis Catholic Church on November 22, 1863. At the time the pension application was made there were two children under the age of 16; William, born February 12, 1883 and Bertha, February 16, 1886.

Because the name is so common, no further information is known.

Snyder, Edwin

GAR member Edwin Snyder is a Pennsylvanian by birth, and was born in Philadelphia on July 22, 1844 to John and Mary Maxwell Snyder. Both parents are buried in Union Cemetery located in the town of White Marsh, in Montgomery County, Pennsylvania.

He stood 5'3", had a light complexion, blue eyes and brown hair when he enlisted on January 22, 1862, and following his service in the 31st Pennsylvania Infantry, he moved to College Point on January 6, 1877. On April 2, 1878 Edwin married Pennsylvania-born Mary Schumann, at St. George Episcopal Church in Flushing. Rev. J. Carpenter Smith, Rector, performed the ceremony.

They lived in College Point in 1880 and are found on page 237A in the Census with the surname spelled *Schneider*. Edwin is 36 and works in the rubber factory, while Mary keeps house. They appear as well in the 1900 Census where he is a rubber polisher.

Both lived on through the 1920 Census of College Point. John died on June 12, 1920 in College Point followed by Mary on February 20, 1921. They lived at 226 10th Street, today's 119th Street.

Snyder, William H.

The family of John and Mary Schneider *(sic)* are enumerated in the 1860 Census of Flushing on page 740. John, 56, and Mary, 30, are both from Pennsylvania. William, their 24 year-old son was also born in Pennsylvania, and he has two siblings, Kate, 11, and Adelia, 2.

Living with the family are Louis Fritz and Hiram Warner. Both will serve during the Civil War.

On enlistment day, June 15, 1861, he stated that he had been born in Philadelphia, was 26, making his birth year ca. 1835. William stood 5'4" with a fair complexion, blue eyes, brown hair and was a cigar maker by trade. His unit was Company C, 74th New York Infantry also known as Sickle's Brigade.

Over the course of his military service he was sick for two weeks in Washington, DC beginning February 14, 1862 and then again the following May 8th in Williamsburg, Virginia where he served as a nurse to the wounded.

William H. Snyder is among the men named in the August 23, 1862 *Flushing Journal* list of volunteers from College Point. He is also listed in Munsell's' *History of Queens County* where it is incorrectly noted he was wounded in both thighs at the Battle of Cold Harbor in Virginia. This battle took place early in June of 1864 and at this time William had been out of the Army for at least 18 months.

His January 10, 1863 Certificate of Disability for Discharge states that he could not perform the duties of a soldier because of *"chronic diarrhea of 7 months standing together with hypertrophy of the heart. Had done no duty of the last eight months. Was hearty and strong when enlisted."*

For whatever reasons, it appears he did not apply for a pension thus nothing else is known of this individual. His mother Mary however, remains in College Point and appears on page 88 of the 1870 Census of Flushing. She is a widow with two children; Adelia, 14 and Oscar, 9.

On page 314C in the 1880 Census of College Point Mary is once again enumerated. Living with her is her daughter Adelia called *Ottilie* and son Oscar. Two grandchildren, John Allison, 5 and Alfred Allison, 8 months, are also listed. These must be children of the daughter Kate who was enumerated in the 1860 Census of Flushing, but she is not found anywhere in the 1880 Census in New York.

Sparks, John

The pension record for this soldier gives no reference to College Point, but his occupation in the 1860 Census of Philadelphia gives us a strong lead; he was a maker of combs and probably had moved to College Point to work at his trade prior to the commencement of the war.

The list of volunteers printed in the August 23, 1862 *Flushing Journal* includes one T. Sparks and a reference to the 10th Regiment. This soldier served in the 10th New York. Every other indication says he was from Pennsylvania.

He was a musician and a machinist born ca. 1827 in Pennsylvania whom the record says enlisted at the age of 20 on April 26, 1861. The age is slightly incorrect as John married his wife, Sarah Ann Ferrel, on November 7, 1848 in Philadelphia and in the 1850 Census there, he and Sarah are listed as being 22, with a one year-old son named Albert.

On November 1, 1850 Sarah gave birth to another son and named him John. Twenty-two years later on October 1st, he is baptized at a Lutheran Church in Philadelphia. Another child, a daughter named Mary Ann will be born ca. 1852, and according to the pension record, is baptized in Philadelphia on May 2, 1869 at the 7th Street Methodist Episcopal Church. No reason is given for the span of years between birth and baptism for either child.

During his years in the Army John contracted chills and fever that lead to, according to the claim, the consumption that ended his life on February 3, 1872 in Philadelphia.

The widowed Sarah appears in the 1880 Census of Philadelphia living with her son John, now 29 and a *"saw smith"*, and daughter Mary who has married Benjamin Scank, a saw handle-maker. They have three children; Sarah, 5, Alfred, 3 and Mary, 1.

Mary Sparks passed away at her daughter's Philadelphia home, 6024 Torresdale Avenue in Philadelphia, on March 3, 1918 at the age of 90, and is buried in Magnolia Cemetery along with Benjamin, her son-in-law, who passed away at the age of 75 in 1926.

Stader, Charles

For reasons unknown, no pension was ever applied for by John Stader, the father of Charles who enlisted in the 39th New York Infantry on May 20, 1861. The 39th, known as the *Garibaldi Guard*, was composed of three Hungarian Companies, three German, one Swiss, one Italian, one French, one Spanish and one Portuguese.

According to his military record, on May 20, 1861, the day he enlisted in Company C of the 39th New York Infantry, Charles was a 21 year-old clerk standing 5'10", with a fresh complexion, brown eyes and dark hair.

Early in July 1863 he was promoted to Sergeant in place of a Sergeant George Bonin who was killed at Gettysburg on July 2nd. At that time he was detached to New York, Riker's Island, to receive a contingent of drafted men.

On December 1, 1863 Charles was reported as *"missing on picket"* and was actually captured the next day at the Mine Run Battle in Virginia. He was sent to Andersonville Prison in Georgia the following February 15th and on July 21st he was admitted to the hospital there where he died of Scorbutus, or scurvy, a prisoner of war, on August 2nd. He is buried in Grave Number 4574 at Andersonville.

His name was included in the June 2, 1866 list of College Point casualties that appeared in the *Flushing Journal* and is etched on the Flushing Memorial to Civil War casualties.

His military file contains two letters written by his father transcribed as follows.

Strattonport August 7, 1864

Colonel William Hoffmann, Esquire, Company General of Prisoners

Dear Sir,

Having been informed that my son was taken Prisoner and that only by you to find out whereabouts he is to be found and let his parents know as soon as convenient (illegible) *to you. His name is Charles Stader... he was enlisted 1861 for 3 years...he was sworn in the service on the 17th May 1861 39th Regiment Company, A, Garibaldi Guard. He then was captured on the 4th December with 34 men of his Rgt. near Court House was brought to Dell's Island, Va. Since that time I did not hear anything of him anymore. Please do your best to find out where he could be and oblige his parents.*

The second letter, similar to the first, acknowledges a reply from Colonel Hoffmann and asks for *"more particulars about my son.... And oblige me and my poor family who all depended on our son and know we cannot find out if he is alive or dead or anything about his whereabouts."*

The letter goes on to name a number of the men who were captured with Charles, *Francis Messing, Nilson Bernhardt, Theodore Reinke, Christian Romany, Charles Schneider, Albert Schwarzenbach and Nicholas Schutz.* Only Reinke and Schutz would survive Andersonville and the war.

A note in his military file indicates that $16.04 was due the government for an overdrawn clothing allowance.

Stader, George

George is the first-born, ca. 1836, son of John Stader. On May 15, 1861, he joined his brother in Company C of the 39th New York Infantry. George was a locksmith, stood 5'11", and had a dark complexion, gray eyes and black hair.

According to his pension record he was at one time *"run over by a provision wagon"* suffering wounds to both legs and recuperated at City Point Hospital in Virginia.

He also became a prisoner of war near Harper's Ferry, Virginia on September 11, 1862, and ultimately was paroled and sent to Camp Chase located west of Columbus, Ohio, from which he was discharged because of his wounds on October 2, 1862.

Following the war George lived at 207 West 29th Street in 1873 and then in 1874 he married a woman named Katherine whose surname is indecipherable in the pension record. The ceremony was performed at a church on Stanton Street in New York City with Rev. John A. Foersch officiating.

Four children were born; George, January 12, 1878, Ann, July 26, 1883, Georgianne, November 23, 1887 and Frank, September 17, 1889. It is possible that at the time she married George, Katherine may have been a widow as in 1880, where George and his family live in New York City, there are two daughters listed; 12 year-old Josephine and 4 year-old Dora. The pension record makes no mention of these individuals, nor does it mention a previous marriage.

George died on September 19, 1904.

Stader, John

John Stader appears in the 1860 Census of Flushing on page 715, a 42 year-old tailor from Bavaria married to Elizabeth who is 43. When the family emigrated is unknown, but in 1860, they have four children; George, 19, Charles, 17, Margaret, 14 and John, 4. George and Charles were born in Nurnberg in Germany.

John is listed in Munsell's *History of Queens County* as having served in the 15th New York Heavy Artillery, but it was actually a 30-day enlistment in the 15th New York Regiment of National Guard Infantry called out from June 6, 1864 through July 7, 1864 to garrison Fort Richmond in New York Harbor.

He remains in College Point where he is found on page 228 in the 1870 Census of Flushing, a 51 year-old tailor with an annual income of $4000.

In the 1880 Census record, where his name is spelled Stadler, he is a widower and still a tailor. Living with him is his son John who works in the rubber factory and the family of veteran Jacob Sutorious who has married his daughter Margaret. His remaining son George has married and lives in New York City with his family. The surname is spelled Stadter.

When and where John Stader died is unknown.

Starkins, John

GAR member John Starkins was born in Great Neck ca. 1842, and appears in the 1860 Census as a blacksmith apprentice living in the town of North Hempstead. His name is mentioned as First Sergeant on page 255 in Roemer's book on the 34th New York Light Artillery. He had attained this rank on October 17, 1863

He, along with Carl Ludwig and Joseph Hibson, were awarded the Congressional Medal of Honor. Starkins' July 30, 1896 Citation reads:

"On the retreat at Campbell Station, Tennessee November 16, 1863, Starkins brought off his piece without losing a man."

John lives in College Point in 1880 and is found on page 305B of the Census married to Catherine, surname unknown, and working in the rubber factory. There are four children; Esther, 13, Henrietta, 10, George, 7, and Elizabeth, 1.

John was born to Prussian-born parents in New York. The record says Catherine was born in Prussia. He died of Brights Disease in Flushing on April 4, 1897 and is buried in Zion Church Cemetery in Little Neck. There is no information in the file indicating when or where Catherine died.

Steinbeck, Julius

Julius Wilhelm Steinbeck was born in a German village called Gera Reiss in Saxony, ca. 1834. He probably came to America ca. 1859, but he does not appear in the 1860 Census. He became a citizen on October 20, 1864.

He enlisted in Williamsburg on May 6, 1861 and stood 5'4", with blond hair and blue eyes. Julius served in the 20th New York Infantry, was discharged on June 1, 1863 and on Sunday, January 15, 1865, Pastor August Ebendick of St. John's Lutheran Church, married Julius to Amelia Behring, she the daughter of Frederick Behring, who also served in the 20th New York. Her brother Paul was a witness.

The fact that Amelia and Paul are siblings confirms that Frederick Behring, whose name is spelled *Behringer* on page 719 in the 1860 Flushing Census, are one and the same, as he has children by these names. Another daughter, Christine, married yet another veteran, Edward Freund.

On page 40 of the 1870 Census of Flushing, there are three children; Paul, 5, born July 9, 1865, Francis, 4, February 1, 1867, and Julius, 9 months old, September 4, 1869. Julius works in the comb factory, having served a comb-maker's apprenticeship in Norway prior to coming to the United States.

Son Francis is not enumerated on page 242D in the 1880 Census of College Point, he having died on April 4, 1871. Additions to the family include; August, 8, born December 11, 1871, William, 7, born November 19, 1873, Caroline or Lena, 4, born December 25, 1875 and Otto, 2, born March 22, 1878. Julius works at the rubber factory.

Caroline died on August 25, 1896, and Hannah lives on until September 7, 1962 according to Julia Steinbeck-Reeves, a descendant.

In 1900 Amelia still lives in College Point and indicates that she had had 9 children of which 6 are yet living. Living with her are Julius, August, William and Hannah.

Through 1910 and in 1920 Amelia remains in College Point and in that Census she is listed with her daughter Lena, no longer living with the Grell family as she was in 1900. She has married Edward Metz.

Julius is an original member of Adam Wirth Post No. 451 and his sons Julius and Paul became active members of the Sons of Union Veterans. Paul also became a well-known carriage designer.

Julius lives until May 20, 1891, whereupon he dies and is buried in Flushing Cemetery. Amelia died many years later on September 5, 1920.

Steinbecker, John

There are two individuals with very similar names in this book.

John Steinbecker, because he enlisted in the 34th New York Light Artillery on September 6, 1861, is among the men included in the *Flushing Journal* list of volunteers from College Point.

Both he and John Steinbrucker, whose story follows, are the same age at the time of enlistment, 31, and both are reported as having deserted. This one truly did on June 25, 1862, and although given an opportunity to return without punishment by his commander, Jacob Roemer, he chose no to do so. Since this person did not file for a pension, nothing else is known.

Steinbrucker, John

John Steinbrucker, his wife Mary and daughter, also named Mary, appear in the 1860 Census of Flushing on page 738. He is a laborer from Bavaria and had emigrated to New York prior to 1857, the year Mary was born.

His name was not included on the August 23, 1862 *Flushing Journal* list of College Point volunteers. It was, however, included in the list of College Point men who had fallen in the war that appeared in the June 2, 1866 *Flushing Journal*. His widow, Mary, whom he had married in New York City on September 10, 1853, filed for her widow's pension benefits on May 2, 1865, one month following his death at Farmville, Virginia on April 6, 1865.

While the record indicates that he deserted a month after he enlisted, such is not the case, as he went to the 7th New York Infantry. His military record indicates that following his supposed desertion, a 36 year-old soldier named Henry Nelly took his place.

One of the saddest coincidences encountered in the research for this book was this man's death, as it occurred within the same time frame as that of Henry Apel. Both Steinbrucker and Apel had enlisted in the 29th New York on the same day and then re-enlisted in the 7th New York where they were serving at the time of their deaths. Both men, very likely friends looking forward to the end of the war, died within days of the cessation of hostilities.

Farmville was a small tobacco town of 1,500 residents in the spring of 1865. Both Union and Confederate soldiers were marching west toward Appomattox where General Lee had hoped to issue some rations to his soldiers, but was unsuccessful, and where the Confederate surrender took place on April 9th.

Sternberg, Casper

Casper Sternberg was born in Hollenstein, Austria on January 3, 1846 and came to America sometime before 1860 where his family appears in the Census of Flushing on page 697. Henry, his father, also known as Jurgon, is a laborer, 48, married to Mina or Wilhelmina. There is an 18 year-old servant named Doras, who is actually a daughter named Dorothy. Casper is 15, Lewis, 12, Charles, 5 and Mathias, 2. The family attended church at St. John's Lutheran.

On enlistment day he said he was 18 when in fact he was only 15, stood 5'5", had a light complexion, blue eyes, brown hair and served as a bugler.

His name appeared in the August 3, 1862 *Flushing Journal* list and while in the Army he suffered a flesh wound to the left side of his forehead during a night raid made by Lee's Army. The wound was caused either by a bullet or a bayonet. He could not recall which.

The pension record says he returned to College Point following his June 21, 1865 discharge and stayed there for three weeks, whereupon he left for Galena, Illinois, worked on Mississippi river boats for the next fourteen years, and never came back.

Sometime ca. 1872 or 1873 he married in Galena and two children were born; Dora, ca. 1878 and Louis, ca. 1880. Shortly after their birth he separated from his wife whose name is not given, and who does not appear in the 1880 Census.

Following his years on the river, Casper moved to North Dakota where at various times he worked as a mail carrier. In 1908, he lived in Towner, in McHenry County where on January 20, 1910, he died as a result of heart trouble.

A single woman, age 40, named Dora Sternberg appears in the 1920 Census in New York City living at 623 West 142nd Street in Manhattan. She is a sales lady in a dry goods store and could be the daughter born ca. 1878. The son named Louis appears nowhere in this Census.

Sternberg, Jurgon

Jurgon, also known as Henry, is the father of Casper whose life is described above. Surprisingly, there does not appear to have been a pension applied for, but it is known that he was admitted to Aquia Creek Hospital at Windmill Point, Virginia on January 19, 1863 and that he died there of Typho-Malarial Fever a week later, on January 26th.

His name is on the August 23, 1862 *Flushing Journal* list and is also etched on the Flushing Monument to Civil War casualties.

From the Battery Muster Roll in his military file dated June 30, 1862, it is indicated he was promoted on May 27, 1862 in place of Sergeant Adam Wirth, he who would die three months later after the Second Battle of Bull Run.

Wilhelmina, his widow, appears in the 1880 Census of College Point living with her daughter Dorothy, herself a widow, and her three children. Dorothy works in the rubber factory. It appears none of her three sons appear anywhere in the 1880 Census.

Stobbe, Nicholas

Nicholas was born in Germany ca. 1824 and appears in the August 23, 1862 *Flushing Journal* list, but not anywhere in the 1860 Census of New York.

On enlistment day, October 16, 1861, he stood 5'5", had a dark complexion, black hair and brown eyes.

He served in the 57th New York Infantry and at the Battle of Antietam, September 17, 1862, Nicholas *"received a gunshot wound to the right leg about three inches below the knee. The brigade was ordered to advance and while they were moving he was shot and ordered to the rear being unable to advance for loss of blood."*

He was treated in the field hospital from that day until October 12, 1862 and at Camp "B" near Frederick City, Maryland until February 20, 1863.

Following his discharge on September 23, 1864 he settled in Middlesex County, New Jersey marrying Appolona, surname unknown, on December 1, 1867 at St. John's Reformed Church in New York City. Rev. Charles Banks performed the ceremony.

In 1880 the family lived in North Brunswick, New Jersey with four children; Charles, born ca. 1869, Nicholas, ca. 1870, Elizabeth, ca. 1875 and Henry, ca. 1876. Nicholas was a manufacturer of bone dust and he tells us also that prior to his entry into the service he was a rubber polisher thus explaining his presence in College Point prior to the war.

Over the years Nicholas acquired a bit of property in and around North Brunswick before his death on January 19, 1896. He is buried in Evergreen Cemetery there, along with his wife who, passed away on February 13, 1906.

Stonebanks, John

John Stonebanks was born in England ca. 1846 and appears with his family at the age of 4 on page 244 in the 1850 Census of New York City. He is the son of Joseph Stonebanks, a 35 year-old carpenter, and his wife Elizabeth, who is 33. He has three siblings; Isabella, 11, Margaret, 9, and George, 3.

The family appears on page 739 in the 1860 Census of Flushing and John has four more siblings, Mary, 11, Truletta, 9, Joseph, 5 and Conrad, 2. His father, still a carpenter, makes a substantial annual income for the time, $15,000.

In another of the war's tragedies, John enlists in the 15th New York Heavy Artillery, actually a 30-day enlistment in the 15th New York Regiment of National Guard Infantry, called out to garrison Fort Richmond in New York Harbor from June 6, 1864 through July 7, 1864.

Toward the end of his service on June 29th, he died in a drowning incident and the obituary that appeared in the July 2, 1864 *Flushing Journal* reads:

"John Stonebanks, a son of Joseph Stonebanks of College Point, was drowned Wednesday afternoon, June 29, 1864 at Fort Richmond. Young Stonebanks belonged to the 15th Regiment which is doing 30 day's guard duty at that place. After partaking of a hearty dinner, he went in to bathe. Shortly after entering the water, he was seized with apoplexy and immediately sank. The wind being high, his body was soon washed ashore, but his life was extinct. His remains were brought to Flushing and buried from the residence of his parents yesterday, July 1. There are many who deeply sympathize with the afflicted parents for the loss of a son who bade faire to be a solace to them in their declining years."

His name is etched on the Flushing Memorial to Civil War casualties.

In 1870 and 1880 the Stonebanks family is strongly represented in College Point, but by 1920 it appears they have moved on.

Stratton, Alfred

Alfred Stratton enlisted in Company G of the 147th New York Infantry on August 19, 1863 at Dunkirk, New York in Chautauqua County, about as far away from College Point in New York State as possible, being on the far southwestern border. Supposedly he is a descendant of the Stratton family that had owned a large part of what is now College Point, but efforts to locate him anywhere in the 1850 Census have been unsuccessful.

Alfred was 18 when he enlisted in 1863 and the surgeon's report in the pension file indicates that on June 18, 1864 *"he was wounded in both arms while charging the enemy's works in front of Petersburg, Virginia"*. The wounds resulted in the loss of both arms for which he received artificial replacements.

Alfred, recovered from his wounds, married Julia Elizabeth Johnson at the Washington Street Episcopal Church in Brooklyn on October 28, 1865. Rev. Wilbur Watkins performed the ceremony and two children were born in the years to come; Alice, October 16, 1867 in Brooklyn, and Henry Draper, December 21, 1871, in Washington, DC to which the family had moved. They do not appear in the 1880 Census.

At some point Alfred had a house built on what is now College Point Boulevard between 25th Avenue and 25th Road. He died in Washington of a severe respiratory infection, consumption, the file says, on June 13, 1874.

Julia applied for a widow's pension on August 17, 1874, and married a second time to John J. Sweeney at Westminster Presbyterian Church in Washington on June 15, 1877.

Straube, Henry

Henry was born in the village of Sehlen in Hesse, Germany on December 12, 1840 and is found in the 1860 Census of Flushing on page 718. He is a 19 year-old laborer, son of Helena Straube from Hesse, and has an older brother named Ralph, 22, and two sisters, Martha, 17 and Catherine, 14.

On May 6, 1861, the day he enlisted he stood 5'6", had light brown eyes and brown hair.

As were a number of other members of Company I of the 20th New York Infantry, he was subject to Court Martial for laying down his arms before the Battle of Chancellorsville, and, in fact, had difficulty when applying for his pension, so much so that a reference had to be made by the Washington Law Firm, H. Spalding & Sons, to the awarding of a pension to Frederick Dockendorf, whose Court Martial had been overturned along with the others who had served in this unit.

The pension record doesn't tell us, but Henry returned from the war following his June 1, 1863 discharge, and married a New York-born woman named Magdalena, surname and date of marriage unknown. Over the following years he became father to Henry; born ca. 1865, Emma, ca. 1867, Katie, ca. 1869, and Edward, ca. 1871. The family appears in the 1870 Census of Flushing on page 237 where it indicates that Henry works in the rubber factory.

They also are enumerated in the 1880 College Point Census on page 240D. Henry still works at the rubber factory. His brother Ralph has stayed in College Point and can be found on page 293A of the same Census, married to Catherine and father to 8 children. He, too, works in the rubber factory.

Henry also appears in the 1900 Census where it is noted he arrived in the United States in 1853. He is a comb-presser and lives with his wife, and children Emma, Kate and Edward.

The pension file tells us finally that he died on Christmas Day in 1914. Henry Jr. becomes an active member of the Sons of Union Veterans organization.

Sutorious, Jacob

Jacob was born on February 16, 1839 to Friederick Louis and Jacobina Katharina Loeffler, in the town of Grossheppach, Neckarkreis, in Wurtemberg Germany. His father was a vinedresser, command councilor and curator of the town who died in 1851. Ten years later in August, Jacob emigrated to the United States and worked as a vine gardener. His mother died in Germany in 1879.

On enlistment day, May 3, 1861, he stood 5'9", had a light complexion, blue eyes and brown hair. In the course of his service in the 34th New York Light Artillery, he injured his right leg at the Pegram House near Petersburg, Virginia, *"while digging a hole, made a misstep and struck right leg with spade while erecting posts to tie horses in making winter quarters."* The injury made him unfit for duty for three months according to the surgeon.

After his June 30, 1865 discharge, he married Margaret Stader on April 2, 1866, a College Point girl, daughter of veteran John Stader and sister of brothers George and Charles who also served. Pastor L. Halfman performed the ceremony in a New York City Lutheran Church located on 84th Street in Manhattan.

Up until some time in 1880 he worked at the Enterprise Rubber Works in College Point whereupon he went to work at the Ansonia Clock Company.

In 1880 he lives with Margaret's parents in College Point and there are five children listed; Elizabeth, born April 25, 1867, William, October 4, 1869, Charles, March 9, 1872, John, May 17, 1874 and Anna, who is 3 months old. Pension data indicates that Anna must have died and another son, George, was born on October 2, 1883.

He is in College Point in 1900 and is working as a night watchman. Living with their parents are sons Charles, now a rubber worker and John, a silk weaver. Son George works as a press boy.

An original member of GAR Post No. 451, Jacob died on November 11, 1919 at his home, 138 13th Street. His son William became an active member in the Sons of Union Veteran's Organization.

In 1920 John, married, lives in Ridgewood, Queens. Charles, George and Matilda, the widow of William, live in College Point.

Thomas, George

A 19 year-old unmarried young man by this name appears on page 752 of the Flushing Census in 1860.

On September 5, 1862 at age 21, he enlisted in Company F of the 163rd New York Infantry in Flushing. According to his pension application, that was where he lived prior to enlistment. On that day he stood 5'8", had a dark complexion, brown hair and blue eyes.

During his time in the Army he received a gunshot wound between his shoulder and elbow.

"It was in the latter part of June, 1864 at a place the Officers called Clover Hill, Virginia. We were on a march toward Richmond when we met the enemy and were fired upon. While throwing up dirt to form breastworks, I was shot in the arm and had to crawl to the rear with some others until reaching the ambulances. After being treated at Mount Pleasant Hospital in the District of Columbia for five days, I was transferred to Fort Schuyler for two months."

He also suffered a rupture building a corduroy road near Fairfax Courthouse, Virginia. Following discharge on June 29, 1865 in Washington, DC, he eventually settled in Little Neck, Long Island.

George Thomas never married and lived out his days at the Soldiers and Sailors Home at Bath New York in Steuben County. He died there on February 20, 1906.

Thompson, Edward

Edward, 19, appears on page 742 of the 1860 Census of Flushing, a day laborer and son of John, 38, from Sweden, and his Irish-born wife, Catherine. Edward has five siblings; Catherine, 11, John, 8, Peter, 5 Elizabeth, 3, and Nicholas, 1, all born in New York.

Edward is named in an article published in the August 16, 1862 edition of the *Flushing Journal* as having enlisted along with Frederick Schuelzgover, William Hoenig, Charles Michel, Henry Wurtz and William Wilson. Wilson deserted, but Edward received a disability discharge on August 27, 1863. He did not, apparently, apply for a pension.

From his military file it is learned that he was a comb-maker when he enlisted at the age of 21 and that he stood 5'6" with a sandy complexion, blue eyes and brown hair. Furthermore there is a record of a disability discharge stating he suffered from *"valvular disease* of the heart with great deformity of the chest contracted since enlistment."

On page 293A in the 1880 Census, a 38 year-old comb-maker named Edward *Tompson* lives in College Point, married to Caroline who is 35. Both are New York-born and living with them is a 54 year-old laundress from Germany named Olivia Wald, possibly Caroline's mother. There is nothing to prove this is the same individual, but he is a likely candidate.

Caroline Thompson is enumerated in the 1920 Census of College Point living on 12th Street in the family of Charles Mollitor, 76, and his daughter Sophia, 39. She is identified as "aunt", probably Sophia's.

Nothing else is known of either Edward or Caroline Thompson.

Thurston, Thomas

Thomas Thurston has no connection to College Point other than the fact that his son, Fred W. Thurston, was a member of the Sons of Union Veterans organization. Fred's name appears in the article, source and date unknown, describing the presentation of a flag to the mother of David Schultz, after whom the Post was named.

For the record, Thomas Thurston served in Company C of the 6th New York Heavy Artillery. A native of Canada, he was a 20 year-old blacksmith on September 12, 1864, the day he enlisted in Tarrytown, New York for a period of one year. Thurston was 5'8", had gray eyes, light hair and light complexion. One month later he took part in and survived the Battle of Cedar Creek in the Shenandoah Valley, Virginia.

Discharged on June 28, 1865, he married Josephine Lenox at All Saints Episcopal Church in Great Neck. Fred was born on May 19, 1869, and was followed by the birth of a sister, Sarah Estelle, born on August 21, 1871.

Thomas Thurston lived his entire life in Nassau County, but for one period of time his son lived in, and was a part of, the fabric of College Point. Fred eventually moved from the town and lived in Great Neck in 1920. His father died on February 17, 1926 in that town.

Todt, Charles

Charles Todt, a 35 year-old merchant, appears in the 1860 Flushing Census married to 27 year-old Mary. He is from Hesse in Germany; she from Hanover. When they emigrated is unknown, but in 1860 they have two children; Charles 5 and Mary, 4. Two servants are also enumerated, John Ziegler and Ann Duke.

The marriage of Charles Todt and Marie Clara Weidman took place in Hanau, Germany, on July 7, 1854. Two other children were born to the couple; William Charles, born July 30, 1865, and Alice Emma, April 30, 1870.

Brickel's 1st Battalion of German Light Artillery was the unit in which Charles served, enlisting on December 18, 1861. While in the service, he contracted typhoid fever and as a result was discharged on a surgeon's certificate on June 7, 1862.

He lived on until September 9, 1876 when he died of yellow fever in Brunswick, Georgia where he is buried. Marie lived in Brooklyn in 1880, where she is enumerated along with the four children. She applied for widow's benefits from 51 Rue Petite Purse in Antwerp, Belgium in 1884, but she was in Belgium is not explained. She was awarded her benefits.

Troy, John

A person by the name of John Troy enlisted in the 34th New York Light Artillery on September 6, 1861 at the age of 20 and the record indicates he deserted shortly thereafter on September 22nd. It is very possible that he is the same John Troy identified as serving in the U.S. Mortar Flotilla in the August 23, 1862 *Flushing Journal* list of College Point Volunteers. His military record includes the note that *"Vigilant measures were used advertising his desertion without success."*

Tyrrell, Wyllis

Sergeant Wyllis Tyrrell, son of Sylvester and Lemira Tyrrell, was born in New Marlborough, Massachusetts ca. 1837, and appears in the 1850 Census where he is listed with his six siblings; Grove, 15, Abigail, 12, Rhoda, 9, Hubert, 6, and Alcina, 3.

At the age of 25 Tyrrell enlisted in Company E of the 11th Connecticut Regiment on October 25, 1861. By occupation he was a mechanic and had a light complexion, blue eyes and light hair, On September 17, 1862, he was wounded in the left knee on the battlefield at Antietam in Maryland. This wound caused lameness, according to a doctor in West Winsted, Connecticut who examined him during his 30-day furlough following the injury. Eleven months later, on August 25, 1863, he died of disease at Balfour Hospital in Portsmouth, Virginia.

In all of the documentation supporting his mother's application for his pension, there is nothing to connect Wyllis Tyrrell with College Point. Nevertheless his name appears on the Flushing Memorial to Civil War casualties, so there must have been a connection; probably work at the comb factory as a mechanic. Coincidentally John Hoelle, whose service is described previously, enlisted in this regiment on the same day.

Tyrrell's parents and remaining family appear in the 1880 Census of Goshen, Litchfield County in Connecticut. Grove had moved out west to San Francisco and is there in 1870. He is also there in 1880, a retired merchant.

In 1900 his mother Lemira lives in College Point. Her daughter Emma, who in the 1880 Census had a married named of Green, but no husband, is now married to one Charles *Grell*. Green and Grell may be one and the same as two of her children listed in 1880 are still living in the family. Caroline Steinbeck, daughter of veteran Julius Steinbeck, lives with the family and is listed as a servant.

Underhill, John

In the 1860 Census of Flushing on page 690, John Underhill, age 17, is living on the College Point/Whitestone border in the family of his New York-born father, Aaron, a farmer, and mother, Elizabeth B. By any standards the Aaron Underhill family is wealthy, owning real estate valued at $60,000 and having a personal estate valued at $10,000 according to the Census data.

He has a 20 year-old brother named Edward and four younger siblings; Maria, 15, Lucretia, 12, Ada, 10 and Walter, 7. Jane Toohey is a 30 year-old servant from Ireland.

On July 11, 1861 John, a boatman, enlists in Company C of the 65th New York Infantry. He is 5'5", gray eyes and light hair with a fair complexion. In his pension application, he indicates that he suffered a rupture during his service and had also contracted rheumatism.

In the 1880 Census there is a 40 year-old John Underhill living in Flushing with his wife Mary, and a 25 year-old woman named Lorena Meade. He is a retail grocer. It is likely, but not definite, that he is the veteran.

The pension file says also that in 1892 he lived at 34 Van Dam Street, and in 1904 on West 51st Street in Manhattan. It is here on March 24, 1904, that John Underhill died.

Vix, George

On page 713 of the 1860 Flushing Census, the family of 47 year-old John Vix of Baden, Germany, is a large one. He is 47 and his name is spelled *Yix*. In addition to his 48 year-old wife Margaretta, there are seven children. Richard, 21, George, 20, Barbara, 19, Mary, 16, Margaret, 14, Matilda, 10 and Louisa, 4. All, with the exception of baby Louisa, were born in Baden. Elizabeth, an older sister born in 1836, is not listed in the family in the 1860 Census, she having married one Conrad Hartmann. Elizabeth was born in the town of Oldshofen, which is in Baden.

On May 15, 1861, George enlisted in Company E of the 29th New York Infantry, served as a drummer, and died at the Second Battle of Bull Run, August 30, 1862. His name is etched on the Flushing Memorial to Civil War casualties.

It is uncertain where he is buried, but in truth it is he, and not Adam Wirth, who was the first College Point man to die in the Civil War. Wirth was wounded at the same battle and died the following September 25th.

In the 1880 Census of College Point, page 204C, George's 76 year-old widowed father appears still working as a gardener. Living with him are his two daughters, Louisa and Christina, who will never marry, and a 15 year-old grandson named Robert Vix. There is no indication as to who his father is, but we know it isn't George.

In 1884 his father, still alive, applies for and receives benefits from his son's pension. Of note is that the pension file contains a number of letters written by George to his parents. The letters are in German and the handwriting is different for each, most likely due to George not being able to write.

A translation of one letter done by Steve Hoffmann, a descendant of Elizabeth Vix Hartman, follows. The letter, written from a camp near Winchester, Virginia, was dated April 18, 1862.

I picked up the pen to write and let you know I am still in good health despite the hardships of the last 40 days. I could not write for the past 30 days, but I hope you received the letter, which I wrote to my brother.

We left Warrenton Junction and reached Warrenton City in the evening. From there we went to (illegible) where we spent three nights in the snow under the open sky, and there were three from the Polish Regiment (58th New York Infantry) frozen to death.

On the fourth day we went on. We saw no enemy soldiers, but as the division moved along, the enemy moved up behind us. They captured four wagons and took some of the stragglers prisoner.

There were farmers everywhere. We went along our way, but those who were too tired to keep up were taken prisoner.

From (illegible) we went to Upperville and found all the farmers assembled. We marched through peacefully and after three hard hours reached Paris where we are staying. We had nothing to eat since we started the march. We only had crackers all day.

The cattle perished during the march so that we had no meat either. That day we marched fourteen miles hungry with our packs and all our belongings. You can appreciate that it was no fun.

We stayed three days in Paris waiting for the bridge to be built over the Shenandoah River, but it was not finished. A raft was built, but as soon as cannon was placed on it, the raft nearly sunk. We now had to make a detour of ten miles with the wagons and artillery. The two brigades moved to where there was a ferry.

No sooner had we arrived when disaster struck. Sixty-four men of the Polish Regiment drowned on a faulty raft. I do not know how it happened. One third of the drowned men were never recovered. They fell into the water and sank. You had to see it to understand. Some of the fellows had artillery pieces on their backs and cartridge bags, which had sixty cartridges inside. Some of them had their rifles on them, which helped to pull them down.

We are now five miles from Winchester where we are supposed to rest. I will not write what I went through, but will tell you about it when I see you.

I will close my letter now. Greetings to all the relatives and friends.

I greet you cordially and remain your son.

George Vix (I hope for a quick reply)

In another July 3, 1862 letter, written to his brother Michael, he said, "*I cannot write to you of all I have seen or heard since the Battle of Cross Keys* (June 8, 1862). *Only 264 men survived and Bernhard Weber lost his left arm.*" He adds, "*I have been thinking of Barbara (his sister) and her husband. I have lost her address and for that reason I cannot write to her. Greet them both for me.* He writes then about the poor mail delivery, saying, "*Last evening 3,000 letters came to our Regiment – they have been left lying for a long time.*

George never did get to tell his family of his experiences.

Vogt, Jurgon

Jurgon Vogt was born on November 29, 1834 in the village of Boesen, Germany where on April 15, 1857 he married Wilhelmina Hentschen, in the Evangelical Lutheran Church. Wilhelmina was born in the same town on November 1, 1835 and baptized Adamine Elsabea. Rev. Schwartz performed the marriage ceremony.

Jurgon arrived in New York Harbor on July 4, 1857 and came directly to College Point where he probably worked at the rubber factory. He enlisted in Company L of the 2nd New York Heavy Artillery, in Flushing on October 1, 1861. At the time he was described as being a farmer, 5'6" with a light complexion, blue eyes and brown hair.

From his original June 21, 1865 discharge form and pension record it is learned that he was wounded at Petersburg, Virginia on August 12, 1864, suffering gunshot wounds to his left side under his ribs and in his left leg above the knee. He was treated at the 9th Army Corps Field Hospital, then the General Hospital at City Point, and finally at Wolfe's General Hospital in Alexandria, all in Virginia.

Following the war he worked in Poppenhusen's factory and became father to John, born May 12, 1864, Henrietta, November 25, 1869, Wilhelmina, January 6, 1872 and Emma, September 1, 1875. Wilhelmina, who was known as Minnie, never married. The family appears in the 1880 Census in College Point where Jurgon worked at the rubber factory.

Jurgon died at his residence, 110 10th Street in College Point, on December 23, 1907. Wilhelmina died seven years later on March 30, 1914. Both are buried at St. Michael's Cemetery in Astoria.

Vollbracht, William

Sons of Union Veterans member George Vollbracht was the son of William Vollbracht, who served in the 45th New York Infantry, and his mother Veronica Vollbracht.

William was born in Germany ca. 1823, and before entry into the service, married Veronica Dietz on January 23, 1853 in New York City. Rev. William Schluter performed the ceremony.

The original Marriage Certificate is included in the pension file, as is the Baptismal record for Anna, one of his daughters.

On enlistment day, September 26, 1861, William stood 5'6", had a dark complexion with gray eyes and brown hair. His disability discharge ten months later came about as the result of an *"aneurysm of the carotid artery caused by a fall in the night at Salem, Virginia while carrying a large kettle of water."*

In 1880 there were five children living in New York City; Ann, 20, born August 8, 1866, George, 16, Catharine, 13, Lizzie, 10, born December 30, 1869, and Augusta, 8, born April 10, 1872. William is a cabinetmaker and son George works on picture frames.

Whether or not the family ever moved to College Point is not certain. William died of stomach cancer on March 18, 1882 and is buried in Green-Wood Cemetery in Brooklyn.

Veronica's application for widow's benefits was denied on the basis that his cancer had not been caused by anything he had undergone in the Army, and his son George became an active member in the Sons of Union Veterans.

Von Kockeritz, Benno

One of the most fascinating names in this endeavor, Benno von Kockeritz appears on the list of College Point volunteers that was published in the *Flushing Journal* on August 23, 1862.

His service in Company L of the 1st New York Cavalry, began on May 29, 1861 and his discharge took place at Oldtown, Maryland on December 5, 1862. The following March 13th he enlisted again, this time in the 13th New York Cavalry. When he was discharged is unknown

He is a 62 year-old widower in the 1880 Census in New York City enumerated under the name *Beringeon Roeckwitz*, thus he is more than likely in the area in 1870, but it is not known where.

Wagner, Henry

Henry Wagner was born in the village of Oberellenbach, Hesse, Germany on March 7, 1838, came to America in 1859, and was working as a comb-maker in College Point on August 22, 1861 the day he enlisted in Company D of the 1st New York Engineers. Standing 5'3", he is described as having a *"white"* complexion, blue eyes and brown hair.

His role in the Army was that of *artificer*, one who would repair the artillery when necessary. He received a disability discharge at Hilton head, South Carolina, as a result of suffering a hernia to his right side while building a pier.

Rachel Herte became his wife on June 27, 1866 at the Adam Leicht House, 281 East Broadway in New York City. Minister Merkel performed the ceremony. Rachel was a widow and had been married to George Gauthier, a *"segar dealer"* who died in 1863. In the 1860 Census of New York City, the Gauthier family appears with a two month-old son named George.

In 1880, on page 281C of the Census, the Wagner family lives in Flushing and Henry is a *"Pedlar of Dry Goods"* with three children; William, born May 23, 1873, Mary Eloise, May 23, 1876 and Eva Elizabeth, June 27, 1878. There is no sign of the child George, and he is not in New York City in the same Census. They also have a servant named Annie Walster.

In 1915, in response to questions asked by the Department of the Interior Bureau of Pensions, it is learned that Rachel died in 1911 and Henry lives with daughter Eva, now married to a man named Henry Noll, on Rocky Hill Road in Queens. Mary Eloise is now Mary Lester and William is married and also living in Queens. In 1920 Henry still lives with Eva and her husband and does so until June 13, 1926 when he died.

Warner, Hiram

Hiram Warner first appears in the 1850 Census of Philadelphia, a 23 year-old comb-maker.

He next appears on page 740 of the 1860 Census of Flushing. He is a single, 26 year-old maker of combs from Pennsylvania. The age is obviously incorrect, as he is at least 33.

He is also named in the August 23, 1862 list of College Point volunteers that appeared in the *Flushing Journal*. The listing indicates he served in the Navy aboard the Gunboat *Perry*.

There is no pension record for Hiram, but page 37C of the 1880 Census indicates that one Hiram Warner, 44, married to Agnus, *(sic)* lives in the town of Menallen in Adams County, Pennsylvania. There are five children; Sallie, 18, Michael, 15, Anna E., 12, Noah D., 10 and Bessie, 1. This could be the veteran, but there is no way to confirm at present.

Weber, Bernhard

Bernard Weber is a 19 year-old barber from Germany living in Flushing with Charles Weber, and found on page 622 of the 1860 Census. The age for Charles, who runs a restaurant, appears to be 20, but that may be an error as the woman whose name follows his, Augusta Caroline, is 38. Four more persons are enumerated. They are Charles; also 19 and possibly a twin to Bernard, Augusta, 16, Edward 14 and a 20 year-old female named Caroline. No relationships are given, but Caroline could be Bernhard's wife.

There is a 30 year-old Bernard Weber married to 29 year-old Caroline in the 1870 Census of Brooklyn, He is a wool merchant from Prussia and Caroline is from England. There are no children, the age is correct and the names could be coincidence.

Bernard Weber's name appears on the list of College Point volunteers that appeared in the August 23, 1862 *Flushing Journal* indicating he served in the 58th New York. His first name is written *Beruh*, and no one by the name of Weber served in that unit. Moreover, only one person by this name, Bernhard Weber, served at all and he was in the 39th New York Infantry. He is probably the correct person.

Bernhard's military record indicates he worked as a clerk at the time he enlisted on May 28, 1861. He stood 5'6" with a fair complexion, blue eyes and light hair. He was shot in the right knee at the Battle of Cross Keys on June 6, 1862, and also spent some time in an unspecified prisoner of war camp.

The Battle of Cross Keys is mentioned in the letter written on July 3, 1862 by George Vix of the 29th New York infantry to his brother Michael in College Point. In it he says that Bernhard Weber had indeed been wounded at the battle, and as a result had lost his left arm. The letter, written in a camp near Middletown, Virginia says also that Weber had suffered a wound to his right knee.

It is important to note also that the letter was one of a number that Vix had written back home to College Point before his August 30, 1862 death at the Second Battle of Bull Run. Written in German, they were included in the application for benefits submitted by his father in 1884. Steve Hoffmann, a descendant of the Vix family, translated the letters quoted for this book.

An application for widow's benefits was submitted on August 31, 1896, and while there does exist an index entry for the application, the file could not be found in the National Archives. The name Leonard appears on the application card as the widow of Bernhard, but that may have been a son. No reason is known as to why the file is not there.

Weiss, Charles

A person named Charles *Wise* appears on the list created by the Provost Marshall's Office in 1863 as living in Strattonport. The military career of Charles Weiss is unclear, but a soldier by this name served in the 11th New York State Militia from June 18 through July 20, 1863.

Whatever unit he served in, it is known that two of his sons, Oscar and Charles, were members of the Sons of Union Veterans.

The family lives in College Point in 1870, enumerated on page 249 of the Flushing Census. Charles builds organs for a living and says he is from Baden in Germany. In this record, a 24 year-old woman named Frederica, from Prussia, is listed as the housekeeper. Oscar is 6, Charles, 3 and Emil is 5 months old.

The family appears on page 312C in the 1880 Census of College Point. Charles is 42, married to Mary, 30 from Wurtemburg. It is not known if Mary is the same person called Frederica in the 1870 Census. There are five children; Oscar, 15, Charles, 11, Emil, 7, Henry, 5 and Minnie, 4, all born in New York. The elder Charles is a saloonkeeper and young Oscar is an apprentice typesetter.

Move ahead twenty years to the 1900 Census and 62 year-old Charles, born in Germany in June 1837, is married to 49 year-old Mary, born also in Germany in July 1850. This family includes none of the children named in the 1880 Census, however there are four additional names; Mary, born in September 1880, Rosa, November 1882, Kate, June 1884 and William, August 1886.

There is a problem in that the number of children borne by Mary, 6, and the number of children still alive in 1900, 5, would not include those mentioned in the 1880 Census leading to a number of questions.

Is this the same individual? Did a first wife, possibly Fredricka, die prior to the 1880 Census? Did he marry a second time to Mary? Is the Census data incorrect?

Whatever the answers, there was a man named Charles Weiss who served during the Civil War and whose descendants were in College Point in 1920, most specifically Oscar, now a full-fledged printer, and his family who lived on 11th Street, today's 120th Street.

Wenzler, Leopold

There is nothing to connect Leopold Wenzler to College Point other than his inclusion on the database of names compiled by Flushing Historian, Vincent Seyfried. Nevertheless his story is told, as much of it as can be known.

Wenzler was born in Germany in the early 1820's and joined the 34th New York Light Artillery at the age of 40 on February 27, 1864. Enlisting in Jamaica, Leopold stood 5'6", had a dark complexion, gray eyes and dark hair.

The records say that upon enlistment Leopold received his $300 bounty paid by Queens County along with an additional bounty of $60, plus $13 advance pay, but probably didn't get to spend it, as on August 18, 1864, he was sent to the Third Division Hospital suffering from chronic diarrhea. He died there on September 1st and is buried at the National Cemetery in Alexandria, Virginia. His effects on the day he died included a cape, one blouse, one pair of trousers and shoes, a knife and a pocketbook. The trousers were bought at auction for $ .60.

It is not known if he was married and there was no pension application ever filed.

Werner, Frederick

Frederick's name appears in the August 23, 1862 list of College Point volunteers that appeared in the *Flushing Journal*.

According to information in his military file, Frederick was born in Prussia ca. 1838, and on enlistment day was 23, stood 5'7" and had a light complexion, blue eyes and sandy hair. He enlisted in the 34th New York Light Artillery on October 6, 1861.

The following notation appears in the file for November/December 1962.

"For merit in action on the 12th and 13th of December 1862 for accurate fireing (sic) at the enemy's works for which he is highly recommended."

He is also mentioned in Roemer's book in two places. On page 139 he writes, *"September 6th the order came for the Battery to start the march over the Cumberland Mountains and follow General Burnside into Tennessee. I was very sorry I was obliged to leave Sergeant Werner behind at Camp Parker for he was a very promising, non-commissioned officer and was likely to be promoted to a higher grade. He was with me in Cincinnati, August 24th assisting in drawing supplies and was taken sick at the same time I was. I tried to persuade him to go with the Battery, but he said he was too sick by far to do so."*

Werner died a week later, September 12, 1863, and true to military regulation a form in file reads, *"Due Gov't. on account of clothing, December 12, 1863, One dollar and fifty one cents."*

No explanation exists as to why his name was left off the Flushing Memorial to Civil War casualties, but his name was published in the *Flushing Journal* on July 8, 1865.

White, Thomas

Thomas White appears in the August 23, 1862 *Flushing Journal* list of College Point men who had volunteered for service. He was 24 years old and his military record indicates he stood 5'10", had a light complexion, brown eyes and hair and was a farmer before joining the Army.

According to his pension file he was born in County Tyrone, Ireland on September 9, 1838, and came to America in 1857 where from Strattonport, on October 1, 1861, he joined the Army and served in the 34th New York Light Artillery.

On November 25, 1868, three years after being mustered out, Thomas married Ellen O'Donovan in the town of Newport, Herkimer County, New York. Father Fitzgerald, a Catholic Priest, performed the ceremony.

Four children were born; William, October 14, 1869, Mary, November 25, 1870, Katie, Augusta 17, 1872 and Thomas, September 14, 1875. The family appears in the 1880 Census of Herkimer County living in the town of Norway. William works in a tannery. In 1882 the family moved to Iowa.

In time Mary married a man named Welsh, and Katie, a man named O'Meara. Katie passed away before her father.

In his pension application Thomas claims to have been twice wounded, once *"in a cornfield on the right of the Richmond Turnpike"* and again *"at Cold Harbor."* Neither claim could be substantiated, but William was able to name the doctors who treated him, so it is likely neither of the wounds were serious in nature, and so did not make it into his file.

He was hospitalized with a fever on September 13, 1863, treated at the Post Hospital in Crab Orchard, Kentucky, and released the next day.

In 1910 he is enumerated in the town of Buck Grove in Crawford County, Iowa, a widower, unemployed and living alone. The pension record says he lived on until October 15, 1919. His son William is a widow in 1920 living in Sioux City with a son named Christos, 11, and two daughters, Esther, 10 and Doris, 5. William is a teamster for a lumber company.

Wieners, Jacob F.

Jacob Wieners was born in New York in April 1844 and was married to a woman named Fredericka, surname unknown. The couple had four children; Jacob F., born in August 1865, Godfrey A.S., September 1866, Freda born ca. 1867, and Selma, in September 1869. He served for 30 days in Company E, 69th Regiment of New York State Militia starting June 22, 1863. Both sons were active in the Sons of Union Veterans.

The family appears in College Point in the 1870 Census. Jacob is 26, a New York-born confectioner married to Fredericka and there are four children; Jacob, 5, Godfrey, 4, Fredericka, 2 and Selma, 1.

Jacob, Freda and the four children family appear in the 1880 Census in College Point along with two servants; Annie O'Neal and Rudolph Miller.

Jacob is the first to pass away and does so on December 20, 1901. Fredericka lives an amazing forty-five more years, dying on January 18, 1945. Both are buried in Flushing Cemetery

The obituary for Godfrey that appeared in the *Long Island Star Journal* on January 15, 1948 tells us that Freda died at the age of 100 in January 1945. She had married Jacob in 1864 and in the summer of 1867, the couple had moved to College Point.

Godfrey, who had been a renowned banker in College Point, lived at 13-45 122nd Street at the time of his death.

Wiessner, Valentine

Valentine, 39, appears with wife Elizabeth, also 39, on page 726 of the 1860 Census of Flushing. He is from Bavaria, the name is spelled *Wiessman*, and there is a 2 year-old daughter named Matilda enumerated as well. He enlisted in Company L of the 2nd New York Heavy Artillery on October 1, 1861 and the official record indicates he deserted during or after the battle fought at the North Anna River in Virginia, May 26, 1864.

His military record indicates this man really did not want to be in the Army. Here it states he had deserted at least once before from Camp Wagner at Tenallytown, Maryland on June 25, 1862, and apparently returned to Strattonport where he was apprehended on or about February 22, 1864.

A $30 reward was given to the Provost Marshall from the 1st District of New York for the arrest and delivery of Valentine back to the unit. The record continues indicating that following capture, he rejoined the unit and took part in the Battles of Spotsylvania, May 12th and 13th as well as North Anna on May 24th, whereupon he deserted once again on May 26th. There is nothing else known of this individual.

Wilhelm, John

John Wilhelm's name appears on the list of volunteers from College Point that was published in the August 23, 1862 *Flushing Journal*. It is likely he was an employee of Conrad Poppenhusen, but his pension record provides not a single clue as to his connection to College Point.

He was a shoemaker, when on March 28, 1859, he married Caroline Veisez in a Catholic ceremony in Hamburg, New York. Father Fullam performed the rite.

The unit he joined on August 1, 1861 was the 68th New York Infantry, otherwise known as the 2nd German Rifles, so it can be assumed he was of German extraction.

In his pension application he claimed that on February 5, 1862 he *"fell into a well while marching from Roach Hill to Hunter's Point, Virginia and suffered a rupture."*

Following his June 25, 1862 discharge, he lived in New York City on both Hester and Chrystie Streets. In the 1880 Census there is a John Wilhelm living in Brooklyn about the right age and married to Catherine. He is a house-framer with a 15 year-old daughter named Caroline.

Finally, while living in the village of Rosehaven in Cumberland County, New Jersey, he died on February 5, 1890.

Wilkens, Frederick

GAR member Frederick Wilkens was born in the village of Bleckide in Hanover, Germany on July 15, 1843 and came to America in 1856 at the age of 13.

Standing 5'4", with brown eyes and light brown hair, Frederick enlisted in Company A of the 39th New York Infantry on May 17, 1861, and was mustered out of service on June 24, 1864.

Following the war he returned to Queens, opened a tailor shop, and married Lucy Ann Holdsworthy, *"one of Whitestone's prettiest girls"* on October 18, 1868 at St. George's Church. The pastor, Rev. Mr. Stevenson, performed the ceremony. Lucy's birth had taken place in Sheffield, England on August 17, 1851.

One child, George, was born August 22, 1869, and appears with his parents in the Census of College Point on page 95 in 1870. Lucy's parents are on page 95 as well. Her father George is 48 and a tinsmith from England. Sarah is her 42 year-old mother and she has two sisters; Martha 13, and Ada, who is 9.

With the exception of a ten-year period between 1880 and 1890 when the family lived in Providence, Rhode Island, the Wilkens family lived in Whitestone at 32 West 18th Street. Frederick was very active in the GAR and served as the Commander from 1912-1913.

In his latter years he was always given the honor of raising the flag at the Memorial Day exercises in College Point.

He died on May 12, 1928, and was thought to be the last active member of Adam Wirth Post No. 451. Actually, Tuffeil Denno and Joseph Roessel lived longer.

His son George went on to become the Superintendent of the Jackson Heights and Douglaston stations of the Flushing Postal District.

Wilson, William

William Wilson is mentioned in an August 16, 1862 article in the *Flushing Journal* as having enlisted in the 61st New York Infantry along with Edward Thompson. Also named in this article are Frederick Schuelzgover, William Hoenig, Charles Michel and Henry Wurtz. The official date in his record is given as August 27, 1862.

His military records indicates he was a mason, 25 years old, 5'7" with a dark complexion, gray eyes and brown hair. He was hospitalized a few times and once, September 13, 1863, due to sunstroke.

William Wilson deserted at David's Island, New York on November 29, 1863 and that is all that is known.

Winkler, John

GAR member John Louis Winkler was born ca. 1829 in Baden, Germany and lived in New York City from 1850 until 1861. On August 9, 1861, the day he enlisted, he was 31, a 5'7" carpenter with a fair complexion, blue eyes and light hair.

Following his March 8, 1862 disability discharge from Company B of the 52nd New York Infantry, he moved to College Point. The family appears there on page 219 of the Flushing Census in 1870. John, a 41 year-old cabinet-maker, has married 44 year-old Emelia, whose maiden name had been Kranz. They have four children; Kate, 16, Caroline, 13, William, 10, and Frank, 4. Kate works in the comb factory. Another daughter named Sophia, born February 1, 1852, is not enumerated, and is very likely married.

The family continues to live in College Point in 1880 with John still at his trade, while Caroline works at the rubber factory, and William at the silk factory.

Emelia died on January 20, 1890 in College Point and John marries a second time to Carolina Braun on November 14, 1897. Rev. Eldenbrode, possibly Rev. August Ebendick of St. John's Lutheran Church in College Point, performs the ceremony. No indication is given as to where.

The pension file indicates John is a widower at the National Military Home in Montgomery County, Ohio in 1906, and that he died in College Point on September 27, 1913. His son Frank lives in the Bronx at the time at 3418 Park Avenue.

Winter, Adam

Adam Winter was born in Germany in the early 1830's, came to the United States early in the 1850's where on August 19, 1855, he married Christina Schellhaus on Pitt Street in New York City. Rev. Stein performed the ceremony.

In 1860 the family is still living in the city with an infant named George. Two women, Anna, 42, and Margaret, 28, are listed as well as a young man named Thomas who is 12.

He is a laborer, and his name is among those published in the August 23, 1862 edition of the *Flushing Journal*. Very likely he worked at the rubber factory. On enlistment day he stood 5'7", had a fair complexion, gray eyes and sandy hair.

The pension information indicates he was frequently ill, and had suffered a buckshot wound to his leg at the first Battle of Bull Run that resulted in frequent ulcers at the site of the wound, so much so that following treatment at a convalescent camp near Alexandria, he received a disability discharge on November 16, 1862.

It is not indicated that he returned to College Point after the war, but Adam and Christina are in New York City in 1880 along with their children. George has been followed by Thomas, born ca. 1860, Henry, ca. 1862, Joseph, ca. 1864, Ameila, ca. 1867, Ferdinand, ca. 1870 and Delia, ca. 1872. Adam is a carpenter, as are George and Thomas. Henry works in a paper factory.

Five years later on September 25th, Adam passed away and is buried in St. Michael's Cemetery in Astoria. Christina lives on until June 15, 1906 and is buried with Adam.

Wirth, Adam

Perhaps the most famous College Point casualty of the Civil War was Sergeant Adam Wirth, born in New York City on October 26, 1841 with a twin sister named Eve, who died the following year on June 11, 1842. His parents were Jacob Wirth, born in Brucksal, Germany on December 14, 1807, and Elizabeth Bauer, whom he had married in a Catholic ceremony on March 2, 1841. Elizabeth was born in Konigsbad, Baden, Germany.

They emigrated to the United States shortly after the wedding, whereupon the twins were born, and then followed by the birth of two more sons; Jacob, on January 20, 1843, and David, September 21, 1844.

Elizabeth died of ovarian cancer in Williamsburgh, Brooklyn on February 23, 1855 and is buried in New York Bay Cemetery in Bergen Hills, New Jersey. Jacob lived on until January 24, 1883. He is buried in Flushing Cemetery along with his grandson, David Wirth, who at the age of 21 months, died in March of the same year. He was very probably the son of his own son David. Jacob, the son born in 1843, who died on July 7, 1892, and is buried with his mother.

The Wirth family appears in the 1860 Census of Flushing on page 699. The widowed Jacob, a shoemaker, lives with his sons and a 51 year-old woman named Magdaline Hum.

On October 9, 1861, Adam enlisted in the 34th New York Light Artillery and on August 30, 1862 in the Second Battle of Bull Run, he is wounded. A month later on September 25th he dies of septicemia at Seminary Hospital in Georgetown, DC, and is buried there at the U.S. Soldier's Home/Military Asylum Cemetery.

His father and brothers are still in College Point in the 1870 Census on pages 221 and 103 as well as in the 1880 Census of College Point. Jacob and his son Jacob are on page 246D. The younger Jacob works at the rubber factory. David appears on page 234C, 34 years old, working also in the rubber factory and married to Charlotta. They have three children; Jacob, 10, Amelia, 7 and Ida, 4.

On February 21, 1884, the GAR Post No. 451, was formed in College Point and named for Adam Wirth, and from the booklet that was prepared for the Memorial Day celebration in 1928 the following quote dated October 14, 1862, appeared:

"The members of this company, having heard of the death of Sergeant Adam Wirth. RESOLVED: That it having pleased Almighty God in His infinite wisdom to take our dear brother and companion to Himself, we desire to express our heartfelt sympathy and condolence with his family and friends in the great loss they have sustained and at the same time to give expression to our sorrow for the loss of one who was beloved by us all. His remarkable courage in the battlefield was only equaled by his uniform attention and diligence in the discharge of his duties in the camp. Upright in his dealings, generous in his friendship, obedient to every command as a good soldier, he was a bright example, as a friend and companion, worthy of the warm attachment in which he was held by all. In his death our battery loses one of its most intelligent and active members, a brother whose memory will be long cherished in the holiest and best sympathy of our common nature."

The Resolution was signed by a number of members of the unit including Captain Jacob Roemer.

Woener, John J.

John Jacob Woener was born in Wurtemburg, Germany ca. 1818. He is found on the August 23, 1862 *Flushing Journal* list of volunteers from College Point. He is listed as Jacob and that was his middle name. When he emigrated to the United States is unknown.

According to his military record, on October 2, 1861, the day he enlisted in Company L of the 2nd New York Heavy Artillery, he was a 44 year-old shoemaker and stood 5'8", with a dark complexion, dark eyes and gray hair. His record adds that on May 15, 1862, he was given a disability discharge *"by reason of deafness and impairment of light of our eye and old age"*. Adding insult to injury, $39.38 was held back from his mustering-out money for clothing he had purchased.

Nothing else is known of this soldier.

Wurtz, Henry

Henry, the son of Jacob and Franziska, was born at Aslar, Germany ca. 1843. The family appears in the 1860 Flushing Census on page 748. His father is a 51 year-old day laborer from Prussia, while his mother, with her named spelled Francisco, is 44 and from Baden. Living with 17 year-old Henry are his two siblings; Mary, 14 and Frederick, 12. There is also a 21 year-old *"factory girl"* named Philipena from Baden.

On enlistment day, August 15, 1862, Henry stood 5'6", had a light complexion and gray eyes. He first served in Company A of the 20th New York Infantry and on May 7, 1863 he transferred into Company A of the 5th New York Light Artillery. Then on January 28th of the following year, he was transferred once again, this time to the 3rd New York Light Artillery.

Henry was discharged on June 24, 1865 and returned to College Point. Less than a year later, he married Barbara Becker at St. John's Lutheran Church in College Point on February 25, 1866. Pastor August Ebendick performed the ceremony with Jacob Wilhelm and Maria Wurtz, his sister, acting as witnesses.

Over the years 16 children are born; Wilhelmina, August 23, 1866, Henrietta, November 4, 1867, Henry, 1869, Charles, November 4, 1870, Mary, November 27, 1871, Emma, ca.1874, William, March 28, 1875, Elizabeth, March 5, 1877, John, September 22, 1878, Henry, ca. 1879, Philip, September 21, 1881, Louise, October 12, 1883, Herman, September 5, 1885 and Pauline, May 1, 1889. Daughters named Babette and Barbara and a son named Heinrich, not Henry, are also born, but the years are not indicated.

In 1870 Henry and Barbara appear with babies Wilhelmina, Henryetta and Henry on page 218 of the Flushing Census. This third child passes away before the 1880 Census is taken where Henry lives at 14 11th Street, a house he bought on August 26, 1870. His family is growing and he works at the rubber factory.

Barbara, but not Henry, appears in the 1900 Census of College Point still living on 11th Street along with children Henry, Philip, Herman, Louisa and Pauline.

In his latter years he suffered from rheumatism with his death occurring in College Point on November 8, 1902. There is no indication of when Barbara died, but their son Charles became an active member of the Sons of Union Veterans.

Zeberbiers, Otto

There is one family by this surname living in College Point in 1860, but the first name is Herman and he is possibly a relative. There is a family in Brooklyn, 6th Ward, page 894, headed by Frederick *Saharberren*, a 55 year-old cabinetmaker from Prussia married to Amelia who is 54. They have a 24 year-old son named Augustus and a 16 year-old son named Otto who is a *segar* maker. This individual is a strong candidate, as the age fits very well, but it will very likely never be confirmed.

According to the record, Otto enlisted in Company L of the 2nd New York Heavy Artillery on October 1, 1861 and as a result, his name appeared in the August 23, 1862 *Flushing Journal* list of volunteers from College Point.

The record concludes with the note that he deserted at Cliffburne General Hospital in Washington, D.C. on October 11, 1862 and nothing else is known of his fate.

Ziessler, Charles

The name Charles Zeseler appears on the August 23, 1862 list of volunteers from College Point that appeared in the *Flushing Journal* as serving in the 29th New York.

The official record indicates that a man named Charles Ziessler served in the 29th New York Infantry, and that he also served in the 1st New Jersey Light Artillery upon reenlistment.

Charles Ziessler was born in Halle in Prussia ca. 1824, and on the day he enlisted he was 37 years of age, 6'2", pale complexion, gray eyes, brown hair and by occupation, a comb-maker, but the word is spelled "*Comm*". Because of his job, he was very likely working for Conrad Poppenhusen.

According to the October 20, 1862 Disability Discharge, Ziessler was on detached service at the Regiment Storehouse in Washington, DC and was reported "*sick to the Regiment since May 18th 1862, but has had this disease, convultions (sic) since August 1st.*"

Dr. August Herman, Assistant Surgeon for the 29th found him incapable of performing the duties of a soldier because of *Epilepsia*, but this did not prevent him from reenlisting in the 1st New Jersey Light Artillery the following December 21st. He was discharged from Sickle US Army Hospital on June 15, 1865.

In Baltimore, Maryland on October 11, 1865, he married Louisa H. Steeger, herself born in Germany on March 29, 1846. Over the years the couple had four children; Anna, born May 20, 1868, Louise, May 22, 1871, Mary, March 21, 1873, and Robert, April 12, 1880.

Louise and the four children appear in the 1880 Census of Baltimore, 4th Ward, Precinct 2, Page 623D, at 39 Albermarle Street in today's Little Italy section of the city. Charles is not enumerated, but the children's birthplaces are; Annie, Pennsylvania, Louise and Joseph, Ohio, and Robert, but 2 months old, in Maryland.

An affidavit prepared by Louisa from her home at 31 South Orange Avenue in Newark, NJ is in the pension file. Writing shortly after his death she says that Charles *"came from Germany just before he joined the army. He was a soldier in Germany before he came here. He served to the end of the War of the Rebellion. I married him immediately afterward after an acquaintanship of short two month. All his parents and sister and brothers in Germany, except one sister who is 20 years younger than he, are dead."*

Charles died on July 17, 1900 at the State Hospital in Morris Plains, New Jersey where he had suffered from senility, dementia and finally pneumonia. Buried in Newark, the record indicates that in life he was an actor; perhaps a clue as to why he was not at home during the taking of the 1880 Census.

Robert reported from his home at 1256 Springfield Avenue in Irvington, NJ, that his mother passed away on November 24, 1927.

Postscript and Conclusion

A few final statistical observations are offered for those who might have an interest in such information.

Of the 226 men profiled here, 83 appeared in the 1860 Census of Flushing living in College Point.

Of the 76 names on the August 23, 1862 list that appeared in the *Flushing Journal*, 15 of them appear in the 1860 Census of Flushing leading to the conclusion that College Point did experience a significant population boom between the taking of the Census and the start of the Civil War.

From this data it can be concluded that 146 men with roots in College Point served in the military. If, as has already been stated, 479 men were of an age to serve, then 30% of College Point's men did in fact, take part in the war in some manner, shape or form.

Overall there were 62 men whose names were included on the original 1884 Roster of the Adam Wirth Post No. 451 of the GAR, and only 10 of these men were in College Point in the 1860 Census.

33 College Point men were wounded during the war and survived. 24 other men from College Point died in the service of their country. Their names follow:

Henry Apel	Louis Bisky	John Buckley
Thomas Conners	John Doherty	Charles Erling
John Hefermehl	Valentine Helfreich	Robert Kanz
John Keppler	George McDonald	Andrew Reinhard
Franz Richter	David Schultz	Thomas Skinnon
Charles Stader	John Steinbrucker	Jurgon Sternberg
John Stonebanks	Willis Tyrrell	George Vix
Leopold Wenzler	Frederick Werner	Adam Wirth

The name of one man, Emil Schubert, appears on the Flushing Memorial to Civil War casualties, when in actuality he didn't die until 1882. A case could be made to add the names of George McDonald, Thomas Skinnon, Leopold Wenzler, Patrick Maher and Frederick Werner to the Monument, but since that is unlikely to occur. Let their valor be recognized here.

While Carl Ludwig and John Starkins are usually mentioned as having been the only local men awarded the Congressional Medal of Honor, Joseph Hibson's name can be added to that list. James C. Cornell's bravery at Petersburg was officially recognized and warranted the award, but that never occurred. Let his recognition be noted here as well.

The country of origin was determined for 217 of the 226 men who served:

140 were born in Germany
 33 in New York
 15 in Ireland
  5 in Pennsylvania
  4 in England
  3 each in Switzerland, New Jersey and Massachusetts
  2 each in Canada and Connecticut
  1 each in Maryland, Louisiana, France and Scotland

Overall, Conrad Poppenhusen employed 65 of the men named in this book either before of after the war. He also provided work along with educational opportunities for their children.

As has been noted elsewhere, a number of men whose names appeared on the 1862 *Flushing Journal* list were never actually found, nor was it possible to confirm their having ever served in the military. For another small percentage of the men, very little information was ever located.

Some had served in the Navy and did not file for pension benefits. Others deserted, or their pension or military file could not be located at the National Archives. Yet others, had a name common to many, and lacking any corroborating information, it was not possible to confirm that a particular individual was the veteran in question.

Dates and data tell only a skeletal portion of the life and times of these men and their families so these stories are incomplete, but they are a beginning for anyone who can trace his or her lineage at least to 1860 and the small town called College Point, in Queens, in New York City. Their stories will continue, to be sure.

In any case, it has been an honor to research and write about the lives of these men, the women they married, and the children they raised. They have become so much more than statistics, and in their memory I quote James Agee's prose poem titled Knoxville: Summer of 1915:

"May God bless my people, my uncle, my aunt, my mother, my good father, oh, remember them kindly in their time of trouble; and in the hour of their taking away."

Index

Connecticut Heavy Artillery

1st   Colvin, John

Connecticut Infantry Units

1st   Gear, Samuel
         McManus, Robert

11th   Hoelle, John
         Tyrrell, Willis

14th   Englehardt, Charles

Delaware Infantry

1st   Dockendorf, Frank
         Miller, Frederick
         Piereth, Valentine

Maine Infantry

13th   Grant, Fred

Massachusetts Infantry

11th   Erling, Charles

46th   Coffin, Lowell

Michigan Infantry

28th   Lindecke, William

New Jersey Infantry

2nd   Marx, Charles   transferred from 15th New Jersey Infantry

15th   Marx, Charles   transferred to 2nd New Jersey Infantry

         Hobson, Josh

New Jersey Light Artillery

1st   Ziessler, Charles   transferred from 29th New York Infantry

New York Cavalry Units

1st	Doherty, Bernard	
	Kockeritz, Benno von	transferred to 13th New York Cavalry
11th	Reinhard, Andrew	
13th	Kockeritz, Benno von	transferred from 1st New York Cavalry

New York Engineers

15th	Fisher, John
	Heyne, Lewis
	Kelly, Cornelius

New York Heavy Artillery

1st	Motz, Henry	
5th	Houser, John	
15th	Buser, Charles	
	Hefermehl, John	
	Hollweg, August	
	Haubeil, Martin	transferred from 74th New York Infantry

New York Infantry Units

3rd	McCormick, Daniel	
4th	McClymont, George	
6th	Drakert, Frank	
	Fritz, Louis	
7th	Apel, Henry	second enlistment after 29th New York Infantry
	Kabisch, Frederick	
	Rhein, Moritz	
	Schermerhorn, Louis (30-day unit)	
8th	Duer, Franz	
10th	Dillen, Michael	
	Egan, Patrick	
	Egan, Thomas	
	Leppert, John	
	Skinnon, Thomas	
	Smith, James	
	Sparks, John	

Index

20th	Dockendorf, Frederick	
	Fahner, Jacob	
	Freund, Edward	
	Horn, Michael	
	Jockers, Adam	
	Lasche, Robert	
	Miller, Louis	
	Muecke, Engelbert	
	Pluemacher, Charles	
	Rausch, Peter	
	Schneider, William	
	Schumacher, Henry	
	Sennewald, Theodore	
	Smith, William	
	Steinbeck, Julius	
	Straube, Henry	
	Wurtz, Henry	transferred to 5th New York Light Artillery
25th	Harrington, Thomas	
29th	Apel, Conrad	
	Apel, Henry	
	Mutz, Gustave	
	Neumann, Edward	transferred from 121st New York Infantry
	Roessel, Joseph	
	Rubel, Henry	
	Schierlitz, Paul	
	Schrader, Otto	transferred to 2nd New York Light Artillery
	Steinbrucker, John	
	Vix, George	
	Ziessler, Carl	transferred to 1st New Jersey Light Artillery
31st	Herbig, Hieronymus	
32nd	Haubeil, Charles	
39th	Noss, Adam	
	Stader, Charles	
	Stader, George	
	Weber, Bernhard	
	Wilkens, Frederick	
40th	Neimeier, Andrew	transferred from 74th New York Infantry
	Young, William F.	transferred from 74th New York Infantry
41st	Schubert, Emil	transferred to 9th New York Light Artillery
	Winter, Adam	
45th	Bisky, Louis	
	Feuerbacher, August	
	Vollbracht, William	

46th	Dockendorf, Joseph	
	Otto, Henry	
48th	Gardner, Rufus	
	Gardner, Savillian	
	Hibson, Joseph	
52nd	Kanz, Robert	
	Winkler, John	
54th	Rausmuller, Charles	
57th	Stobbe, Nicholas	
58th	Ackerknecht, Frederick	
	Behring, Frederick	
	Bockler, Chrisostomus	
	Franke, Anton	
	Gunzert, Theodore	
	Helfreich, Valentine	
	Kanz, John	
	Koch, Charles	
	Richter, Franz	
61st	Conners, Thomas	
	Thompson, Edward	
	Wilson, William	
63rd	Dougherty, John	
	McDonald, George	
65th	Underhill, John	
67th	Fowler, George	
68th	May, William	
	Pfortner, Max Vonder Holle	
	Matthew, Johann	
73rd	Newman, George	
	Thomas, George	transferred from 163rd New York Infantry
74th	Haubeil, Martin	transferred to the 15th New York Heavy Artillery
	Maher, Patrick	
	Montgomery, George	never found
	Neimeier, Andrew	transferred to 40th New York Infantry
	Quaid, T.	never found
	Snyder, William	
	Young, William F.	

Index

79th	Baumeister, Z.	never found
	Briody, Richard	
	Broid, J.	never found
	Schultz, David	
82nd	Dietrich, George	
83rd	Montanye, Washington	
90th	Mahlenthal, Emmanuel	
103rd	Baumann, Frederick	
121st	Newman, Edward	transferred to 29th New York Infantry
131st	Griffin, Michael	
	Lutters, Ernest	
133rd	Hoenig, William	
	Horstmann, Charles	
	Schultz, Franklin	
147th	Stratton, Alfred	
158th	Kulle, Albert	
162nd	Landt, Henry	
163rd	Thomas, George	transferred to 73rd New York Infantry

New York Light Artillery Units

2nd	Schrader, Otto	transferred from 29th New York Infantry
3rd	Wurtz, Henry	transferred from 5th New York Light Artillery
5th	Wurtz, Henry	transferred from 20th New York Infantry
9th	Schubert, Emil	transferred from 41st New York Infantry
29th	Todt, Charles	transferred from 32nd New York Light Artillery
32nd	Todt, Charles	transferred to 29th New York Light Artillery

34th   Mustered in as Co. L, 2nd New York Heavy Artillery

Baumann, John
Becker, Ludwig
Berndt, William
Bracken, John
Brill, Jr., Christian
Brill, Sr., Christian
Cooper, William
Cornell, James C.
Foster, Samuel

Frank, Lewis
Frey, Joseph
Green, John
Griffin, Albert
Heilmann, John Peter
Johnston, Daniel S.
Kaufmann, John
Kiernan, John
Kiernan, Patrick
Ludwig, Carl
Ludwig, William
Miller, Louis
Mahoney, Michael
Nau, Michael
Palmer, Samuel
Reinheimer, Daniel
Richard, George
Schaefer, Nicholas
Schaefer, Peter
Schumacher, Frederick
Starkins, John
Steinbecker, John
Sternberg, Casper
Sternberg, Jurgon
Troy, John
Vogt, Jurgon
Wenzler, Leopold
Werner, Frederick
Weisssner, Valentine
White, Thomas
Wirth, Adam
Woener, John
Zerberbier, Otto

New York National Guard

5th	Johann, Matthew
13th	Dillman, Henry
69th	Wieners, Jacob F.

New York State Militia

11th	Weiss, Charles
15th	Beresheim, Jacob
	Beyerly, Peter
	Buhl, Peter*
	Cordier, Daniel
	Ehm, Jacob
	Fink, John
	Freygang, Charles

Gentner, Nicholas

Glaeser, Charles
Hebel, Jacob
Metzger, Charles
Motz, Jacob
Naumann, George*
Piereth, Christian
Plitt, George
Propfer, Augustus
Schultz, Henry
Stonebanks, John

* The service of these men preceded the war

Ohio Light Artillery

Farrell, Henry

Pennsylvania Infantry

31st	Snyder, Edwin
45th	Keppler, Jacob
210th	Hickman, Richard

United States Artillery

1st	Motz, Phillip
5th	Lark, Joseph

United States Engineers

Bertschinger, Gustav
Lark, Peter

United States Marine Band

Benz, Louis

United States Navy

Arnold, William
Buckley, John
Emmerich, John
Harrington, Thomas   transferred from 25th New York Infantry
Harvey, Andrew
Lane, Charles
McGowan, William
Michel, Charles
Schultz, George
Troy, John
Warner, Hiram

United States Signal Corps

        Beardslee, Frederick

Vermont Infantry

9th   Denno, Tuffeil

Wisconsin Infantry

35th   Lasche, Robert   transferred from 20th New York Infantry